Thinking About Religion in the 21st Century

A New Guide for the Perplexed

Thinking About Religion in the 21st Century

A New Guide for the Perplexed

George C. Adams, Jr.

IFF
BOOKS

London, UK
Washington, DC, USA

CollectiveInk

First published by iff Books, 2024
iff Books is an imprint of Collective Ink Ltd.,
Unit 11, Shepperton House, 89 Shepperton Road, London, N1 3DF
office@collectiveinkbooks.com
www.collectiveinkbooks.com
www.iff-books.com

For distributor details and how to order please visit the 'Ordering' section on our website.

Text copyright: George C. Adams, Jr. 2023

ISBN: 978 1 80341 468 3
978 1 80341 469 0 (ebook)
Library of Congress Control Number: 2023903057

A CIP catalogue record for this book is available from the British Library.

Design: Lapiz Digital Services

UK: Printed and bound by CPI Group (UK) Ltd, Croydon, CR0 4YY
Printed in North America by CPI GPS partners

Previous Books by George C. Adams, Jr.

The Deathbed Sutra of the Buddha or Siddhartha's Regrets
Washington: O-Books, 2014
ISBN: 978 1 78279 612 1

The Structure and Meaning of Badarayana's Brahma Sutras:
A Translation and Analysis of **Adhyaya I**
Delhi: Motilal Banarsidass, 1993
ISBN: 81 208 0931 9

Contents

Chapter 1 Why This Book?   1

Deconstruction   **15**
Chapter 2 How to Think About Traditional Religions   17
Chapter 3 How to Think About Sacred Texts   28
Chapter 4 How to Think About Ritual   41
Chapter 5 How to Think About Doctrine   49
Chapter 6 How to Think About Religious Diversity   64

Reconstruction   **77**
Chapter 7 The Myth of Scientific Materialism   81
Chapter 8 Basic Epistemology: How We Know
        What We Know   99
Chapter 9 A State of Transition   107
Chapter 10 Perennialism: What We Already Know   113
Chapter 11 Consciousness   138
Chapter 12 The Sense of Moral Goodness   164
Chapter 13 Religious Experience   176
Chapter 14 Making Sense of Suffering   197
Chapter 15 The Question of Meaning   211
Chapter 16 Putting It All Together   221

Endnotes   260
References   276

Chapter 1

Why This Book?

A Note of Apology

Over 150 years ago, the Danish philosopher Soren Kierkegaard (speaking through his pseudonym Johannes Climacus), in the preface to his renowned masterpiece, *The Concluding Unscientific Postscript*, took time to apologize for adding to what he referred to as the "paragraph parade."[1] Writing at a time when book publishing was becoming quite commonplace and writers of all sorts were churning out books at a never-before-seen pace, Kierkegaard felt a bit guilty at adding to what he perceived to be a glut of unnecessary verbiage which added more confusion than clarity to the religious and philosophical issues of the time. Kierkegaard believed that much that was being published at that time had little merit, and was being produced more for publisher profit and author egotism than for actual enlightenment of the general population. In such an environment, despite being convinced that he had something important, relevant, and profound to say, he nonetheless felt compelled to apologize for contributing yet another lengthy tome to what could be described as a bad case of writing and publishing dysentery.

While the short, simple, elementary work that follows can hardly be compared to Kierkegaard, I nonetheless feel a bit of the same guilt that the Dane experienced back in the mid-19th century. This is a book about contemporary spirituality, and there certainly is an abundance of books out there about contemporary spirituality: in Kierkegaardian terms, there is a "paragraph parade" of books on spirituality, and not every entry into that parade is a worthy one. Today, an Amazon search of "spirituality" yields over half a million results, and

I'm sure that that number will increase dramatically by the time you begin to read this book (and even further by the time you finish it). Indeed, it seems that we have an abundance of gurus, masters, theologians, philosophers, spiritual teachers, etc., each offering some sort of insight (often accompanied by a specific plan) into how to live a spiritually meaningful life in contemporary times where the value of traditional religion is increasingly questioned. From the big names (often with an Oprah-ish connection) such as Eckhart Tolle, Deepak Chopra, Wayne Dyer, Michael Singer and others, to hundreds or more of second- and third-tier authors who offer seminars, retreats, web-based teaching and counseling, and produce book after book from lesser known publishers, to the countless self-published gurus who crank out books and work the lesser known spiritual circuits, we are seemingly flooded with a bounty of profound (or is it superficial?) spiritual guidance.

In the context of such a paragraph parade, why this book?

A Perplexed Friend and the Purpose of This Book

In part, I felt compelled to reluctantly make yet another contribution to the paragraph parade because of my conversations with a good friend, and the frustration that I felt in seeing him struggle with religion.

My close friend, Jonathan, is a successful physician. He is an exceptionally bright, insightful, thoughtful, middle-aged man, widely read, highly intelligent, conversant in what seems to be an unlimited range of fields: medicine (of course), history, geography, economics, politics, literature, technology, science, and on and on. He is an exceptionally rational and open-minded person. But in addition to all this, he is one of the most kind, sincere, gracious, humble, virtuous, compassionate persons that I have ever had the good fortune to meet over the span of six decades. Jonathan has, in the purest sense, a "good heart." When asked what was the essence of Buddhism, the Dalai Lama is said to have once replied, "A good heart." While some may find that that sounds a bit simplistic, I would suggest that it's actually a very profound answer. A truly good heart, difficult as it is to define, and hard as it is to find embodied in an actual person, is indeed something that is spiritually rare, and Jonathan possesses this quality.

And yet, for all his intelligence, open-mindedness, and good heart, there is one thing that Jonathan will have no part of: religion. Jonathan finds religious beliefs to be not just laughably irrational and absurd, but morally and intellectually offensive. He finds the Biblical accounts of miracles such as the parting of the Red Sea to be preposterous in the light of contemporary science (in which he was thoroughly trained). He finds accounts of a vengeful Old Testament God authorizing the murder of women and children to be morally repugnant: how could a morally good person profess allegiance to such a bloodthirsty entity? And given that in his job as a pediatric surgeon, he sees the horrible things that happen to innocent children and families on a daily basis, he sees no reason to believe that there is any transcendent, spiritual goodness or meaning in this universe.

So why do I write of Jonathan, and what does he have to do with this book? Quite simply, Jonathan is representative of a widespread trend in our culture, one that has spread throughout all levels of society, creating what is a veritable "silent spiritual majority."

Specifically, he is representative of the countless numbers of intelligent and good-hearted people who want nothing to do with "religion" of either the traditional or New Age sort. And they adopt this position out of what is actually a noble motive: they are trying to be intellectually and morally honest with themselves. They refuse to acknowledge the validity of ideas that simply don't make sense to them; they refuse to ground their hopes in stories and symbols that simply don't have any meaning to them; they refuse to profess allegiance to or admiration of a deity that acts in a manner that is inferior to the moral standard that they expect of not only themselves but even their children. They believe that they cannot be religious if being "religious" means sacrificing their intellect and professing belief in a person successfully commanding the sun to stand still in the sky or a paradisal realm that is "up there" or a creation that takes place in a mere seven days and in contradictory sequences that do not exactly correspond to the scientific evidence. They believe that they cannot be religious if being religious means sacrificing their moral sensibility and accepting the goodness of a God who authorizes the slaughter of an entire village of men, women, and children, or a God-man who kills a plant solely because the plant cannot satisfy his hunger (Mark 11:12-14) – and of course, for countless other reasons, found in the sacred texts of many of the world's religions.[2]

But they also cannot embrace "religion" if that means acceptance of nebulous notions that are grounded in wild speculation disguised as scientifically-rooted empirical experience. They cannot accept the existence of spiritual realities whose existence is explained in writings that are weak in evidence, juvenile in logic, and, psychologically speaking, seemingly rooted more in contemporary expressions of wish-fulfillment than in reality of any sort. In other words, they cannot accept the current religions rooted in the past, but neither can they accept the religions of the many versions of the "new spirituality," generally lumped together under the "New Age" label, that have appeared over the past several decades.

Perhaps without even realizing it, they have adopted the worldview of secular naturalism: the only existing reality is the realm of time, space, mass and energy (the "physical world"),[3] and the only valid means of knowledge about the world is through scientific rationalism. Believing that scientific naturalism is a "proven" perspective, they attempt to be honest with themselves by holding positions that are consistent with that naturalism, and religion (as they understand it) is not consistent with that naturalism. In a world that appears to them as devoid of any sort of transcendent meaning or value, in a spirit of authenticity they try to maintain the only source of dignity that is left: being honest with oneself, even if that does involve the acceptance of a rather bleak understanding of reality.

In a certain sense, my friend is representative of what might be considered the contemporary version of "everyman," or, more properly put in gender-neutral terms, "everyperson." They are representative of a general worldview, of a general way of looking at reality, that is shared by much, and perhaps most, of the population of at least the industrialized "first world," and most likely, humans across the globe who live in any culture which has been significantly touched by scientific naturalism, secularism, industrialization, and the related philosophical elements of modernity. They represent a worldwide sense of doubt about the tenable nature of traditional religious beliefs, whether those beliefs have originated in the Western Abrahamic traditions or the various Asian traditions. They represent intelligent, thoughtful, well-intentioned men and women of the modern world who cannot reconcile intellectual and moral integrity with religious belief as they understand it, and hence they go through life with no religious belief at all, choosing the path of atheism or agnosticism or, perhaps even more likely, making no choice at all but rather trying to just not think about such matters.

Of course, at this point one might simply say, "So what?" Some people hold a religious perspective, others do not. In our supposedly post-modern world, where there is room for diversity without (or almost without) limits, why should this be a problem? Believers and nonbelievers, secularists, and religionists, scientists and mystics: why not just rest content with that diversity?

Quite simply, the problem is that those who adopt this stance that intellectual and moral integrity in the contemporary world are incompatible with religious belief are: 1) simply wrong; and, 2) unnecessarily denying themselves the benefits of a spiritual worldview, a perspective that offers a level of depth, meaning, and insight into existence as an embodied human creature that secularism simply does not and cannot provide. We are suggesting that there are real, unique, and profound human "goods" that flow from a belief in Spirit. We are further arguing that belief in Spirit, divested of the symbols and myths of 2000-year-old religions (more on this later) *does not require any sort of sacrifice of intellectual or moral integrity*, and indeed, quite the contrary, an honest, open-minded, rational assessment of that which we label as "reality" strongly suggests the existence of Spirit. We further argue that an honest examination of the nature of our experience as beings of embodied consciousness clearly demonstrates the existence of a human capacity to empirically gain experiential access to that Spirit. And we are even further suggesting that reflection on the nature of human values and morality likewise suggests the existence of a spiritual dimension to existence.

In a sense we are saying that, far from being an anachronistic embarrassment which the honest contemporary human cannot accept, the existence of Spirit is a position that any intellectually, empirically, and morally honest person can embrace without reservation. The purpose of this book is simply to flesh out and defend that assertion, and in doing so hopefully free the countless intelligent, honest, and good-hearted Jonathans of the world to recognize that they are free to both retain their intellect, honesty, and morality *and* to accept the presence of Spirit.

But to adopt such a receptive and appreciative perspective on religion, *a radical shift from the traditional view of religion is required*. If (like Jonathan) one's only way of thinking about religion is in the context of existing traditional religions, then the transformation that we are advocating regarding how one views religion is not likely to happen. Rather, it is necessary to set aside all of one's preconceived ideas about religion and start again from scratch, so to speak.

And one way to start fresh is to adopt a "Big Picture" view of religion, looking not at any single religion in isolation, and indeed not looking at religion in its multiple current expressions in isolation, but rather looking at religion from the perspective of the evolution of the human species, and in fact, adopting an even more expansive Big Picture, looking at it from the perspective of the evolutionary history of the universe. Such a perspective is not dependent on consulting sacred texts or understanding church doctrines or accepting the authority of religious leaders. Such a perspective is based on simple observation of the factual dimensions of the world in which we have evolved, and is completely compatible with the scientific mode of knowledge that often is cited by nonbelievers as forcing them into disbelief. In other words, how does human knowledge in general, and spiritual knowledge in particular, fit in the grand, cosmic evolutionary process? In the truly Big Picture – or the biggest that our species can comprehend – where does religion fit in?

Of course, at best, we can only speculate, but a reasonable description of such a Big Picture perspective on religion (and the one which our entire argument is rooted in) might look something like this:

Approximately 14 billion years ago, the realm of time, space, matter, and energy came into existence in a singularity event which scientific cosmologists refer to as the Big Bang. From this initial event, over the span of billions of years, ever more complex entities evolved. Elementary particles combined to produce simple elements, which in turn combined with other elements to form various compounds. Eventually simple molecules emerged, and from those simple molecules, life evolved on at least one planet, Earth (and in all probability, on many others – but that's not our concern here). Once established on Earth, living entities continued this evolution into increasingly complex forms, producing multicellular organisms and eventually the more complex organisms that led to the emergence of organisms with sufficiently complex neurological mechanisms to allow them to experience awareness of their environment.

Initially, in nonhuman life forms, this consisted of a rudimentary "awareness" which sensed and responded to, though in all likelihood was not "conscious" of, various sensory qualities: light, sound, heat, etc. But with the emergence of humans, we find neurological systems that have attained a level of complexity that made possible the awareness or experience of not only the sensory qualities of the environment, but also various non-sensory, intangible aspects of the world. These objects of awareness are often described as "abstract," but that doesn't mean that such entities are nonexistent. Humans developed the capacity, for instance, to conceive of number – not just as in a number of specific objects, such as four apples, but the *concept* of fourness, independent of its relation to any set of objects representative of fourness.

Humans also developed an awareness of abstract qualities such as goodness, truth, and beauty. Indeed, with reference to these three, humans clearly had evolved an awareness of a dimension of existence that the rest of the evolved world did not have. In a sense, human consciousness evolved to the point where, unlike nonhuman forms of consciousness, it had the capacity for awareness of non-sensory realities, including those which we might designate as "spiritual" in nature. This included a sense of the presence of unseen realities – understood in a plethora of different ways by various early human peoples – but all consistently expressing the sense that there is "something else" other than the material realm, and that that "something else" was of the greatest importance in how humans lived. And with this came the evolution of the concept of "meaning" in life – again, a mode of consciousness that we do not perceive in other species which lack the evolved brain complexity of humans. And this notion of "meaning" in life was sensed as being intimately connected to that transcendent Something Else.

What we are talking about here is the emergence of religion at a point in human history, made possible by the evolving complexity of the human brain. Of course, we can only speculate in the vaguest terms about how, when, and where this might have happened: as humans became human, what happened in the emerging human psyche to lead to the capacity to experience non-sensory and "spiritual" realities, a capacity that apparently is not present in other species? How, when, and why did the notion of a spiritual reality first appear in the human species? How and why did humans end up with this notion that is not found, in any sense whatsoever, in any other species? When and how did the thought or awareness or perception of "Spirit" – of whatever sort – first occur in the human brain? When and how did human beings first conceive in the mind the notion of an invisible, or spiritual, realm, one that was not subject to the suffering and decay of the material realm?

And what happened in the brain, when that first sense of the spiritual occurred, or what had evolved in the brain which allowed the first sense of a spiritual reality to occur in the human mind?

When did those things happen? And was it a *thought* or something more like, in keeping with historian of religion Mircea Eliade, an *experience or feeling or sentiment* of the sacred? Did someone say, "You know, I've been thinking – maybe there's an invisible dimension in addition to this dimension we're in now." Or... *did early humans experience something* – something of a numinous, mysterious, sacred quality, which they subsequently attempted to describe and communicate in symbols, from the Neolithic cave paintings to the great theological treatises of the Middle Ages?

What we are suggesting here, of course, is a position which often gets skirted in the world of academic scholarship. Is religion nothing more than the product of human imagination – did we just make it all up? Or, as we are suggesting, is religion the product of an experience of or a sense of something that is actually *there*, however elusive "there" might be? Put differently, did early humans create an illusory notion of spiritual reality, or did they perceive or experience a spiritual reality that did indeed exist, and was accessible to them in various ways dependent upon their ability to perceive it (which, of course, would include the evolutionary stage of the development of their brain and consciousness)?

But perhaps both can be true: it seems quite obvious that much of what we call "religion" is indeed the product of a particular culture and a particular time period – in other words, human beings do indeed "make up" or construct much of the detail that goes into what we call religion. But that does not negate the possibility that those human constructions are an attempt to make sense of something that is indeed experienced or sensed as a real presence. And, being the sort of imaginative and creative creatures that we are, we have to elaborate on it and dress it up in all sorts of wonderful, wild, and confusing ways, with doctrines, rituals, myths, and everything else that goes into this thing called religion.

Indeed, one might ask: if religion is only the product of human speculation and creative imagination regarding the notion of a spiritual reality, *where did the idea of a spiritual reality come from in the first place?* Where and how did we first get that notion of spiritual reality that we subsequently played with and decorated in countless different ways over centuries and centuries?

So to briefly summarize the position that will be presented in more detail in the course of the book: it is not necessary to sacrifice one's intellectual or moral integrity to believe in a spiritual dimension of existence. Quite to the contrary, cognition, empirical experience, and moral intuition all point more toward the existence of a spiritual reality than they do to the atheistic alternative. One can be honest with oneself, intellectually, experientially, and morally, and maintain belief in Spirit by whatever name one chooses to call it. However, such honesty does require making a distinction between spiritual truths and the symbols and myths through which they have been expressed in pre-modern cultures.[4] Many treasured symbols and stories, if treated as literally true, must be abandoned as literal truths and understood as representations of a spiritual reality for which our post-axial culture has not yet developed a "new story" with new symbols, and as such remains somewhat elusive and mysterious. But better to honestly lay claim to that elusive mystery than to engage in an act of self-deception in clinging to ways of thinking about and expressing Spirit[5] that no longer make sense in today's world.

Before proceeding, however, a brief note would be in order regarding who should *not* read this book. Many people are quite content with traditional modes of spirituality. They accept traditional texts as authoritative, and find comfort, solace, and guidance in their pages. They find that orthodox beliefs and practices provide a meaningful and reassuring perspective on life and its many vicissitudes. That's quite comforting, and it is not my desire to in any way disturb the confident faith of those who find traditional religions to be credible and effective. If you are content in your faith as a Christian, Jew, Muslim, Hindu, Buddhist, Jain, Daoist, Confucian, or any other existing religious tradition, then you're not likely to find much useful material in what follows. To those content believers, I would simply suggest that you not read this book.

But for those who look at the traditional faiths and simply cannot buy into them, I hope you will read on.

A Note on Style

There is a certain sense in which this book doesn't have anything new to say at all. Indeed, given the abundance of spirituality-oriented books that address the notion of an evolutionary shift from an outdated mode of spirituality and consciousness to something new and revolutionary, one could argue that there's not much more that can be said on the matter that doesn't amount to simply repeating, in a slightly modified form, what has already been put forth by others.[6]

Nonetheless, this book does have a unique objective, in that it attempts to examine these issues in a manner that is likely to be positively received by a broader audience. There are many books out there for traditional believers; there are many books out there for New Agers. But where are the books that openly explore the potential for new spiritual possibilities without being weighed down by either allegiance to past traditions or blithely chasing, with little sense of critical assessment or discrimination, virtually any spiritual path that runs counter to traditional religion? This will attempt to be such a book, threading the needle between the two extremes of overcautious traditionalism and careless innovation.

At the present time, works on the validity of a religious perspective and the emergence of a new spirituality tend to be of two types: popular spirituality books and scholarly/academic books. Books written from a nonacademic, spirituality-based perspective, abound in number and popularity. Tolle, Chopra, Singer, and many others do indeed find a large audience, but I would argue that they do so at a price, and that price is intellectual and logical rigor. As inspiring as such works might be at times, to the reader who has even a modest familiarity with world religions, philosophy of religion, history of religions, and related fields, these works are also extremely frustrating at times, in that the authors do not present their positions in a manner that represents sustained and rigorous logical thinking, and at times they contort factual information to suit their own needs.[7] As such, their positions are often not taken seriously by not only the scholarly community but, even more importantly, just the intelligent lay reader. Looking for an alternative to what they rightly perceive as outmoded forms of spirituality found in the still-dominant organized religions, these everyday people in search of spiritual alternatives are not likely to be convinced by writings that simply don't reflect an even modest level of reasoning and common sense. My friend Jonathan, for instance, who is most decidedly not a professional philosopher or theologian, cannot be convinced to take seriously the arguments of these new spirituality icons since the weaknesses in their positions are so obvious.

On the other hand, the intelligent lay reader is not likely to find much of value in academic works dealing with contemporary spirituality since academic works, by their very nature, are not intended for a broad audience. Full of lengthy analyses, innumerable footnotes, and multiple references to obscure scholarly works that are not likely to be familiar to the non-scholarly reader, such books provide a valuable perspective but only for a limited audience.

So the intelligent lay reader is often left with little to choose from, caught between the intellectual unsoundness of new spirituality authors and the intellectual overkill of academic works.[8]

The present work attempts to address this need by offering intellectually sound, rationally serious arguments that will be convincing to the thoughtful lay reader who wants to retain her intellectual and moral integrity, but without the unnecessary verbiage and related clutter that characterizes so much academic work. We will attempt to present an intellectually credible case for a new, emerging spirituality, but in a manner that is also clear and comprehensible. We will present a case for spirituality that is intended for the "everyperson" of the early 21st century.

As such, this work is not intended for quite the same audience as the writings of the celebrity spiritual writers such as Tolle, Chopra, etc., in that the focus will not be on the cultivation of any sort of exceptional, non-ordinary spiritual experience. We will not be advocating a non-dual enlightenment experience. We will not be recommending the necessity of mystical experiences. We will not be speaking of past-life, shamanistic, meditative, or entheogens-induced experiences that are posited as the alternative to no longer credible traditional religions. Of course, we are not denying the reality or value of such experiences, and in various ways we will touch on such experiences as they fit into our exploration.

But this is not a book for those who are looking for a path to something extraordinary and transformative. Rather, in presenting what we hope will be a convincing exposition to "everyperson," we will be looking primarily at the everyday experience that every person is familiar with. In fact, we will be arguing that the reality of Spirit can be found in the very ordinariness and preciousness of everyday life, when that everyday life is looked at without the multiple unconscious prejudices of either scientific naturalism or traditional religion. In a sense, we are simply saying to the ordinary person: cast aside the preconceived notions about reality that you have been exposed to through the competing, but equally misguided, poles of traditional religion and scientific naturalism, and you will see the obviousness of Spirit in its full simplicity, goodness, and beauty.

Deconstruction

Chapter 2

How to Think About Traditional Religions

If we were living in Medieval Europe and someone asked what would happen if they climbed in a boat on the shore of the ocean and sailed West as far as possible, the reasonable and obvious answer would be that the boat would eventually fall off the edge of the Earth and all would perish.

If we were living in ancient Greece and someone asked why the sun moved across the sky, the reasonable and obvious answer would be that the sun god was riding his golden chariot.

If we were living in Biblical times and someone asked why rain fell from the sky, the reasonable and obvious answer would be that God makes it fall.

If we were living in ancient India and someone asked why society is divided into different classes, the reasonable and obvious explanation would be that there once was a Cosmic Person (*mahapurusha*) who had been sacrificed, with his various parts creating the different social castes.

If we were living in ancient China and someone asked what the weather would be like tomorrow, the reasonable and obvious response would be to put a turtle shell over a fire and observe the pattern of cracks that formed on the surface of the shell.

If we were living as late as the 17th century in Europe, and someone asked what could be done to cure a sick person, the reasonable and obvious answer would be to drain some blood – *lots* of blood.

If any of these questions would be asked today, in the 21st century, and someone gave the same response, such a response would no longer be deemed "reasonable and obvious." Quite to the contrary, it would be labeled uninformed, irresponsible, stupid, crazy, etc. And, to make a point that hopefully will seem ridiculously obvious to the reader, *why* would it be the case that an answer that was reasonable and obvious to our ancestors would be considered absurd and ridiculous to us today? Because *human knowledge has evolved over time*. What the human species knows about the nature of things and how they work in the 21st century has changed considerably since what was known in pre-modern times. We simply know more today than we knew in times past, in virtually all fields of knowledge: science, medicine, engineering, agriculture, and on and on. We simply do not think the same way that we thought 2000 years ago. Or at least, in most areas we don't...

And that brings us to religion – perhaps the one area of human understanding where much of the human race continues to think in the same way that humans thought two thousand years ago. Why is it the case that Christians and Jews look to writings that are over 2000 years old for knowledge about the nature of God or the Transcendent or Spirit? Why do Hindus and Buddhists, following traditions that are perhaps slightly less text-dependent than the Biblical faiths, nonetheless look to writings that likewise were written over 2000 years ago? And even in the more "recent" religion of Islam, why do Muslims believe that the knowledge of God as found in a book that was assembled in the 7th century is the only valid source of knowledge about God? Really, when you step back and contemplate this practice of 21st century people habitually and without hesitation looking to ancient books for knowledge about something that is presumed to be a present-day reality (God), the practice might appear to some to be a bit bizarre.

Physicians and other health care providers don't look to the writings of Galen (2nd century) when they are looking for guidance on how to treat an illness. NASA doesn't consult Ptolemy (2nd century) for astronomical guidance when planning the complex task of launching a satellite into orbit. If you're planning on taking a trip to China, you don't do so based on a map from the time of Marco Polo (13th century). And so on and so on. The point is obvious, and yet precisely because it's so obvious, the continuation of the practice of people in the 21st century consulting 2000-year-old writings is all the more peculiar.

Of course, one could rightly point out that knowledge about "worldly" realities, or aspects of reality found in the ever-changing matrix of time and space – in other words, knowledge about *things* – is different than knowledge about God or the Transcendent. This is certainly the case, and this distinction has a number of important implications, which we will explore later, for how one thinks about religion in the 21st century. But the fact that there is a difference in the nature of our knowledge about the material world and our knowledge about Spirit need not logically lead to the conclusion that knowledge about worldly realities changes and evolves over time whereas knowledge about God is static and confined to books written in the pre-modern era. Of course, one could adopt the traditional position of the Abrahamic traditions (which, unless otherwise noted, we will use to refer to Judaism, Christianity, and Islam), and contend that knowledge about God is the product of revelation which is a one-way transmission, coming only from God to humanity, and that transmission ended over 2000 years ago (or, in the case of Islam, 1400 years ago). That is a position that one might hold as a matter of faith, but it is not a position that can be derived from any sort of observation and analysis of religion in general. Maybe knowledge about God is indeed limited to what God chooses to communicate to humanity, and, maybe God did choose to stop that communication a long, long time ago (although it seems rather odd that an omnipotent and benevolent Spirit would choose to do that). But that position is based on faith, derived from those very texts, and as such is something of a tautological position, along the lines of "We believe that knowledge of God only comes from the Torah/Bible/Qur'an because the Torah/Bible/Qur'an says so."

Actually, none of those texts say anything of the sort, but that's a point we don't need to argue here. Rather, the point is that people from a given religion can choose to define their ancient texts in such a manner, but they are doing so solely on the basis of faith, and a blind sort of faith at that. Our exploration of how one can think about religion in the 21st century is being made independent of dependence on such faith-based assertions. We are simply saying: look at what's there – at yourself, at the Earth, at the Cosmos – and from that starting point let's consider what seems to be reasonable when thinking about religion. And from that starting point, there simply is no justification for thinking that religious knowledge must be limited to information found in old – *very* old – books.

Of course, this is not to suggest that existing sacred texts have no value or that traditional faith has no role in 21st century spirituality. For many believers, these ancient texts continue to be profoundly meaningful, and the ideas expressed in those texts about the nature of God and God's relationship to the Universe and humanity continue to provide a valuable guide for leading a spiritual life even in today's world.

However, we also have to acknowledge that there is a substantial population of thoughtful, intelligent, well-intentioned people who do not find the traditional way of thinking about religion, rooted in a one-directional revelation captured in a single text written many centuries ago, as credible, or even consistent with their own moral and spiritual intuitions. It is to this latter audience that this book is addressed.

The traditional understanding of religion, including the belief that an ancient scripture is the sole valid source of knowledge of God, assumes something that we are choosing to deny, namely that *religion doesn't change*. But it does! It changes, very slowly perhaps, over the span of centuries, but in very recognizable ways. In other words, just as the human awareness of other aspects of reality has changed over time – and changed in a progressive manner, such that it would be justified to say that it has, admittedly in fits and starts, evolved – likewise human awareness of the spiritual nature of reality has evolved over time. And the challenge that we are addressing here of 21ˢᵗ century humans looking to 2000 years old texts for knowledge about Spirit is rooted in the widespread *failure to recognize the evolving nature of religious wisdom*.

The sense in which religion has evolved over the span of human existence has been well-documented by many scholars, anthropologists, theologians, and cultural historians. Indeed, an entire field of study in graduate work, History of Religions, developed in the mid-20ᵗʰ century in response to this recognition of identifiable patterns of change in human religion over long spans of time.[9] Just to cite one example of such scholarship (although perhaps the most influential one), consider the work of the German philosopher, Karl Jaspers.[10]

In 1949, Jaspers coined the term "Axial Age" to describe a period of human history, running from approximately the 8ᵗʰ century BCE to close to the beginning of the Christian era, during which there was a radical shift in religious consciousness in civilizations across the globe. Religion prior to this period tended to be fairly uniform in the various cultures covering the Earth; but during this period, these civilizations dramatically modified their understanding of the sacred into a religious perspective that was significantly different from what had been present in the previous 20,000 or more years of human religious thought and behavior.

Specifically, Jaspers demonstrated that prior to this Axial Age, in what we will call pre-Axial religion, we find that religion throughout the world tended to contain some combination of the following elements:

- Belief that Spirit was found in multiple entities, some being presences in nature, others being personified deities in a "heavenly" realm.
- Sacrifice was the primary behavior that established a relationship between the spirits and the human realm. Animals, plants, and even humans were sacrificed to the sacred powers in the belief that in return for such sacrifice, the spirits/gods would bestow benefits on the sacrificing parties.
- The human relationship with the sacred was understood primarily in terms of power; divine beings were powerful beings who were approached with fear and trembling.
- Divine beings often acted in a very capricious manner, displaying qualities such as anger, jealousy, favoritism, etc. Gods, in other words, were not seen as exemplary beings.
- Morality had little to do with how humans related to the realm of the spirits.
- Acting in a religious manner was largely a matter of following rules about giving to the gods what they wanted in order to avoid divine wrath and hopefully (though not in any guaranteed sense) secure divine protection.

In a nutshell, in the pre-Axial era humans recognized the presence of an invisible, powerful spiritual presence in the world, but they understood this spiritual reality as something that was primarily a source of power, and something that was related to through the performance of sacrifices. Moral qualities (kindness, generosity, compassion, justness, etc.) were neither seen as part of the nature of spiritual reality nor an important aspect of religious behavior.

And then things dramatically changed, over the span of about five centuries (a remarkably short time in the larger context of the history of the human species) – in China, in India, in the Mediterranean civilizations – in a remarkable manner which would result in a radically different type of spirituality. This change would produce the great World Religions that are still with us today: Judaism, Christianity, Islam,[11] Hinduism, Buddhism, Confucianism, and Daoism all emerged during this period, in what Jaspers coined "Axial Age" religion, based on the notion that it seemed as if humanity was collectively pivoting on an axis and turning to a very different understanding of the spiritual dimension of reality.

More specifically, it was during this period that we see a shift away from understanding the sacred as a capricious and threatening power and toward a perception of Spirit as the unitive embodiment of all perfections. During the Axial Age, belief in multiple sacred spirits or deities tends to move toward a sense of the unitary nature of Spirit. In the monotheisms of the Abrahamic traditions, in the non-dualism of the Hindu Brahman, in the all-encompassing Buddhist concepts of Shunyata, Tathata, and Dharmakaya, and in the Chinese Dao, we see an evolution away from a sense that the sacred is a scattered reality to an awareness of some sort of unity or oneness. This is the period of the rise of monotheisms in the West and the rise of non-dualisms in the East. In the Mediterranean world, the old gods clearly are in the process of receding by the time you get to the Temple period in Judaism, while in Asia the multiform sense of deity never completely disappears but rather becomes incorporated in the larger picture as part of a larger Oneness.

But along with this movement toward an awareness of the unitary nature of spiritual reality, we also find a dramatic shift in the understanding of the qualities of that sacred reality. *Spirit becomes moral* during the Axial Age. Sacred reality is no longer characterized by capricious, petty, insolent, vindictive behavior, but rather is understood as the repository of moral perfection. Rather than gods acting like immoral humans, the Axial Age sees a morally perfect spiritual reality which is the source of all human virtues. Spirit is now associated with love, compassion, kindness, justness, and other moral virtues. And given this new awareness of the sacred, humanity's understanding of how it should relate to the sacred also changes. *Sacrifice is gradually replaced by virtuous behavior* as the fundamental spiritual practice. Whereas in pre-Axial religion, morality was at best secondary to the performance of ritual sacrifices, in Axial religion the role of sacrifice gradually diminishes and is replaced by the importance of leading a life based on moral virtues.

If we look at religions across the globe in, say 3000 BCE, we find people offering sacrifices to a collection of rather unpredictable spiritual beings in return for protection from harm. If we look at religions across the globe in the first century CE, we often (although not exclusively) find people endeavoring to lead virtuous lives in accordance with the will of a benevolent and all-powerful deity or force.

Of course, this short account of the shift from pre-Axial to Axial religion is an oversimplification of the complexities of religious life during that period, but the point that we're trying to make, even in this simplified account, is that *religion changed*, and changed dramatically during this period. And, to finally return to the point that led us to a consideration of the Axial Age religion, if we have definitive evidence that human awareness of the sacred changed radically in the past, *why should we assume (as many apparently do) that the human understanding of Spirit stopped evolving around 2000 years ago?* Human awareness of the sacred dimension of reality clearly changed radically from the birth of human self-awareness to the beginning of the Christian era... and if so, why should we think that that evolving awareness would have stopped at that point? That much of the world's population subscribes to this scenario of a religious awareness that is stuck somewhere around the first century or so is clearly demonstrated by the manner in which people from all of the major faiths look to texts that were written during the Axial Age for knowledge about God/Spirit. When a Christian looks to the Bible for an understanding of the nature of God, she or he implicitly affirms that the portrayal of God in that 2000-year-old book is more valuable, meaningful, valid, etc., than what a person living in today's world can know about God. The Buddhist who looks to the teaching of the Buddha from the 6th century BCE commits the same error, knowingly or not, of acting as if human insight into the nature of the sacred can only be found in books that record alleged teachings from 2500 years ago.

Frankly, this might appear to an objective outside observer to be a bit bizarre. There is no compelling reason to presume that human religious consciousness developed and changed dramatically up until 2000 years ago, and then ceased to develop at all. Human awareness of spiritual reality, like all kinds of human knowledge, evolves over time, influenced by a myriad of cultural and contextual factors. But it does change. It does evolve. Human beings have changed since the first century; our awareness of the sacred has changed as well. It makes no more sense to consider the Bible or the *Bhagavad Gita* as the sole authoritative source for spiritual knowledge than it does to consider Ptolemy's work as a valid source for knowledge of astronomy or Galen's work as a guide for the practice of 21st century medicine.

In this context, we argue that the problem with the widespread disbelief that we find today is not religion itself, but rather adherence to an antiquated type of religion which is no longer credible to much of the 21st century population. And as we shall lay out in subsequent chapters, the challenge is to construct the elements of a religion that *is* credible to someone who is fully informed by a 21st century sensibility, both intellectually and morally. As philosopher J.L. Schellenberg asks, "Is there a form of religion appropriate to our place in evolutionary time?"[12] In the following pages, we hope to convince the reader that there is, even though its contours are in a very early stage of development and will require development and elaboration in the coming years, decades, and centuries (religion changes, but it changes *slowly*).

So this – finally – brings us to the larger point of this chapter: *it's OK if you can't accept the stories in those ancient religious books.* It's OK if you just can't accept the ideas found in those ancient texts. You don't have to feel guilty about reading the story of Jonah in the belly of the whale and saying, "That's ridiculous." In fact, we would suggest that it's a good thing to openly admit that you cannot accept it. It's always a good thing to be intellectually honest with yourself, and unfortunately many people continue to sacrifice their intellectual honesty because they mistakenly feel that to question the literal veracity of anything in the Bible (or Qur'an or Gita) would be irreligious or heretical. And many others, refusing to sacrifice their intellectual honesty, sacrifice their religious faith instead, believing (again, mistakenly) that being religious requires assent to everything that is found in these ancient texts, as if the only alternative to believing in a literal interpretation of the sacred text is to reject religion completely.

But such a sacrifice is unnecessary, as we shall see as we work our way through the chapters of this book. For now, it will have to suffice to say, and to say definitively and boldly, that being religious does not mean accepting all of the contents of a book written 2000 years ago, and being religious does not need to involve even the slightest sacrifice of one's intellectual integrity: spiritually speaking, one can, so to speak, have one's cake and eat it too. We can maintain our intellectual integrity *and* be religious believers – but only when religion is understood in a manner that is freed from its historical tether to words written centuries ago.

Just as our Axial Age ancestors gradually set aside and rejected the spiritual concepts of pre-Axial religion *but still remained religious,* albeit in the context of the new, Axial Age religions, so we should feel confident that we can set aside the concepts of the Axial Age spirituality which served humanity well for 2000 years but may have reached the end of their relevance, while we remain "believers," but believers of a somewhat different sort: believers in a *post*-Axial Age spirituality that is only in the early stages of emergence from the Axial traditions that it is evolving out of and slowly replacing.

So how does one think about "religion" in the 21st century? Perhaps it's easier to respond to "How does one *not* need to think about religion in the 21st century?" And the answer to that question is: one does not need to think of religion as an unchanging set of beliefs, communicated a very long time ago, and found in a very old book. As to the positive content of what it means to think about religion in the 21st century, we'll be looking at that in the pages ahead.

Chapter 3

How to Think About Sacred Texts

To some, the alternative approach to understanding religion as the product of a prolonged evolutionary process that has been presented above may seem quite objectionable to traditional believers because it situates religion in a space that is not necessarily grounded in a sacred text of some sort. The Christian might be disturbed at the suggestion that it's not necessary to assent to whatever is found in the Bible. The orthodox Jew will be offended at the suggestion that the holy Word of the Lord as found in the Torah can be disregarded. The devout Muslim, especially of the fundamentalist persuasion, is likely to be intensely outraged and condemn this author for heresy for suggesting that a religious person does not need to assent to every passage found in the Qur'an. Asian traditions tend to be considerably less defensive about challenges to the literal interpretation of their sacred texts, but nonetheless it is likely that there will be Buddhists and Hindus who read this and are troubled by the assertion that one can lead a legitimately spiritual life without agreeing with the full content of texts such as the Pali sutras (the oldest Buddhist texts, and presumably the closet thing we have to the original teachings of the Buddha) or the Vedas (the oldest Hindu texts, believed to be delivered to the ancient sage Manu from the gods).

We are suggesting that it's possible to look at sacred texts differently, in a manner that preserves one's intellectual and moral integrity while still recognizing that there is much of value in these books which have retained their influence over the span of many centuries. Of course, talking about sacred texts or Holy Scriptures is a complicated and daunting task, given that sacred texts differ from one tradition to another and that the content of such texts sometimes consists of a bewildering array of quite different types of material. With regard to the first point, for instance, there obviously is a difference between a book like the Bible, which (even if, as a whole, it is interpreted as the Word of God) contains the voices of multiple writers, and the Buddhist sutras, which are understood to be the sayings of one person, the Buddha (with a few exceptions which are attributed to a disciple). Then again, we have the Qur'an, which is understood by Muslims as being the words spoken by the Prophet Muhammed, but dictated to him by the angel Gabriel, based on (in some Muslim theologies) a heavenly version of the very same text.

With reference to content, the difference is obvious between the Buddhist sutras, which for the most part simply contain teachings, with little reference to and no importance placed on, events, and the Bible, which contains all sorts of diverse material. In the Bible we find creation stories, laws, histories, genealogies, hymns (Psalms), moral aphorisms (Proverbs), philosophical speculation (Ecclesiastes, Job), and theology.

In light of the diverse nature of sacred texts, we need to be cautious about making generalizations, but in the remarks that follow we believe that the observations can be applied across the board to texts from different traditions.

First, it's important to note at the outset that our intent here is not to completely negate the value of traditional sacred texts, but rather to frame our understanding of those texts in a broader context that takes into consideration the historical and cultural perspectives that are an integral part of the contemporary intellectual, spiritual and moral consciousness. Sacred texts should be looked at with complete intellectual honesty, and this means that, regardless of whatever spiritual inspiration might have been involved in their creation, they also are the product of the same sort of influences that all texts are subject to: the influences of the culture they are written in, the historical circumstances prevalent at the time of their production, the personality (or personalities) of their author(s), etc. Hence, we are saying that *sacred texts do not need to be interpreted literally.* It's OK to say that you don't believe that the sun stood still in the sky during Joshua's attack on Jericho. It's OK to say that you don't believe that the Buddha traveled from India to Ceylon by levitation. It's OK to say that you can't believe the Torah's account of God commanding the Hebrews to kill all of the men, women, and children in a Canaanite village. It's OK to say that you don't believe that the Quranic passage in which Muhammed states that it is acceptable to hit your wife before going to bed is a revelation from God. Indeed, one might understandably ask, what kind of God would countenance such things? *It's OK to say all this, and still be a believer in the existence of a spiritual reality. Being a believer need not be tied to blanket acceptance of texts that are two millennia old.*

Setting aside the requirement of a literalist interpretation of sacred texts frees us from the two main problems that lead many people today to shun such works: the sacrifice of the intellect and the sacrifice of moral integrity.

The first common hindrance to accepting the value of sacred texts is an intellectual one: sacred texts sometime contain statements that reflect a view of reality that has been convincingly demonstrated to be antiquated and/or false by modern science. This is not to say that science is the final arbiter in defining the nature of reality, but within the sphere that it legitimately operates (space/time, material reality, the realm of "stuff"), science does indeed function as the definitive source for establishing truth about the nature of that dimension of reality. Science tells us things about the nature of the physical universe, truths about time, space, matter and energy, which we have good reason to believe are indeed universal truths, applicable to all times and all places. Consequently, when we read in sacred texts accounts of events and descriptions about the nature of the world that run counter to scientific knowledge, we understandably are inclined to reject those texts. To do otherwise could only be done at the price of sacrificing our intellectual integrity.

An intellectually honest person in the 21st century simply cannot accept as true such notions as that the world was created in seven 24-hour days, the sun stood still during the battle of Jericho, a body of water parted to allow one tribe to pass through and then reconnected to drown the pursuers of that tribe, and so on and so on. We use examples here from the Bible since we assume that that is the sacred text which most of our readers are familiar with, but similar examples could be cited from the Qur'an, *Bhagavad Gita*, Buddhist sutras, etc. Put simply, the 21st century person who wishes to preserve his/her intellectual integrity should not accept those accounts in these ancient texts which simply contradict or defy the nature of the reality as revealed to us by science.

But there is another, equally disturbing aspect of sacred texts that presents a challenge to the contemporary reader, and that is the challenge to one's *moral* integrity. There are accounts of events in sacred texts that are presented as reflecting the will of God, events that are portrayed in a spiritually positive light, but these events are morally repugnant to contemporary consciousness, and it is the moral repulsiveness of these passages as much as the intellectual falsity of other passages that drives the modern reader away from them.

The contemporary unbeliever looks, for instance, to the account of God commanding the Hebrews to enter into a Canaanite village and slay everyone – men, women, and children[13] – and reacts along the lines of, "If this is what God is like, I want nothing to do with Him. I will not lower my sense of morality to that level." One sometimes reads sacred texts and comes away with the sense that the spiritual being portrayed in the text is morally inferior to humans. One comes away with a sense of being morally superior to the Being portrayed in the text as the maker of the universe. Quite understandably, who would want to make a commitment to a being whose moral constitution seemed to be characterized by violence, jealousy, pettiness, vengefulness, and other such qualities that mere mortals recognize as qualities that one should strive to eliminate?

But that is precisely what we are saying: *you don't need to interpret these books literally.* When you find something that is objectionable, whether from an intellectual or moral point of view, reflect on it carefully, and if in all honesty you still find it objectionable, then dispense with it. Just as Muslim astronomy from a thousand years ago had valid observations mixed in with serious errors, likewise sacred texts from centuries ago contain perspectives on the nature of reality and the nature of human moral behavior that in some cases are still legitimate, and in other cases are simply outmoded and have no place in the spiritual worldview of contemporary believers. Separate the wheat from the chaff, and do so without hesitation and without guilt. It's OK to say that you just don't buy into certain parts of sacred texts.

However, to say that a sacred text should not be interpreted as the literal word of God which must be accepted in its entirety without the slightest alteration, is not to discredit that text completely. Quite to the contrary, a text can be recognized to be the product of various worldly influences, full of factually false information, and full of events that are morally offensive to the contemporary reader, and still contain profound, sublime, and entirely legitimate insights regarding matters of spirituality. In other words, with regard to the authority of sacred texts, we're not dealing with an either/or scenario, as in either a text is literally the Word of God and is 100% authoritative, or a text is not literally the word of God and has no authority at all. Rather, we are suggesting that an intellectually honest assessment of sacred texts reveals that they are indeed, at least in part, human products influenced by cultural and historical factors, *but they still have value as special resources for our understanding about the nature of the Sacred.*

So even after recognizing that they are imperfect, inconsistent, and even sometimes contradictory products of the human effort to articulate that which cannot be easily and clearly articulated, the value of these ancient texts remains. Indeed, to one who wishes to dismiss the likes of the Bible and Qur'an entirely, it is reasonable to ask *why* these texts have been around so long if they are so obviously flawed. Their persistence over centuries and across multiple cultures would seem to suggest that there is indeed something special about these books.

The question of how and why these texts have maintained their authoritative nature is a complex one, and thoroughly exploring that issue is beyond the scope of this work. However, a few points can be made which hopefully will encourage the present-day skeptic to recognize that, not only did it make sense for our ancestors to revere these texts as revelations, but it also makes sense to continue to look to them for spiritual guidance, even after we have rejected a literal mode of interpretation and recognized that there is content in these texts that cannot be accepted by the contemporary believer. In other words, there's no need to throw out the proverbial baby with the bathwater.

For starters, it's important to consider that ancient texts use language which made sense to the authors of those texts, even if that language seems rather odd to us today. Living in a culture in which kingly rule was the only known model for political authority, it makes sense to use kingship and all that it's associated with as a set of symbols to describe the greatness of God. Indeed, a writer can only draw from the cultural experience and related symbols that are available to him/her. We need to look at ancient texts with a certain historical understanding that allows us to accept that the language used by the authors was, in a sense, the best that they had to work with at the time. And we need to look beyond the specific word/symbol and ask, *what was the meaning that the symbol was attempting to convey?*

When we start looking for the meaning behind the symbols, rather than taking the words of ancient texts in a literal and non-symbolic manner, a whole new world of interpretation opens up, and we can see that there are deep spiritual truths expressed in the language of the ancient authors. Consider, for instance, the story of Abraham.

God asks Abraham to leave the security of his settled home in Ur, and travel far away to Canaan, where God promises that he will deliver a son to Abraham and his wife, Sarah. Through this son, God promises to create a special, chosen people who will prosper for many generations in the land of Canaan. Abraham and Sarah dutifully leave home and travel to Canaan, but they experience doubt and despair as the years go by, far past the age of childbearing, and no children are born to them. Has God broken his promise? But they are filled with joy when, well into their 90s, Sarah conceives and bears a son, Isaac. And yet, just when it appears that God has faithfully fulfilled his promise, he issues a shocking new command: Abraham is told to sacrifice Isaac, his only son, the son promised by God, the son through whom God had promised innumerable blessed future generations. Abraham dutifully takes Isaac to the top of a mountain, builds an altar, straps Isaac to it, prepares the wood for the fire, and is about to light the sacrificial fire which will kill his only beloved son when – *finally* – God intervenes. At the last moment, God speaks to Abraham and retracts the command to sacrifice Isaac, who is replaced by a lamb that supernaturally appears as his substitute.

What is the modern reader to make of this story? Most likely, at first glance, it evokes a sense of revulsion. For starters, there is the apparently capricious nature of this God, who changes his mind and seems to be toying with these people. He asks Abraham and Sarah to leave the security of their home in return for the promise of a new land and a blessed son. And yet he then makes them wait and wait and wait – to the point where they have aged beyond childbearing years, and hence would have good reason to believe that God had lied to them. It was a false promise. Imagine the many decades of hope mingled with doubt, followed by the eventual resignation of despair that the couple must have experienced. And then, to make matters simultaneously better and worse, Sarah conceives. Certainly the prospect of finally having their son must have been joyful, but would there not have also been thoughts along the lines of: God, why did you wait so long? Why did you put us through so many years of doubt? Why did you destroy all our hopes before delivering what you had promised? And then, as if God's behavior wasn't bad enough already, he adds to his repertoire of horrible behavior by commanding Abraham to sacrifice Isaac, about which any sensible and sensitive contemporary reader will ask: What kind of God would ask a father to murder his only son? Especially a son greatly treasured because he had arrived so unexpectedly late in life? Especially a son who had been promised by God? The traditional believer might try to lighten the blame on God by pointing out that, at the end of the story, God revokes the command to sacrifice Isaac. But to the modern reader, doesn't that make God's behavior even worse? Does God not appear to be something of a sadist, leading Abraham to the brink of the murder of his only son, and then at the last moment saying, "Oops, just kidding"?

So clearly there is much to be morally offended by in this Bible story. And yet, one might ask, why then is it there? How could a story of such a capricious and malevolent deity find its way into a sacred book and remain in that book – indeed, even be treasured as a foundational story in that book, for generations afterward?

This is a tricky issue, with many dimensions for exploration. For starters, there is the need to recognize that every sacred text (as with any human text) is generated in a particular cultural setting, and consequently with ideas, values, and beliefs that are unique to and deeply embedded in that culture, even while simultaneously expressing broader and perhaps universal truths. Indeed, one of the challenges in reading sacred texts in a mature and insightful manner is the challenge of sorting out the timeless wheat from the cultural chaff, so to speak, or wading through often various cultural peculiarities in order to dig down to the broader, more culture-free insights that functioned as the basis for identifying the material as worthy of inclusion in a sacred text in the first place. In the case of Abraham, the 21st century reader needs to temper his/her revulsion at the notion that God would command Abraham to sacrifice his son with the recognition of the reality that sacrifice of the first-born was a not uncommon practice in cultures from that time and area. We cannot retroactively apply our 21st century mores to a story that is perhaps 3000 years old, although we certainly can and should read such a story in the context of the moral and spiritual perspective that we currently share, thus creating the challenge of, again, sorting out the wheat from the chaff.

But understanding, appreciating, and deriving meaning from ancient sacred texts involves other and more subtle approaches as well. This includes recognizing that the point of a story is often not the story itself – the actual facts – but rather the meaning conveyed by the events of the story. Indeed, recognizing that a sacred text is not exactly meant to be a history book but rather uses stories to convey spiritual truths that transcend history is a key to appreciating the value of these texts that we might otherwise find strange and ethically repugnant if interpreted as literal accounts of actual events. Looking again at the story of Abraham and Isaac, we can interpret it as a tale of a sadistic God who toys with his faithful servant, or we can look at the events of the story as merely a medium for the sake of expressing a larger truth, namely that sometimes spiritual faith requires us to remain faithful to God even when doing so requires us to do something that we do not want to do. Faithfulness to God can be hard, but it is precisely the perseverance shown during that hardship that strengthens faith and our closeness to Spirit.

The German theologian Rudolf Bultmann referred to this mode of interpretation as "demythologizing," which essentially involves looking beyond the specifics of the story (the myth) to the message that is meant to be conveyed by the story. For Christians, this can be applied to various aspects of the life of Jesus. A modern reader might find it difficult to believe in the notion of God becoming human and literally entering into the womb of a woman and being born as a human being. But if one looks beyond the mythic details to the message that Christians derived from the Incarnation, we find the notion that the essential nature of Spirit is love, and what better way could one find to mythically express the love of God than in the notion that the omnipotent, pure, perfect Spirit would suffer the pain and indignity of entering into the realm of blood, flesh, and tissue for the sake of bringing salvation to humankind? Again, one does not need to accept the story as literally true to appreciate the beauty of the message expressed in the myth.

This mode of interpretation is perhaps illustrated nowhere better than in the classic Aesop's fables. Needless to say, it's pretty unlikely that Aesop ever witnessed a race between a tortoise and a hare, or indeed if anyone ever witnessed such an absurd spectacle. But the *event* is not the point: rather, the point is the *meaning* conveyed by the story, a meaning that expresses a truth about how life works that, in a sense, is just as much a "reality" as any actual race could ever be. Not true in a literal, historical sense, but deeply true in an existential sense.

Of course, the reader might ask: Then why didn't they just say what they meant? Why create these convoluted stories when they could have just stated the meaning in simple terms, such as God is Love?

This is a complex and challenging question, and once again, it requires us to put ourselves in the shoes of those who wrote and collected the texts, recognizing that in certain ways their way of perceiving the world was different from the way that most 21st century humans perceive it. Specifically, we need to recognize that in pre-modern cultures, the distinction between what was "real" and what was "not real" was not nearly as carefully defined as it is for us today. We make a clear distinction between myth and historical fact, but that is a distinction that apparently was not made in many pre-modern cultures. As Reza Aslan states,

> like most people in the ancient world, (they) did not make a sharp distinction between myth and reality; the two were intimately tied together in their spiritual experience. That is to say, they were less interested in what actually happened than in what it meant. It would have been perfectly normal – indeed, expected – for a writer in the ancient world to tell tales of gods and heroes whose fundamental facts would have been recognized as false but whose underlying message would be seen as true.[14]

Put a bit differently, the distinction between fact and meaning was not a hard and clearly defined one in pre-modern cultures. Things that "happened" were understood in the context of a meaning that they expressed, and the details of the "actual" event were not as important as the broader meaning expressed in the event. Consequently, changes in the account of the details of an event over the span of years or, even more so, generations, was not seen as problematic, since the meaning, not the event, was what was important. This is, of course, a very different way of thinking about reality than what we are accustomed to in contemporary times, but it is a way of looking at what happens in the world that was universal in pre-modern cultures (see, for instance, the work of historian of religion, Mircea Eliade, or mythologist Joseph Campbell).[15]

This perspective on how pre-modern people thought about "reality" does not, of course, explain in detail how any particular sacred text came into existence. But it does provide a general framework for understanding how certain writings were able to acquire and retain the status of "sacred" even though they contained internal contradictions, lacked historical grounding, conflicted with known facts, etc.

In the face of the persistence of these sacred texts over the span of, in some cases, over 2000 years, we would do well to treat them with due respect, even if our reaction to parts of them is a bit incredulous or even at times offended. We should recognize that, however opaque the value and meaning of the text might be to us today, there was some reason that those words came to be granted the status of a sacred text and retained that elevated status over many generations. As indicated in the earlier part of this chapter, as spiritual persons we do not need to blindly accept the teachings found in a book merely because previous generations have identified it as in some sense revelatory or sacred, but at the same time we should maintain a sense of respect toward these texts and recognize that there is something there worthy of our attention.

So how should one think about sacred texts in the 21st century? First, it's OK to recognize the human origins of sacred texts, and secondly, it's OK to not interpret them literally. It's OK, in the context of a contemporary intellectual and moral perspective, to sort through sacred texts and distinguish between those parts which are no longer tenable and those parts which have enduring meaning and value. Being religious in the 21st century means adopting a critical, but nonetheless appreciative, approach to these ancient documents, recognizing that while there may be ways in which they point us to a sense of the spiritual dimension, there are also parts which no longer are meaningful or acceptable to 21st century believers.

Chapter 4

How to Think About Ritual

So sacred texts continue to exist and continue to be revered, often in an uncritical, "blind faith" style, despite the various insights of literary criticism, comparative religions, and other fields that have called into question such an uncritical acceptance of these texts as an infallible direct communication from the divine. But sacred texts are not the only aspect of traditional, Axial Age religion that has persisted despite greatly straining the credulity and sensibility of thoughtful people who are open to the sacred but unwilling to sacrifice their intellect and common sense in the process: ritual has also survived. Ritual in a bewildering assortment of expressions and modalities. Ritual that believers cling to with deep faith and affection, but often little understanding of the meaning or origin of the actions that they are taking. To the contemporary seeker incorporating what we know as citizens of the early 21st century, how do we make sense of this thing called ritual? How do we think about ritual in the 21st century?

Some would argue that, at least within the Biblical religions (Judaism, Christianity, and Islam), it is ritual which often is the factor that initially turns potential contemporary believers away from the faith. Even to one who is willing to adopt the broad, open, non-literalist approach to belief and sacred texts as described above, the thought of engaging in a series of repetitive movements and vocalizations with no clear understanding of the purpose and no confidence in the efficacy of said rituals is enough to keep such potential believers away from embarking on the spiritual quest within the ritual-laden traditional religions.

So what is ritual, and what is the source of its survival? And more importantly for our purposes, how can one think about ritual today in such a way that it does not function as a deterrent to the thoughtful and well-meaning person who is looking for a spiritual path that does not involve a sacrifice of the mind or heart?

Perhaps by way of a preliminary remark, it should be stated that we won't be saying as much about ritual as we will about other aspects of religion, for the simple reason that this author confesses that he is one of those who simply don't "get" ritual very well. I've spent years participating in all sorts of rituals – mostly Christian (Lutheran), but also Buddhist and Hindu – and I have to confess that, whatever ritual is supposed to do, just doesn't happen for me. So please interpret the following remarks accordingly, and I'm afraid that you might have to look elsewhere for a better example of a contemporary way of understanding ritual.

So what do we mean by ritual? Despite the seemingly endless variations, the practice that we identify as ritual can be described as a pre-defined set of formal movements and vocalizations. In terms of body movement and position, this can include standing, sitting, kneeling, prostrating, walking and running (the Zen practice of *kinhin*), hand gestures (the sign of the cross), facing a specific direction and/or person or object, and countless other pre-established, stylized movements. Vocalizations can include practices such as singing, chanting, recitation, responsive reading, shouting, praying, etc. Order and precision are important parts of ritual, so timing, spatial orientation, and accurate repetition are all important elements. All sorts of objects can be incorporated into rituals: water (a universal part of ritual), wine, incense, smoke, fire, feathers, etc. In all cases, however, a common thread in all aspects of ritual is the absence of spontaneity and improvisation. Ritual is not a spontaneous outpouring of words, gestures, music, etc. Rather, ritual derives its authority and power from its established order, structure, and predictability.

But defining ritual is really not the issue: I suspect that the reader knows ritual when she sees it. The question for our purposes is, what's behind ritual? Why do religious people do such things? And is there any way that the contemporary semi-believer can make sense of this stuff?

Of course, there is no simple answer to the question of why ritual is a universal element of religious behavior, and students of religion (many of them practitioners as well) have offered many theories. In some sense, the certainty of ritual for believers of a tradition ("it's always been done this way, and always will be done this way") offers a sense of assurance in a world of constant change and uncertainty. To the extent that belief in God involves belief in an unchanging reality, ritual is in a sense a physical and visible manifestation or symbol of that unchangeable nature. In some cases, ritual enhances the awareness of the divine by functioning as a remembrance, and sometimes reenactment, of an important sacred event (as, for example, in the Christian Eucharist which is both a remembrance and reenactment of the Last Supper). In other cases, rituals are performed simply because the community believes that God has commanded them to do so, as, for instance, in the Muslim practice of *salat,* or five times-daily prayer. In Confucianism, the consistent, precise, and detailed performance of ritual is an important aspect of maintaining a right relationship with the larger cosmic order, or Dao, and a manifestation of the Confucian virtue of *li,* or propriety.

Andrew Newberg, a neurologist who has attempted to develop an understanding of how brain activity and spirituality interact, has used brain imaging made with scanning devices such as MRIs in an attempt to identify what happens in the brain when humans participate in various aspects of religious behavior, including ritual.[16] His explanation of the relationship between brain activity and religious ritual is rather complicated and quite hypothetical. For our purposes, going into the details of what Newberg has observed in the brains of individuals participating in ritual activity is not necessary, but what is important is his belief that humans are "hardwired" to be religious, and part of that hardwiring includes the satisfaction that comes from ritual. In other words, when we participate in repetitive, formal, stylized gestures and vocalizations accompanied by cognitive representations that relate these actions to something that has deep meaning, there are certain neurological events that occur in the brain that are innately appealing to the human consciousness. Our brain has evolved in such a way that ritual behavior triggers certain activity in the brain that is experienced as desirable.

That ritual is a "natural" part of the human makeup is supported by the survival of ritual even in nonreligious institutions, and even more so its survival in completely secular and even anti-religious cultures. The presence of rituals in secular aspects of our life is so obvious and in such abundance as to hardly require examples: playing the national anthem at the beginning of a sporting event, singing the school alma mater at college functions, pledging allegiance to the flag to begin the school day or a government meeting, fraternity rituals, the elaborate protocols for installing new rulers, even in Communist societies, and countless other occasions where a repetitive, highly structured, pre-established behavior with no obvious utilitarian value is routinely practiced in nonreligious elements of societies across the globe.

The enduring nature of ritual was sharply illustrated during the more strictly Marxist years of the former Soviet Union, where we find a society that was overtly anti-religious engaging in public rituals that venerated past leaders, historic events, and state ideology through displays of repetitive acts that were thoroughly soaked in the essence of ritual.

But getting to our main objective, which is not to speculate on the origin, nature, and function of ritual, but rather to consider how the contemporary semi-believer should look at ritual, what can we make of this complex and somewhat puzzling aspect of religion?

In simple terms, I would suggest that we really don't need to make anything of it. Ritual exists, and some people are attracted to it. Others are not. For some, and for a multitude of different reasons, ritual provides a means of feeling closer to sacred reality, however that might be defined. For others, however, ritual offers no such connection to spiritual reality. It leaves them unmoved. The sights and gestures and sounds and smells and various accoutrements seem empty of meaning.

But before dispensing with ritual as a nonessential element in the emerging new spirituality of the 21st century, we should pause to consider another possibility: perhaps even though it is the case that existing ritual is no longer meaningful to many semi-believers, the emergence of a *new* set of rituals might recover the sense of meaning and emotional connection with the sacred that once was associated with traditional rituals. Ritual is always derived from or connected to a belief system. Existing ritual is connected to the belief systems that developed in Axial Age religions. For example, the Christian ritual of the Eucharist is derived from the belief that the only Son of God instituted this practice at the Last Supper. For those who no longer find the anthropomorphic symbolism of a Son of God or a kingly God in a human body to be credible, or for those who question the historicity of this founding event, that ritual loses its meaning.

But if, as we suggested earlier, we are moving out of Axial Age spirituality and into a yet-to-be defined post-axial spirituality, perhaps it is the case that a *new* set of rituals will emerge from the belief system that evolves in this developing post-Axial spirituality. If this is the case, the problem is not so much that ritual in general has lost its impact, but rather that the rituals connected to a no longer tenable way of thinking about the sacred have lost their impact, leaving open the possibility that ritual could once again be meaningful if derived from a tenable belief system. Indeed, the survival of some sort of ritual would be expected in light of Newberg's theory that the brain is hardwired to develop and respond to ritual. However, that response to ritual is always in tandem with a tenable belief system, and to the extent that most existing rituals are attached to outmoded Axial Age concepts of Spirit, ritual (of the religious type) will only regain its hold on the human psyche when a new set of rituals have emerged out of the still evolving concept of Spirit in post-Axial spirituality.[17]

So perhaps there are two questions to consider: How to think about existing ritual and how to think about the potential for an emerging post-Axial spirituality ritual. With reference to the first question: ritual is a human product, created in the context of a specific culture in a specific time period in which specific, culturally-conditioned beliefs serve as the underlying basis for that ritual. Simply recognizing that ritual is a human creation, albeit a very special human creation to the extent that it is inspired by some sort of awareness of the sacred, removes the aura from ritual and hopefully removes the fear that there is something terribly wrong with not performing it. As we've said above, it's OK to stop thinking of the sacred in Axial Age anthropomorphic terms, and as a corollary to that position, it's OK to break away from Axial-Age-based ritual. No guilt, no sense of impending doom, no sense of being spiritually negligent need accompany the abandonment of traditional ritual. It made sense at one point in human development; it doesn't seem to make as much sense at this point in human development in which many people now find themselves. "Spiritual but not religious" is often used with reference to beliefs, but it applies equally to ritual. One can recognize the reality of Spirit in terms that are meaningful and believable to the human species in the early 21st century, without feeling any commitment to the multitude of ritual acts which may have had a deep sense of sacred importance to earlier generations, but which to many contemporaries no longer function to connect them to an awareness of Spirit.

As to the future of ritual in a world of post-Axial spirituality, who knows what will evolve over the decades or even more likely, centuries, as the transition to "what comes next" in human spirituality emerges. Some have speculated that the new spirituality will largely be ritual-free, seeing ritual as the vestige of the slowly dying remnant of an earlier period in the development of human consciousness. Others, pointing to the perseverance of ritual in secular societies and the evidence (admittedly somewhat weak because of its highly speculative nature) that the brain is hardwired to respond positively to ritual, suggest that rituals of some sort will always be present in human spiritual life, even though the rituals of the new spirituality have not yet developed and are likely to be quite different than those associated with traditional religion.

So how should the 21st century citizen who is open to a sense of Spirit but unmoved by existing religions think about ritual, in such a way that there is no sacrifice of her intellectual or moral integrity?

Simply accept that it's OK to abandon the ritual of existing religions if they are no longer meaningful to you, without guilt or fear of damnation. Remember that these rituals developed in a cultural setting where they were meaningful (and still are meaningful to many people), but that cultural setting has changed dramatically. So it's OK to set aside those rituals, but be open to the appearance of new expressions of ritual which will be more attuned to the beliefs of a post-Axial, 21st century, global spirituality.

If ritual in its present form seems empty and pointless to you, that's OK... don't do it. But be open to the possibility that new rituals will eventually emerge to replace those which can now be set aside.

Chapter 5

How to Think About Doctrine

Every contemporary religion claims to offer a true understanding of the nature of God or Spirit, an understanding of God that is known by means of a sacred text or texts, and a set of rituals that are believed to place one in a right relationship with that God. We've looked at those aspects of religion above, and suggested how the contemporary person of faith can, without abandoning either her intellectual integrity or her sense of leading a spiritual life, set aside much of what is taught and required by current traditions. But, of course, there are other elements to traditional religion, and as we continue our deconstruction of the components of traditional, Axial Age religion, the component that we will examine in this chapter is doctrine or dogma.

In a technical sense, and depending on which specific religion or denomination that we're looking at, doctrine and dogma are not exactly the same thing. One might argue, for instance, that by codifying in a detailed, systematic, and legalistic manner a wide range of beliefs that a Catholic must accept, Roman Catholicism is much more of a dogmatic faith than, say, an evangelical church that preaches the need to simply accept Jesus Christ as one's personal savior but doesn't formally articulate much in the way of required beliefs beyond that fundamental one. And in between, we have the "creedal" churches of mainstream Protestantism (Lutheran, Presbyterian, Episcopalian, Methodist, etc.) which, while insisting on a somewhat smaller set of required beliefs than is the case in Catholicism, treat the elements of the Creed (originally the Nicene, but today more commonly expressed in the Apostles) as required belief in a manner that clearly functions with the strength normally associated with dogmatic Catholicism.

For our purposes, however, we will not quibble about the subtle and often fluid differences in meaning between dogma and doctrine. We'll stick with "doctrine," recognizing that in many cases in everyday thinking doctrine and dogma are treated synonymously, and at least for our purposes can be used interchangeably.

So what do we mean by doctrine? As we'll use the term here, doctrine is simply a set of beliefs taught by a religion as definitively true, and necessarily accepted for participation as a member of that faith, and perhaps most importantly, necessarily believed in as a condition for salvation.

Religious doctrine has a close relationship with sacred texts. In many cases, doctrines are claimed to be drawn in a direct and explicit manner from a sacred text (e.g., the Christian doctrine of the virgin birth drawn from two of the Gospel narratives – even though, curiously, it's not even mentioned in the other two Gospels). In other cases, doctrine is seen as a logical extension of an idea that is clearly *implied* by the sacred text. Most mainline Christian churches, for instance, consider belief in the Trinitarian nature of God as Father, Son and Holy Spirit to be an essential dogmatic belief that all Christians must accept, and yet there is no explicit statement in the Bible that describes God in these precise terms. Christians (Unitarians excepted) argue, however, that the Trinitarian nature of God is so clearly implied by passages in Scripture that its doctrinal status cannot be questioned.

But whether or not one is convinced that the doctrine of the Trinity is found in the Bible becomes somewhat irrelevant if, as we've discussed above, the infallible, divinely-inspired nature of the Bible (as well as other sacred texts) is no longer considered to be the mandatory starting point for one's religious faith. If the words of the Bible come directly from God, or have supernaturally inspired their authors to write infallibly, then the doctrine that flows from that sacred text does indeed command a certain authority. But we're suggesting just the opposite: a reasonable and honest assessment of the Bible reveals it to be a human product – often inspiring (though occasionally very disturbing) – but nonetheless, a fallible human creation. Consequently, the doctrines that are based on that sacred text are equally subject to interpretation and error. Like the Bible, church doctrine can contain inspiring ideas that reflect meaningful ideas about God, morality, the human spirit, etc., but that is all that doctrine represents. At bottom, it's a human product. In a sense, *it represents the best that people living in a specific place in a specific time in a specific cultural context could come up with in trying to explain the inexplicable, in trying to demystify that which is, by definition, always a Mystery.*

Of course, merely by virtue of its age and, for most believers, the hiddenness of its origins, doctrine often acquires a sort of sacred aura. The Apostles and Nicene Creeds, one or the other recited weekly in mainline Christian churches throughout the world, are treated with great solemnity and seriousness, almost perhaps with the same sense of reverence that is given to scripture. Human nature is such that we tend to naturally elevate the status of things that are old… in a sense, the older, the more venerated. To some extent there is a logic in this phenomenon: if an idea or set of ideas (doctrine) has persisted for centuries (indeed, in some cases for over two millennia), that persistence alone would seem to be solid grounds for taking that set of ideas very seriously. But taking a set of ideas seriously, and considering them to be infallible or of divine origin, are two quite different things. The philosophy of Plato and the epics of Homer have similarly withstood the test of time, but we don't therefore conclude that they are supernatural communications from above. We recognize that they are human creations from many centuries ago, and that is precisely how we should perceive doctrine.

The human origin of doctrine becomes what some might characterize as embarrassingly apparent when one actually examines the history of the development of the Christian creeds. The Nicene Creed did not come into existence until a church council was convened by the emperor Constantine around 325, and further revisions were made several decades later at the Council of Constantinople in 381. The Apostles Creed is often considered to have earlier origins, perhaps going back to the second century, but no historical reference occurs to it until 390. Even if we accept the chronologically generous interpretation that an early version of the Apostles Creed existed in the late 2nd century, that dating concedes that the creed did not exist until almost two centuries after the time of Jesus. If being a Christian is dependent on assenting to the Apostles Creed, where did that leave the followers of Jesus for those first two centuries, when no such creed existed?

While the actual origins of the Apostles Creed are obscure, the Nicene Creed is another matter. Its origins date back to 325, when the emperor Constantine called a church council in which leading bishops throughout the Roman Empire gathered together to sort out what exactly constituted being a Christian. At that point in the early history of Christianity, there were multiple interpretations of what a person needed to profess in order to be a true "Christian." Indeed, as Biblical historian Bart Ehrman points out, during the early centuries of the Christian era, prior to the coalescing of spiritual and political power in the figure of the Pope and institution of the Roman Catholic Church, it would be more accurate to speak of *Christianities*, in the plural, rather than a single monolithic Christian faith to which all Christians professed allegiance. Rather than a single, universal, uncontested definition of what constituted Christian faith, in those early centuries there were multiple interpretations of what one needed to believe to be considered a "Christian."[18]

Constantine, in fact, called together the council in 325 out of concern that infighting among the many different groups calling themselves "Christian" was exacerbating the instability of an already unstable Roman Empire. At the time of the first Council, many Christians throughout the Roman Empire understood Jesus as a divine being sent by God, but they did not think of Jesus himself as God. These believers, known as Arian Christians, were followers of the theology of Arius, and constituted a large part of the Christian population of the Empire. By contrast, many believers within the church hierarchy followed the theology of Athanasius, Bishop of Alexandria, who argued that Jesus himself was God, fully God and fully human at the same time.

These differing interpretations of the nature of Jesus led to a long, contentious, and acrimonious church council, at the end of which the Arian interpretation was identified as "heresy" and the Alexandrian interpretation came to be understood as the "orthodox" Christian faith. Our point here is not to explore the details of the theological debate at that council, but rather to point out that what eventually became defined by the Church as "orthodoxy" or "right belief" was in fact the product of a very human and very political process. Christian doctrine, as it has come to be understood by all of the mainline denominations of Christianity today, did not supernaturally come down from Heaven, but rather was the product of a hotly contested debate in the fourth century, long after the time of Jesus. The undeniable historical roots of orthodox doctrine clearly undermine its claim to be deserving of universal assent. Quite to the contrary, what we now call orthodoxy was simply the winning argument in a debate; if circumstances had been different, the content of orthodox Christian doctrine might be quite different today.

The aura that surrounds doctrine is further diminished when one considers that that aura is to some extent a vestige of the authoritarian manner in which adherence to orthodox belief, or doctrine, was enforced for many centuries. This is difficult for 21st century citizens to appreciate, given that in the contemporary West there has developed a separation between church and state that allows for the relatively free exercise of religious belief (or disbelief) and prohibits government enforcement of the beliefs of any specific religion. This church/ state separation is, however, a peculiarly modern phenomenon: for many centuries, the ties between the Christian Church and the apparatus of state authority were exceedingly close and sometimes indistinguishable. For over a thousand years in Europe, belief in the orthodox doctrines of Christianity was enforced by the state or, in some cases, by a Church granted permission to use state-like authority and any means necessary, including imprisonment, torture, and death to punish those who openly proclaimed beliefs other than orthodox doctrine. During these many centuries in the history of Christianity, far more was at stake in the matter of doctrine than merely one's private religious beliefs. Rather, the stakes involved the safety, security, livelihood, and very existence of a person (and his/her family). In such a context, extended over such a long stretch of time, it is easy to see how accepting orthodox church doctrine came to be seen as a life or death matter, and rejecting orthodox doctrine became an act associated with danger to one's very existence.

After the Council of Nicaea, for example, the triumphant Roman Church vigorously persecuted those who continued to assert the Arian position, doing so with the full cooperation of the Roman authorities. Several centuries later, throughout Europe, we have the example of the Inquisition, where professing a doctrine other than that of Christian orthodoxy often led to torture and death.

One of the most egregious examples of the abuse of authority by the Church for the sake of enforcing orthodox doctrine was the so-called Albigensian Crusade. Many readers are likely to associate the Crusades with Church-supported armies raised to win back the Holy Land from Muslim rule. However, one Crusade was launched against other Christians. Specifically, a group known as the Cathars had achieved considerable popularity in southern France by the 12th century. Emphasizing a simple lifestyle, asserting a set of Christian doctrines that in some areas departed from orthodoxy, and rejecting the religious and temporal authority of the Roman Catholic Church, the Cathars thrived in many towns in southern France, supported by both nobles and the general population. After unsuccessful attempts at eliminating the Cathar "heresy" through less forceful means, the Church eventually launched a formal Crusade against these fellow Christians, a Crusade that included the torture, pillaging, and large scale slaughter of thousands of Cathar Christians, all in the name of enforcing belief in what the Church considered to be correct *doctrine*.

Other examples could be cited (the persecution of Luther and Calvin by the Catholic Church and rulers, and, in turn, the Lutherans' and Calvinists' persecution of Anabaptists, for example[19]), but the point should be clear by now: the historical price of not accepting orthodox doctrine was so high that one can easily see how accepting orthodox doctrine became as important as accepting the validity of scripture, and conversely rejection of orthodoxy became an act that could result in dire consequences. With such associations attached to orthodox doctrine for so many centuries, it's not difficult to see how a certain aura has remained attached to orthodoxy. Even in the 21st century where no such danger attaches to dissent from orthodoxy in Christian countries, the lingering sense that doctrine is something that should not be lightly challenged remains.

But leaving aside the impact of the air of false authority that doctrine has retained even after the end of the days of its rigid enforcement, there are other factors which diminish the aura of authority that has surrounded doctrine for many traditional believers. As is the case with sacred texts, doctrine can sometimes seem to be simply outdated, in the sense that it is constructed using a language that might have been meaningful when the doctrine was created, but no longer carries the same meaning in today's world. Doctrine is expressed in language, and that language consists of symbols, and those symbols grow out of and are embedded in social and historical circumstances which simply do not carry the same meaning for the contemporary person as they did for believers in the pre-modern world. Doctrine is, in a sense, an attempt to use language to describe that which is beyond language. It is the use of symbols drawn from our culturally and historically-limited spatiotemporal existence to point toward a reality (God, Spirit) which transcends that existence. Religious language, and the doctrine that is created from it, are a natural product of the culture in which it arises. The use of certain words seems natural and the meaning of symbols obvious to those who are immersed in that symbol-creating culture.

In a culture in which monarchy was the only known form of government, the use of terms drawn from monarchical government (God as King or Prince, sitting on a throne, ruling over subjects) is a natural and spontaneous way to describe the sense of power that is intuitively associated with experience of Spirit. But those words are *only* symbols: they point to a reality (God), but they are not the reality itself. One of the problems with doctrine and its calcification into rigid dogma is the confusion of symbol and reality. To say that Jesus sits at the right hand of God the Father might be a reasonable way of saying something about spiritual reality for people who are living in a culture in which anthropomorphic expressions of Spirit are still dominant, but to use such mundane symbolism in today's culture might strike the contemporary believer as rather perplexing. We just don't think of Spirit as something which assumes a bodily position, or can be characterized as located in a spatial sense. Such symbolic language might have made sense in earlier days, and indeed it apparently made much sense when Christian doctrine was developed 2000 years ago. But those symbols just aren't meaningful today, and – to get to the larger point – *it's OK to reject doctrines that are written in language that no longer conveys the symbolic meaning that it did to previous generations.* It's OK to reject doctrines written in a language that uses symbols that no longer possess the capacity to point to that ultimately indescribable reality which is God or Spirit. If doctrine uses outdated language/symbols, it's understandable that the contemporary believer cannot assent to that doctrine, and indeed rejection of such doctrine is an expression of intellectual and spiritual honesty.

But even aside from the above considerations which diminish the sense of having a duty to accept doctrine, there is another, broader consideration (and one which we will examine in more detail when we reconstruct what constitutes reasonable belief in the 21st century) that calls into question the value of doctrine. Looked at from a perspective free of human biases, what exactly is happening when an assertion about God/Spirit is made? In essence, an entity known as a human is making a definitive statement about an entity that is spiritual. Put a bit differently, an entity in space and time is claiming to be able to make a definitive statement about something whose existence transcends the bounds of space and time. Put even more specifically (and accurately), *an entity composed of matter/energy, situated at a single point in a vast cosmos, at a specific moment in time in a temporal realm stretching back for unfathomable years, is making a definitive assertion about a reality that transcends the cosmos.* One might reasonably ask on what grounds such a tiny being (compared to the immensity of the cosmos) existing for a flicker of a moment (in the context of the vast expanse of time) should have the audacity to proclaim that, from such a limited and parochial perspective, it could make any claims whatsoever about the universe as a whole, to say nothing of claims about a non-spatiotemporal reality (God/Spirit). In a sense, doctrinal statements about spiritual matters reflect the epitome of human *epistemological arrogance*, as chunks of temporarily coalesced matter/energy, in a fleeting moment of conscious existence, make proclamations about the entirely of space, time, and... of all things, God.[20] In a sense, this is rather comical, equivalent perhaps to ants performing calculus or fleas building nuclear reactors. When we recognize our extraordinarily small place in the universe, declarations of the sort that are found in doctrine appear utterly embarrassing. Again, one more reason to not take doctrine too literally, and to feel no qualms about not assenting to it in a strict, dogmatic sense.

Nonetheless, imperfect as it may be, humans communicate through language, which is to say, through verbal symbols. Sometimes the symbols and their referent are rather direct and unambiguous, in which case language is very effective: "This is a pencil" (for an English speaker) is pretty easy to understand and not likely subject to misinterpretation. But when we use language to refer to less tangible referents, things get a bit less firm: "I feel anxiety" carries a meaning that listeners would have a general sense of, but the precise nature would be a bit up in the air: Is it a reference to worry, dread, concern about a specific issue, or a generalized sense of uneasiness? It's hard to communicate precisely when we're talking about something that is not an external physical object. Feelings can't be seen, they have no measurable properties that all can observe, they're something happening internally and by virtue of that certain "hiddenness" from public view can only be guessed at in an approximate sense.

If the communication of feelings demonstrates the limitations of language, how much more so is that limitation demonstrated when we attempt to communicate about something that has no spatiotemporal presence whatsoever, something that is not "of this world" as the saying goes, something that is, by definition, beyond description by the use of language.

Nonetheless, while all of the above brings out the limitations of doctrine and provides ample grounds for a highly skeptical attitude toward traditions that assert the necessity of accepting doctrine as proof of one's spiritual status, on the other hand it would be quite unfair to fail to acknowledge that doctrine does serve a purpose, and a purpose that, historically speaking, has been quite important. It may be the case that human creatures making verbal assertions about the ultimate nature of spiritual reality seem rather arrogant and presumptuous, but there is the question of what is the alternative. In other words, to communicate we have to say *something*. Complete silence would be even less effective than saying something that is only a dim symbol of that to which one is pointing.[21] Human creatures communicate via language; hence, we need to say something, however ineffective and even misleading that communication might be.[22]

Throughout the long history of human awareness of the sacred, we have struggled to use the weak but only available vehicle of language to communicate about the nature of the spiritual dimension, using symbols which, in the given culture and epoch in which they were developed, made sense as pointers to that sacred reality which was beyond language. These symbolic pointers carried great meaning and offered tremendous comfort and security to those who used those symbols. Even if, today, we find that those specific symbols have lost their ability to point to the sacred, we should nonetheless appreciate how deeply important these symbols were and still are to those who continue to find them meaningful. The same can be said of the sacred stories which were constructed with those symbols. The stories today may seem to have lost their meaning, but we should recognize that to many the stories continue to function as pointers to a sacred reality.

To the struggling contemporary believer, the story of God asking Abraham to sacrifice his son, Isaac, may seem like a story about a sadistic God who commands a father to kill his son, only to revoke that command at the last moment. To the believer, however, behind the details of the story is a larger meaning, namely an example of faith that is so strong that it does not waiver even when challenged by the dread and despair that must have been experienced by Abraham. Likewise, the parting of the Red Sea by Moses is seen by many today as an unbelievable story of a supernatural act that defies the laws of science (as well as depicting God as a rather savage figure who gladly destroys one people while saving another). But to the believer for whom this story retains its symbolic meaning, this is a moving example of the power of God over and against the oppressive institutions of human society.

Along these same lines, one can also look at doctrine. The doctrine of the Incarnation, for instance, strikes some 21st century thinkers as difficult to make sense of on multiple grounds: How could God reside in a body of flesh, blood, bone, excrement, etc.? And why would a God choose to do so? If it's said that God took on human form to offer himself as a sacrifice for the sins of all humankind, one might reasonably ask why God couldn't have just forgiven those sins without entering into a human body. And then there are the more strictly logical problems posed by the doctrine of the Incarnation. Jesus is said to be God incarnate, fully God and fully man, but then how do we explain the New Testament passages in which Jesus prays to God... is he praying to Himself? In one case, Jesus prays to God, asking that he be spared from the ordeal of the crucifixion that he is about to experience, but logically speaking this would seem to be a case of God asking God for a favor... a bit of a paradox, to say the least.

Much the same could be said about other traditional Christian doctrines – the Trinity, the virgin birth, the resurrection, etc. In each case, it's easy to see why the contemporary seeker who wishes to maintain his intellectual dignity balks at assenting to these doctrines. But one needs to step back from a literal reading of these doctrines and stories, and recognize the spiritual truth in them that provides the basis for their continued viability among traditional believers. Granted, at a surface level these ideas may appear to be irrational and illogical, but the point is that there are values and spiritual ideals expressed in these doctrines, and it is this non-literal spiritual content that accounts for the persistence of loyalty to what otherwise appears to be rather unbelievable ideas.

Earlier in the twentieth century, the German theologian Rudolf Bultmann wrote about the need to "demythologize" Christian doctrine in order to be liberated from the no longer credible literal interpretations and in turn be opened up to the deeper spiritual meaning behind the literalism. That's precisely what we're talking about here with reference to how one looks at doctrine.

The incarnation, for instance, is usually presented as a doctrine that asserts the literal truth of God having somehow entered into a human body. Many nontraditional believers find this to be impossible to understand, for reasons that should be obvious. However, aside from the literal interpretation of the doctrine, there is also the meaning that is conveyed in the concept of Incarnation. Specifically, the concept of Incarnation is used to convey God's love of the creation. Or, to put this in non-Axial, nontheistic terms that are more likely to be meaningful to the reader, Incarnation conveys the sense that the mysterious and indefinable Spirit that is utterly different from the realm of time and space actually has a deep concern for that realm of time and space. *To Spirit, the Universe – including humanity – matters.* In fact, it matters in a very profound sense. In Christian mythological terms, it matters so much that the pure and perfect God would, for the sake of humanity, enter into the impure form of flesh, blood, bone, and all that goes with a human existence. The literal sense of the doctrine may indeed seem rather strange, but the meaning conveyed by the doctrine is quite sublime and moving.

While the Christmas story is an event, more than a doctrine per se, it is the basis for fundamental Christian doctrinal beliefs regarding Jesus as the Messiah, born of a virgin, sent to save humanity from sin, defeating death and bringing the gift of eternal life. Looked at as a literal account of an incident that occurred in history, the contemporary observer is understandably doubtful about the "veracity" of this story. And yet, one could argue that there is a "veracity" to the story that runs deeper than the veracity of historical truth. The Christmas story might not contain *historical* truth, but for the believer it contains a universal *spiritual* truth about the inconceivable love of God for creation, a love that is expressed in the notion of a pure and perfect Spirit sacrificing its own perfect nature out of love for creation. The contemporary nontraditional believer, finding notions of Immaculate Conception and virgin births and angels singing to shepherds difficult to accept, is apt to throw out the proverbial baby with the bathwater by rejecting the value of the Christmas story solely on the grounds that it does not express a historical truth: perhaps it expresses far more than that.

But that brings us back to our earlier dilemma, namely the perpetuation of religious traditions that use symbols that no longer make sense to much of modern humanity. Concepts such as God assuming human form or a pregnancy brought about by means other than human sexual intercourse functioned as effective symbols for the expression of spiritual truths in the ancient world: they just seemed to make intuitive sense in that time. But in our post-Axial world, those symbols no longer carry that intuitive sense that they once did. And the dilemma that we are in is partly explained as the result of *the old symbols having lost their ability to point to the sacred* and a *new set of symbols to perform that same function not having yet emerged...* but more on that later in the book.

So how should the perplexed would-be 21st century believer view traditional doctrine? What should be done by the contemporary seeker, secretly guilt-ridden over his rejection of these ideas that so many have held dear for so long?

If nothing else, our examination of the nature of doctrine hopefully validates the notion that, in simple and straightforward terms, *it's OK to say, I just can't believe that.* Not in a disrespectful sense, and quite the contrary, in a deeply respectful way that recognizes that these ideas once carried a deep intuitive meaning to many people. But like everything else in religion, doctrines change, symbols change, what's "believable" changes, what "works" in pointing to the sacred changes over time. Doctrine, like sacred texts and ritual, is a human product, and as such one should respectfully but honestly acknowledge what no longer is believable to one. It doesn't mean that you're not trying to lead a spiritual life; it doesn't mean that you're doomed to damnation; it doesn't mean that you're not an earnest person with a good heart who has a sense of a sacred presence in life. It simply means that you're being honest with yourself, and that you're ready to move on to a type of spirituality that in significant ways differs from that of the traditional Axial traditions.

Chapter 6

How to Think About Religious Diversity

Over the past century and a half, some remarkable changes have occurred in our awareness of religion as a global phenomenon, and that evolving knowledge has had profound theological and philosophical implications for how we function as members of religious communities. Learning about other religious traditions isn't just an exercise in objective academic learning: it's an experience which, if we are to be faithful to our sense of intellectual integrity, forces a reconsideration of how we perceive our own Western, Biblical tradition. Once you're exposed to the wider world of religions across the globe, retaining the exclusivist belief that salvation is found in one and only one religion becomes an option that is difficult to accept if one also wants to remain intellectually and spiritually honest.

Well into the 19th and early 20th centuries (and even into the 21st century at the level of those who haven't had the opportunity to become familiar with world religions) there was a widespread and confident sense in America that there was an obviously superior religion (Christianity), and that religion was the one "true" religion, the sole path to salvation.

Indeed, prior to the late 1800s, in predominantly Christian countries the world of religions was neatly and confidently (and, in retrospect, with a strong dose of cultural and imperialist arrogance and condescension) typically divided into, depending on how things were broken down, one, two or four categories. The simplest way of looking at religion globally separated the world's religions into Christianity (which was true) and everything else (which was false, wrong, misguided, etc.). A slightly more nuanced perspective employed three categories, adding Judaism to Christianity as the "Biblical" or "Abrahamic" tradition, which, of course, was considered to be obviously the one true tradition (with the understanding that Judaism had been superseded or fulfilled by Christianity) and everything else, which was designated as paganism, heathenism, and other condemnatory labels. Biblical religion (true) and paganism (false) formed a neat binary way of thinking about religion (and is still a functional perspective today among some evangelicals, conservative Catholics, etc.).

Some of the more thoughtful early scholars of the religions of the world recognized that Islam also shared much with Judaism and Christianity, in a way that was not shared by Asian religions. Hence, Islam was often granted its own separate status, leaving a tripartite classification of the world's religions: Biblical religions (Judaism and Christianity), Islam (often incorrectly, and to a Muslim, offensively, referred to as Mohammedism), and everything else. Biblical religion, Mohammedism, and paganism served as a threefold scheme for understanding religion that persisted at both the popular and, to a large extent, the scholarly level, into the twentieth century.

But as early as the 18th century, changes were occurring in the Western world which would eventually demonstrate that this simple categorization of religion was grossly inadequate, being both inaccurate and condescending. Increased ease of long distance travel gradually made it possible for direct contact between Westerners and practitioners of the "heathen" religions found in Asia, Africa, and other parts of the globe. With improvements in long-distance transportation, first by ship and later by train, time and safety no longer functioned as serious impediments for cross-cultural contact between Europeans and countries such as India, China, Japan, and others. Such contact was, of course, not always welcome inasmuch as it often came with the burden of colonialist expansion and oppression, but regardless of the intentions behind European colonialism, a positive outcome was the increased direct experience of non-European cultures, including their spiritual traditions. With British expansion into India and adjoining territories, for instance, the British were no longer dependent on third and fourth hand accounts of the complex spiritual traditions that came to be known as Hinduism and Buddhism. British Europeans (as well as the French, Portuguese, Dutch, and others) had the experience of directly observing and interacting with practicing Hindus and Buddhists.

In addition to the role of improvements in transportation technologies, the impact of new printing technologies played a crucial role in correcting the naïve and misguided Western perception of "heathen" religions. As the modern printing press became more efficient, less costly, and spread beyond the West, sacred texts from "heathen" traditions became available to Westerners to a previously unknown degree. In earlier times, for instance, Buddhist texts were preserved on handwritten scrolls and Hindu Sanskrit texts were retained as the exclusive property of Indian Brahmin priests. With improvements in printing (aligned with greater Western familiarity of languages such as Pali and Sanskrit), copies of the sacred texts of Asian religions, translated into European languages, became available to the general public for the first time.

Direct experience of a spiritual tradition – whether through actual observation or through reading the tradition's sacred texts – is a very different thing than a thirdhand account made by an already biased church source. Consequently, the misguided perception of these non-Biblical religions rapidly changed over the course of time. Clichés and stereotypes, usually created by Westerners with a bias toward the "obvious" superiority of Christianity, slowly became replaced by a more accurate, comprehensive, and less biased understanding. The "strange" religions of "the East" slowly lost their utter "otherness" and gradually became recognized as legitimate spiritual traditions that shared many of the same values and insights as were found in the Biblical religions of the West. Non-Biblical religions were seen to have moral codes, rituals, spiritual practices, and doctrinal belief sets that were deserving of respect. With increasing familiarity with other religions came the recognition that not only were they structurally similar to the Biblical religions (moral codes, dogma, ritual, theology, spiritual practices, etc.), but in many cases the content was also quite similar. Ideas that had been seen as unique to Christianity and proof of its superiority turned up in all sorts of unexpected places. In Confucianism, there is a version of the Golden Rule, written perhaps five centuries before the time of Jesus. In Buddhism we find the moral ideal of universal compassion, extending the range of moral concern to all living beings. The role of divine grace is seen in both the Hindu Vaishnava tradition and the Buddhist Bodhisattva figures. In the Hindu theological tradition devoted to the worship of God in the form of Vishnu, we find medieval discussion of whether salvation is dependent entirely or only partly on the grace of God, a discussion comparable to that which began in Christianity in its earliest days and extended through medieval scholasticism and into the Reformation. Issues debated by the likes of Martin Luther and John Calvin had been explored in India two centuries earlier by Vaishnava theologians such as Ramanuja. In Buddhism, we also find the tradition of Bodhisattvas, beings who assume a Christ-like commitment to delay their own entry into Nirvana and instead vow to remain in the world of suffering and death until all living beings are liberated.

We could go on and on regarding the many aspects of non-Biblical religions that Westerners of the 19th and early 20th centuries came to realize reflected a level of spiritual and philosophical depth that the Christian world had previously assigned to only itself. To cite only a few additional examples: the contemplative practices of Zen Buddhism, the self-discipline of Hindu sannyasins, the cosmic sense of the sacred in the

Brahman of the Upanishads, the intimate sense of the love of God in the Krishna tradition, the poetically-expressed spiritual appreciation of the natural world in Daoist classics such as the *Dao de Jing* and the Neo-Confucian tradition, the complex and subtle Buddhist psychology (in an epistemological sense, at times expressing psychological insights that would not appear in the West for another 2000 years).

In these and many other ways, the value and depth of the non-Biblical religious traditions of the world were, in a sense, so directly thrown in the face of the Christian West that it was no longer possible to retain that naïve typology that separated the world into "true" Biblical religion (with, of course, the understanding that Christianity had superseded Judaism, and Islam was simply a misguided variant of Biblical religion) and "false" heathenism. An intellectually honest perspective now had to recognize the value of these other religions, and that in turn led to the need to reexamine the very nature of Christianity, since it was a religion that claimed to be the exclusive path to salvation.

This new understanding of non-Biblical religions during the late-19th/early-20th centuries was not confined to the halls of the academe, although it did have a significant influence in college curricula. "World Religions" became a new concept, something that one could study as a legitimate expression of religion – in contrast to the past practice of studying "paganism" or "foreign" religions. During the 20th century, World Religions became a standard subject of study, expressed in not only individual courses but entire departments. The very notion of how one studied religion in a university setting changed, as "Theology" departments, rooted in the notion of Christian superiority and exclusiveness, became replaced by something new (new then, commonplace now): "Religion" departments.[23]

As things changed in academic circles, parallel changes took place at the popular level. Books on World Religions in general and specific Asian traditions became best-sellers. Edwin Arnold's 1879 *Light of Asia,* an extended poem telling the story of the Buddha, was embraced enthusiastically by a wide audience at both the scholarly and popular level. Bookstores devoted more and more shelf space to Hinduism, Yoga, Buddhism, and Asian classics such as the *I Jing, Bhagavad Gita, Lotus Sutra,* and *Analects of Confucius.* Notable spiritual leaders from Asia toured America and Europe, speaking to large and appreciative audiences. Eventually, spiritual teachers brought their traditions to the West, establishing centers of Hindu, Buddhist, and other types of teaching and practice in both urban and rural settings.[24]

The net impact of this greater and more accurate awareness of non-Biblical religions was a challenge to the Biblical, and especially Christian, claim to exclusiveness. The idea that God spoke only to a specific, select group of people (first the Hebrews/Jews, then later their spiritual heirs, Christians) and that spiritual salvation was achievable through allegiance to only one spiritual tradition (Christianity) might have been easier to buy into when most Westerners had only a vague sense of a heathen Other as the only alternative to the Christian path. But once one acquires an accurate and thorough familiarity with other religious traditions, containing as they do ideas and practices that to a reasonable and open-minded observer appear to be as morally and spiritually edifying as those found in Christianity, believing that salvation comes through faith in Christ alone becomes less easy to accept. Once Western-generated caricatures of non-Biblical religions are replaced by accurate knowledge of those traditions, it challenges credulity to continue to accept the notion that God chose one person in one place in one period of history to bring salvation to the entire species.

Of course, within the tradition there have been attempts to preserve the uniqueness of Christianity and its exclusiveness claim to be the only salvific path. One approach is to explain away the elevated spiritual aspects of non-Christian religions as the product of cross-cultural contact that led, in a sense, to the theft of Christian ideas and ideals which were then grafted onto non-Christian traditions. That cross-cultural exchange has occurred throughout the history of Christianity is clear, but to explain away the appealing aspects of non-Christian traditions on this basis is to ignore timelines. The Confucian expression of the Golden Rule was formulated 500 to 600 years before the time of Jesus. It was during this same period that Buddhism developed the figure of the Bodhisattva savior figure who sacrificed his/her own welfare for the sake of the spiritual deliverance of all living beings. If any borrowing occurred, perhaps it was in the other direction, given that these key ideas found in Christianity are found centuries earlier in Asian traditions. To cite another example, a doctrine of grace is clearly expressed in the Hindu text, the *Bhagavad Gita*. The dating of the *Gita* is not firmly established, but many scholars believe that it was written in the 2nd or 3rd centuries before Christ, once again demonstrating that a non-Christian religion (Hinduism) had no need to borrow from Christianity an idea that probably appeared in the Christian world later than it did in India.[25]

In Christian theology, one of the titans of 20th century Protestant theology, Karl Barth, attempted to preserve Christian exclusivism by a peculiar argument in his multi-volume monumental work, *Church Dogmatics*. In a lengthy section titled "Revelation as the Abolition of Religion," Barth argues that Christianity (along with its predecessor Judaism) is unique, in that it represents a communication, or revelation, from God to humanity, whereas all other religions are efforts at communication from humanity to God. Given the fallen nature of humanity in contrast to the majestic greatness of God, all human efforts to understand the nature of God, to communicate with God, and most importantly, to achieve rightness with God (salvation) are doomed to failure. However, all is not lost, since

God in his mercy has freely chosen to communicate the path of salvation to us, in the person of Jesus Christ. What humans cannot do, God can do. Christianity is the spiritual tradition that originates in a salvific act of revelation from God; all other traditions are human-created religions that fall short of mending our relationship with God. So, basically, the religions of the world can be distinguished between the true, God-generated *revelation* (Christianity... and its predecessor Judaism) and the false *human-generated* religions.

In a simpler form this notion that Christianity is like no other religion has become a common theme throughout the Christian, and especially Protestant evangelical world.

An objective observer with a familiarity with world religions is unlikely, however, to find this a convincing argument. As we have discussed above, the theological, moral, and doctrinal components of Christianity are found throughout other religions, in many cases having appeared in those traditions prior to the beginnings of Christianity. How would one sensibly explain that spiritual truths supposedly revealed by God only to the people of first century Israel had just coincidentally already been developed, without the benefit of revelation, by the populations of China, India, and other cultures? Does there not seem to be something a bit arrogant in Christians asserting that the same idea (divine grace) as found in their tradition is "true" since it was revealed by God, while asserting that divine grace as found in, for example, Vaishnava Hindus or the Buddhist Pure Land and Bodhisattva-centered traditions is a mere human invention? It strains credulity to accept such an interpretation, and it is an interpretation which we suggest should promptly be abandoned by anyone desirous of maintaining their intellectual integrity when thinking about religion in the 21st century.

So where does all this leave us with regard to how to think about religion in light of our 21st awareness of the religious traditions of the world? Clearly, an educated understanding of the major religious traditions makes accepting any one religion's claim to be the exclusive possessor of spiritual truth and the exclusive path to salvation highly untenable. In specific terms, this means rejecting the claim of the Abrahamic religions (including Islam) to be the sole source of salvation. Whether it's the Jewish people as God's one Chosen People, faith in Jesus as the only path to salvation ("No one comes to the Father but through me"), or the Muslim declaration of Muhammed as the final Prophet and the Qur'an as the final revelation which supersedes all that preceded it and all claims to religious truth that followed it, all such claims to exclusive possession of salvific truth cannot be embraced by anyone who has become familiar with the spiritual content of the other, non-Biblical religious traditions. To assert exclusivity in the face of such evidence is spiritually arrogant, condescending, and insulting.

But how, then, should we think about religion if we are left to sort through this bewildering diversity of traditions and claims?

For starters, it would be helpful to set aside the notion, deeply rooted in Christianity and Islam, that religious truth must be thought of in the binary terms of true and false, with the related binary distinction of one true religion and all others false. This is a residue of Biblical thought, going all the way back to the earliest Biblical stories in which the God of the Hebrews is portrayed as a jealous God who insists on loyalty to him and him alone. Rather than an either/or view of religions, perhaps a both/and perspective is more sensible and defensible to the 21st century seeker.

Perhaps the best way to illustrate this alternative perspective on religious diversity is through the rivers/ocean analogy. If I wanted to reach the Atlantic Ocean, there are many different rivers that I could follow (the Hudson, the Susquehanna, the Delaware, among many others), all of which would lead me to the same body of water, the Atlantic. There are, in other words, many paths to the same destination. In order to reach my destination, it's not necessary to take one and only one path.

Similarly, why not look at the diversity of religious traditions as simply many paths which lead to the same spiritual destination? Why should we assume that it is the case that there is only one path to salvation, liberation, enlightenment, or whatever one chooses to call that final highest goal? Each religion offers a different path, sharing much in common with other paths, but also adding its own unique emphasis. In Judaism we find an emphasis on social justice and the transcendent nature of God. Christianity, along with the bhakti tradition of Hinduism, emphasizes the role of divine grace. In Islam we find a spiritual path centered on the oneness of God and the need to subvert all other allegiances to God. In Daoism there is an acute sensitivity to the natural unfolding of a sacred presence that is larger than our own individuality. In Confucianism the path is followed with a strong sense of the importance of moral responsibility and familial connections. In Buddhism we find a focus on the development of a quiet but mindful interior state that allows us to avoid those things that distract us from remaining on the right path.

We could go on and on, but the obvious point is that there doesn't need to be a conflict or contradiction between these different paths (unless, of course, the tradition itself proclaims that it is the exclusive path, as in Christianity and Islam). Each of the religious traditions can be seen as one of many rivers leading to the same destination, the ocean of spiritual liberation. Each of those traditions has its own specific nuances and biases, just as one would expect given that each has developed in a specific, limited, confined set of cultural and historical circumstances. But each, in its own way, offers a partial glimpse at how to reestablish our relationship with the sacred. Rather than make the unnecessary assumption that one path is valid and all of the rest lead to a dead end, a wiser and more mature perspective on religious diversity recognizes that there are many paths and sub-paths to choose from, including the option of spending a little bit of time on this path and a little bit of time on that path. The awe-inspiring nature of the transcendence of God that one can get from Islam can be appreciated alongside the Vedantic sense of the immanent presence of God/Brahman in all things, and both can be intertwined with the Buddhist and Daoist awareness of the nature of the sacred that is so profound and mysterious that it cannot be described by any words.

So far we have been exploring the problems with religious exclusivity from the historical-comparative perspective: once you have a broader, more accurate understanding of the world's many religious traditions, it's difficult to retain confidence in the notion that any one religion is the exclusive path to salvation.

But one can look at this same issue of the weakness of the exclusivity claim from a very different perspective, independent of historical and comparative considerations. Specifically, one can approach exclusivity from an epistemological perspective and arrive at the same conclusions as we arrived at using the historical-comparativist approach.

We'll keep this brief at this point, since epistemology will become a key component of our exploration of reconstructing a credible, believable perspective on religion in part two of this book. Briefly, however, epistemology is a branch of philosophy that deals with the question of how it is that we know anything. With reference to the epistemological implications of our exploration of the question of how one should look at the diversity of religions, one might approach that question as follows:

All human knowledge is gained through various perceptual and cognitive processes that are rooted in the brain. In other words, what we know about "Reality" or "Truth" is entirely dependent on what we can know using the human brain, whether that be through direct sense perception or through reasoning from those sense perceptions.

But consider what the human brain is: a rather tiny, 2 or 3 pound collection of cells (call it matter, matter/energy, or whatever you wish… it remains a tiny little thing in the larger scale of the universe), an organ that has developed in a species that has existed for a very short period of time at a tiny point of space on a planet we call Earth. Considering that that is what the brain is, indeed that that is all that the brain is, does it not seem almost preposterously arrogant for humans to assume that, dependent on that tiny piece of mush, we should be able to arrive at definitive, comprehensive, and irrefutable truths about all aspects of everything that exists, including spiritual reality? Does it not seem a bit of a stretch to proclaim that the understanding of spiritual reality attained through the use of a small chunk of matter that has developed under rather parochial circumstances represents some sort of universal truth?

With all due humility, the answer, of course, is certainly not! And we will explore this matter in more detail in chapter eight below.

So with reference to the question of how to think about the multiplicity of religions in the 21st century, the bottom line is: *do not* think in terms of exclusivity, but think in *inclusive* terms of many paths to the same goal. Don't think of religious truth as something that has been handed down to one person or group of people at one time or one place. Don't think along the lines that there is a "right" religion or religions and "wrong" religion or religions. Set aside the unfounded devotion to exclusiveness that has been such a dominant part of our religious history, especially in the Abrahamic religions, and instead, recognize that spiritual truth is something far too mysterious and grand to be captured by any single person or group of people, something so vast and transcendent that it cannot be limited to any one of

75

the many human attempts – all partial at best – to understand it. Recognize that, as we have suggested above, there are many paths to the same destination, and even though those paths might become divergent and even contradictory as a result of years and years of cultural accumulations which taint the core truth, all of those paths do indeed contain some kernel of spiritual wisdom.

But that's not to say that in thinking about religion we should be confined to thinking about existing religions – the "old" religions, so to speak, mostly with origins that date back 2000 years or more. Once we open up to the possibility that spiritual wisdom is not the privileged position of any existing religion, there emerges the possibility of entirely *new* ways of thinking about spirituality. Perhaps the best way to think about religion in the 21st century will turn out to be quite different from how pre-21st century humanity thought about religion. Perhaps we are, so to speak, at the cusp of a new Axial Age,[26] in which a new understanding of religion, *respecting the old but not being confined by it*, must emerge. To that reconstruction of religion in the 21st century we now turn.

Reconstruction

Preface to Reconstruction

The basic premise on which we are operating in this short book is fairly simple, and is twofold: First, it is quite justified for a person in the 21st century who is endeavoring to be intellectually honest and morally sensitive to choose not to believe in religion as it is currently manifested in the various organized religions throughout the world (which is not to imply that 21st century humanity is in any sort of New Age-ish, Aquarian state of Enlightenment, but rather is simply an objective observation that derives from the point at which humanity finds itself in terms of the long evolutionary path of both cognitive and moral development: 21st century humanity really is different in some (although only some) ways from humanity of 2000 years ago when these religions originated, but we are nonetheless a limited, flawed, imperfect species that will hopefully continue to develop).

That's the negative side of the premise, which we've covered in the first part of the book. Now we're ready for the second part of the basic premise, which is: It is quite justified for a person in the 21st century who is endeavoring to be intellectually honest and morally sensitive to choose to be religious, but being "religious" or "spiritual" (terms we are using more or less interchangeably, at least for now) in the 21st century means something quite different from what it has meant to human beings over the past two millennia. It's OK to reject religion in its traditional form (part one above), but it's OK to accept religion in its 21st century, post-Axial Age manifestation, even though (as we are about to see in the coming pages) that manifestation is still vague, elusive, hard to articulate, and at times perhaps even contradictory. So having dispensed with the old, it's now on to the new, on to an understanding of what it means to be religious in a way that is intellectually and morally sound to human creatures in the 21st century.

Before we begin to get into details, however, a few words of caution are in order. What follows will not always be neat, tidy, and easy to latch onto. Dissecting existing religions and justifying our moral and intellectual skepticism about them is one thing; articulating what the alternative might be is another matter. Indeed, it is a matter that at times can be elusive to the point of exasperation, and it is a process that will take us down (for better or worse, by necessity) the path of explorations into philosophical, scientific, and cultural issues that may seem to constitute a substantial digression from our stated purpose. In order to argue for an understanding of religion that is legitimate for the 21st century man and woman, it will be necessary to delve into much that is not religion. But the end product of this journey hopefully will eventually lead us to where we need to be, and the reader is encouraged to persevere through what at times might be rather dense and seemingly irrelevant material for the sake of eventually recognizing that there is a logical and morally and intellectually sound justification for religious belief in our time.

So set aside all of your preconceptions about what religion is or is not, open your mind to an alternative way of thinking about and relating to God/Spirit/Meaning – all of the big questions – and be prepared to explore something new. This will not be "that old time religion."

Chapter 7

The Myth of Scientific Materialism

So immediately you might ask: Why are we talking about science if this book is supposed to be about religion?

The answer is quite simple: a commitment to a "scientific" understanding of reality is one of the most significant barriers to embracing a religious perspective in today's world. Even if it is often in a fairly adversarial sense, science and religion are intimately linked, so if we are going to eventually move toward an understanding of religion that is acceptable in our time, we need to first examine and unravel this curious relationship between science and religion. In a sense, we need to discredit one of the main reasons for rejecting a religious perspective ("it's not scientific") before moving forward to the articulation of what a credible and convincing religious perspective in the 21st century might look like.

In examining this relationship between science and religion, we will discover two things: first, the scientific understanding of the nature of reality is not what most people think that it is – much has changed from the days when science and materialism went hand in hand; and second, the very notion that a scientific perspective is necessarily the superior or sole valid perspective is itself quite dubious. Science is one of many ways of understanding reality, or the totality of what is real, and as we shall see, its claim to be the most valid one is without support.

But first, let's acknowledge the reality of the conflict between science and religion that has been particularly prominent in Western culture over the past several centuries. Any discussion of the conflict between science and religion usually begins with the treatment of Galileo by the Roman Catholic Church in the early 17th century. Galileo, observing the moon and other heavenly bodies through the newly refined instrument of the telescope, declared that the planets were not perfect spheres, the orbits of the planets were not geometrically perfect, the surface of the moon was a pockmarked mess of topographical imperfections. And, of course, while Galileo demonstrated the imperfections of the heavenly bodies, the likes of Copernicus and Kepler had earlier shown that the planets did not move in perfectly symmetrical orbits, and, worst of all, the heavenly bodies did not circle around the Earth.

From a religious perspective, why would the Church care about astronomical observations? Quite simply, because these observations challenged religious belief in the perfection of the Heavenly realm. In the pre-modern mind, Heaven was indeed "up there," where the stars, sun, and moon also reside. Heaven, as the dwelling place of God, was necessarily a perfect place: perfect bodies moving in perfect motion (perfect circles). Galileo challenged all this by proclaiming that, through empirical observation (the foundation of science), the Heavens could be proven to be quite imperfect, just like the Earth.

The challenge from Copernicus was a bit different. The traditional Biblical model of the universe saw Earth and humanity as the centerpiece of God's creation. Copernicus demonstrated that, far from being the centerpiece, the Earth was simply one of many bodies drifting through space, just like all the rest. So in a sense, both Galileo and Copernicus, through empirical observation and logical/mathematical deduction (the dual essence of the scientific method), had dethroned humanity. The Earth was no longer the unique center of the universe. The methods of science (empirical observation and rational analysis) were asserting a view of reality that was in conflict with, and radically undermined, the religious view derived from the Church's interpretation of the Bible. For Galileo (and others) this led to all sorts of conflicts with the Church, include

Galileo's house arrest for the latter part of his life. In a broader sense, however, it marked the beginning of a climate of mistrust and suspicion (and at times, outright hostility), found in both prominent figures and everyday citizens, between science and religion. The knowledge of the nature of reality as obtained from religion (via Biblical revelation and Church dogma) was different from the knowledge of reality as obtained from scientific observation, and consequently the Church and the scientific community began a battle that, in various ways, they continue to wage to this day.

Galileo and Copernicus challenged the religious view of reality by demonstrating that the place of the Earth in the universe was nothing special: Earth was not the center of the Universe, and all heavenly bodies did not rotate around it. But their observations, challenging as they were to the traditional Bible-based view of reality, did not directly address the role of humanity. Based on the findings of the astronomers alone, the Earth could no longer claim a special place in the Universe, but the human species could still claim its superiority as God's special creation, even though it now found itself living in a not-so-special place. Earth had been dethroned by science, but humanity had not, at least not in a direct sense.

But this is where the next great source of conflict between religion and science arises, and indeed remains a hotly contested issue even today. Galileo may have only dethroned Earth, but in the 19th century the naturalist Charles Darwin dethroned humanity, and in doing so incurred the wrath of religious believers with an intensity that had perhaps not been seen since the time of his fellow scientist Galileo three centuries earlier.

More specifically, by offering scientific evidence for the evolution of the human species from earlier life forms, Darwin challenged the Biblical doctrine of the direct creation of humanity (and, for that matter, all species) by God. The Biblical account of human origins assigned a glorious place to humankind as the cap of God's creation. Humans were indeed something special, a species created "in God's image." Darwin's theories challenged all that, and he did so with meticulously documented scientific evidence derived from his observations as a naturalist. From Darwin's point of view, the origin of the human species was in the same primal mud and goo that gave birth to the earliest life forms. The origin of humanity could be explained without positing an act of God. Adding further insult to the believer in the divine origin of humankind, Darwin demonstrated that the *process* by which the human species came into existence was not guided by some divine hand but rather was the result of random events (mutation) and a viciously competitive struggle for survival. The result of the Darwinian explanation of human origins was the dethronement of the human species: what Galileo had done for the Earth, Darwin did for humanity. The Earth is not in a special place in the universe, and human beings are not the special product of a unique act of creation by a wise and benevolent deity.

Of course, the debate between scientific evolutionists and religious (usually, but not always, Christian) creationists continues to this day, as does the animosity between the two factions. And in a more general sense, as science over the centuries demonstrated the capacity to explain more and more (no, babies are conceived as the result of the union of a sperm and ovum, not as the result of a creative intervention by God; no, hurricanes occur as the result of atmospheric forces, not as the result of an act of an angry God; no, eclipses occur due to the movement of bodies in space, not because God is displeased with humanity and sending us a warning; and on and on on), that hostility increased accordingly, eventually to the point where, by the early 20th century, there is an assumed irreconcilability between the religious and scientific perspectives. To be a "man of science" meant rejecting the primitive superstitions of religion. To be a true religious believer meant accepting certain ideas about the nature of reality as a matter of faith, regardless of the scientific claims. And this is perhaps where we are now, at least with many contemporaries who wish to maintain their intellectual integrity: one cannot be a religious believer, since to be such entails rejecting the clear and obvious truths of science which contradict the religious view of reality.

But that's where we make a mistake. Yes, there has been a long history of conflict between religion and science, and yes, there are indeed many aspects of a scientific understanding of reality that are different from a traditional, Axial Age religious understanding of reality. But recall what we established in the first part of this book: a religious view of reality does not have to be the religious view of the existing 2000 year old religions. It's OK to think about spirituality in a different way. In fact, in order to be intellectually and morally honest, it's *necessary* to think about religion in a different way. And when we think about religion in a different way, in a way that makes sense to humans beings in the 21st century (the details of which we'll be exploring later), *then the conflict between religion and science largely disappears.* In other words, once one is liberated from the old ways of thinking about religion, much of the conflict with science disappears and at least becomes easy to incorporate into one's post-Axial spirituality.

But before we get into how that new spirituality is compatible with science, there's another twist to the story: science itself has changed dramatically, and an accurate picture of the current scientific understanding of reality changes how we look at that conflict. It's not as bad as we might think. So first, a brief look at the current scientific view of reality.

When we talk about a "scientific view of reality," however, we could be talking about two different but related things. On the one hand, the scientific view of reality refers to the view of reality that results when one employs the principles of science.

Generally speaking, this is a view that is variously characterized as materialism, physicalism, or sometimes naturalism.

However, what makes that view of reality "scientific" is that it derives from a set of epistemological principles (rules for determining how we can know what is true) that are referred to as "scientific." In general, the scientific approach to knowing what is real is based on what is observable through the senses, quantifiable, predictable, etc. So the "scientific" view of reality is actually twofold, consisting of a *method* of acquiring knowledge and the consequent *body of knowledge* that one comes to know as a result of following that method.

In the following chapters we will examine and call into question both of these understandings of the "scientific" view of reality. Neither the method of knowing employed by science nor the conclusions drawn through that method are necessarily the *only* valid means of acquiring knowledge about the way things are. This is an important point, since for the 21st century citizen, the certainty of the scientific worldview, or more specifically, scientific materialism, has become a given, a truth so obvious that it should not be questioned. And to the extent that that scientific worldview does not include a God or spiritual reality, it logically follows for the 21st century citizen that the nonexistence of God must likewise be obvious and should not be questioned, at least not by someone who is well-informed and intellectually honest.

But as we shall see, there are many holes in this argument, holes which dethrone the scientific worldview as the sole arbiter of what an intelligent person in the 21st century should believe. These holes in the scientific worldview do not "prove" the opposite, namely that there does exist a spiritual reality (although there are countless authors who do indeed make such an overreaching claim),[27] but they do open up the possibility that there is more to reality than that which can be known through the principles of science, and once we have that opening, the path to a spiritual view of reality is easily traveled.

So let's begin by looking at the scientific worldview, after which we'll examine the principles behind that worldview.

One of the most common arguments against religious belief goes something like this: science has proven that all that exists is matter – cold, heartless matter. Science has developed the ability to scan the entire universe, and what has it found: nothing but matter. It's a physical world, and that's all that it is. There's no God out there, no soul, no immaterial spiritual realm. The scientifically verified material nature of the universe is proof that God (and any sort of spiritual reality) does not exist.

Such an assertion might have been consistent with the scientific understanding of the world at one time, but the belief that the scientific view of reality is simply one of a universe filled with matter is no longer the case. In fact, what we will call the "traditional" (as opposed to the "contemporary") scientific understanding of "what's out there" has been outdated since early in the 20th century. It's quite odd, and a curious social phenomenon, that over a century has passed since scientists themselves ceased believing in the traditional materialist model while the general public continues to assume that that model is as solid and unquestioned as scientists prior to the 20th century thought that it was. There's a curious parallel here to the public delay in catching up with the scholarly understanding of the Bible. Just as Biblical scholars have viewed the Bible as a fallible, human-created text for over a century while believers continue to see it as an inerrant text delivered from Heaven, similarly scientists recognized the flaws in the materialist view of the universe over a century ago while the public continues to accept this long-discredited perspective. In both areas, this is finally but slowly starting to change, as Biblical scholars like Bart Ehrman begin to popularize the scholarly understanding of the Bible, while a cottage industry of scientific authors[28] is popularizing quantum theory and its various implications which undermine the traditional view that the universe is nothing but stuff.

So briefly, what we do mean by the traditional scientific understanding of reality? Quite simply, it is the belief that we live in a universe of matter, in which all things can be reduced to small particles (atoms), which in turn are composed of a structure of smaller particles (protons, neutrons, electrons, and many more). These small material particles combine in various ways to produce the various larger structures that make up the entire universe. The diversity of these combinations of atomic and subatomic particles might be incomprehensibly complex, to the point of astonishing the human observer, but nonetheless the bottom line is that with reference to what is real, it's all matter. We live in a universe of physical stuff.

What's more, this physical stuff acts in a specific, predictable, orderly way, according to what we call the laws of physics. In this orderly universe of stuff, things happen in a predictable manner according to universal laws that govern the transformations of material particles. This is the Newtonian clockwork universe of the 18th and 19th century scientists, in which the universe essentially functioned as an orderly machine, with its various parts always acting in a manner consistent with the laws of physics. And in this universe, there was no sign of, and no need for, anything along the lines of a God, soul, or spirit. The traditional scientific view of reality was therefore a soulless, mechanistic, materialist view.

In the context of such a scientific view of reality, it's not surprising that many men and women of intellectual integrity felt that they had to abandon their religious belief (although, as we shall see later, it doesn't necessarily follow that a physicalist universe necessarily implies the absence of God). It just seemed to many like the only honest option. Science had scanned the universe, and found nothing but – stuff.

And then everything changed, and changed almost overnight. Not in the general public, but within the scientific community itself. And that change occurred as the result of the discovery of an entirely new dimension of the natural world, the dimension of *quantum physics*.

Our purpose here is not to provide a detailed account of the principles of quantum physics. That would be quite impossible, partly because I am not a physicist, but perhaps even more so because even quantum physicists acknowledge that quantum theory produces such an incredibly strange understanding of the nature of the realm of material reality that even quantum physicists don't entirely understand it. They can explain how it works, and do so with great precision, but they can't explain what it is or why it works the way that it does. As Richard Feynman, generally regarded as one of the most significant figures in the development of quantum theory, famously said, "No one understands quantum mechanics."[29]

So the best that we can do is lay out some of the most basic insights of quantum theory and then explore what the implications are (and are not) for our larger discussion of the relationship between science and spirituality.

Quantum physics, or quantum theory, refers to a description of how things work at the level of the very, very small – at the level of not just the atom, but the level of subatomic particles. In the traditional scientific model, an atom was conceived of as a tiny particle composed of other tiny particles: a tiny bit of matter, the nucleus, around which are orbiting other tiny particles, known as electrons. This tiny piece of matter, the atom, is the building block from which everything else in the universe is made, and countless numbers of atoms combine in countless forms to produce the immensity and diversity of larger structures in the universe, from a simple compound to a vast galaxy.

But the problem with this model is that it's not true. Really, that's not just an exaggeration: it's not true, and scientists have acknowledged that it's not true since the early 20th century, when the field of quantum physics was born.

Quantum physics tells us that the universe is made up of something very different from the orderly, predictable "stuff" of classical physics and traditional science. At times, what quantum physics tells us seems difficult if not impossible to believe, since it challenges our basic beliefs about space and time, and, in a sense, the very notion of logic and rationality.[30]

If you're not already familiar with quantum physics and you're starting from scratch, so to speak, disregard any preconceived meanings you associate with the word "quantum," which in a sense is a somewhat confusing word to be used as the label to designate this entire view of the nature of reality that we are about to examine. If you're familiar with Latin, you are likely to see "quantum" and think "quantity," as in a discrete, defined amount of something. That was indeed what the word referred to when it first was used during the early days of quantum physics, when it referred to the idea that electrons move in distinct packets of energy (quanta) rather than in a graded, progressive pattern. Subsequent discoveries in the field, however, went far, far beyond the orbital movements of electrons, but the initial "quantum" label was retained for this new field of physics that offered a radically new and strange picture of the nature of reality. A new label might have been useful and more accurate (sometimes you'll see references to "the new physics," but that really doesn't tell you much), but "quantum" stuck, so that's the label we'll have to use. Some would use "particle physics," since quantum theory originated with observations about how reality works at the level of atomic and subatomic particles, but it's generally conceded that the quantum nature of reality applies to the larger macro-world as well, even though we're not able to experimentally verify that (yet). So when you see quantum theory, quantum physics, quantum world, etc., disregard the traditional "quantity" meaning of quantum, and just think of something along the lines of physics as it's now understood by the scientific community.

So what exactly does quantum physics tell us about the nature of the physical universe? Well, for starters, it tells us that what we think of as the "physical" world isn't exactly "physical," at least not in the traditional, established, popular understanding of the word. In fact, quantum physics has decisively demonstrated that matter is a rather puzzling thing, so puzzling in fact that it defies logical explanation.

More specifically, quantum theory asserts that, at the level of atoms and smaller, "matter" sometimes behaves as a particle, but at other times behaves as a wave. This is quite strange, given that a particle is a discrete entity that exists at a specific point in space and time. It has location and specific size. It can be distinguished from other particles. But a wave is quite the opposite: it does exist in a single place, but is diffusely spread out over a broad area, such that there is no single, specific location that one can point to and say, there it is, that's the wave. This paradox can be demonstrated with electrons through the well-known "double-slit" experiment, in which electrons are shot through a barrier with two parallel slits and their arrival after passing through the slits is recorded on a plate on the other side of the slits. We won't go into the details of the experiment, although it's fairly simple, easy to perform, and always produces the same results.[31] The results of the experiment demonstrate what appears to be an impossibility: sometimes electrons pass through the slits as particles, but other times electrons pass through the slits as a wave. If this seems difficult to comprehend, it is. In fact, there is simply no logical way to explain how an electron could be both a particle and a wave. That the dual nature of the electron exists is beyond dispute, but no one has yet explained *how* it could exist in two irreconcilable forms.

So this "physical" universe that pre-quantum theory science had confidently declared to consist of simple, predictable, orderly "matter" is really no such thing. The physical universe, however vast it might be, is made up of particles, and the nature of those particles is something of a mystery, and a very strange one at that.

But it gets even stranger: whether or not matter takes the form of a particle or a wave appears to be the product of whether or not it is observed. This is rather odd, so take a moment to let it sink in. When we perform the double-slit experiment, if we observe the electron as it passes through the slits, it acts like a particle; but if we don't observe it as it passes through the slits and only observe the pattern that it forms when it arrives at a recording plate, then it acts like a wave. This is quite peculiar, and it inserts an element that physicists are often quite uncomfortable with: consciousness. In some as yet unknown manner, the act of observing matter appears to determine the form that the matter adopts (particle or wave).[32]

As if this isn't already a rather weird description of what traditional science considered to be an easy-to-understand aspect of reality (matter), it gets even stranger yet. At the level of electrons (as well as photons and other similarly small entities), particles can exercise instantaneous influence on each other, even when separated by vast distances, with no known physical means for doing so. Einstein called this phenomenon "spooky action at a distance," and refused to accept its reality, but experiments from the 1960s onward based on the work of physicist John Bell and others have consistently proven that such "spooky action at a distance" does indeed occur. This means that when something is done to one particle, another "entangled" particle with which it was once paired, but which is now far away and completely unconnected with its former partner, immediately responds in a specific manner to what was done to its twin. One can ask, how can that happen? How can two physical things that have no physical connection engage in instant communication with each other? Again, as with the particle/wave duality, the answer is: no one knows. We don't know how and why it happens, but we know that it does happen.

And then things get even stranger: through what is known as a "delayed choice" experiment, physicists appear to have demonstrated the seemingly impossible truth that at the level of quantum reality, two entangled particles can interact in a manner such that one particle appears to cause its entangled partner to retroactively change its state! Again, we're not going to go into the details of the experiment, but those wishing for a more detailed and convincing account can find excellent, accessible descriptions for non-physicists in Jim al-Khalili's book and elsewhere. What's quite clear from these experiments, however, is that entangled particles seem to interact with each other in a manner that is independent of unilinear time, or at least time as we currently understand it.

Yet the strangeness continues even further! When we look at the structure of matter at the level of the atom, we find that there's really nothing there that corresponds to our notion of a solid world of physical reality. In fact, if we look at an atom, we find that it is largely empty space. This is rather peculiar, when we consider that everything in the physical world is composed of atoms, atoms themselves occupy what is mostly empty space, and yet the macro-level world as we experience it in everyday life seems to be quite solid. It's not: it's mostly empty space. In fact, it's empty in yet even another sense: not only is there a vast distance between, say, the nucleus and the electron, but the very notion that the protons and neutrons that compose the nucleus, the electrons, and the various other subatomic particles are solid, definable entities is false. In fact, everything at the subatomic level exists in a state that is peculiarly elusive when we try to describe it in the language of macro-level reality. Something is there, but it's not exactly solid particles, at least not in the sense that we mean solid at the level of everyday experience. Some would argue that it's more accurate to refer to whatever it is that exists at the subatomic level as packets of energy, rather than particles. Some would say that, rather than a subatomic reality of discrete particles, what's really there is something more like a vast "quantum field," in which the solidity of the material world disappears and is replaced by a seething, and yet quite predictable, cloud-like field of energy which in its constant state of flux is incessantly creating and dissolving the "stuff" of the material universe, the stuff that makes up the particles which make up the atoms which make up the seemingly solid material world which we experience as human creatures.

Of course, that's really quite peculiar, but then that's the point of what is so mind-boggling about quantum and particle physics: the "real" world, the "material" world which science reveals to us, the "physical" universe that is part of our everyday experience – all of it is *radically* different than what we commonly think that it is, both from an everyday perspective and also from the traditional, pre-quantum scientific perspective. The "physical" universe is not at all what we think that it is, not at all what traditional, pre-quantum science claimed that it was. In fact, the "physical" universe is not really "physical" at all!

So the material world which is the domain of scientific knowledge is actually quite strange, perhaps even strange beyond human comprehension and the capacities of human conceptual thought and language. But, you might reasonably ask, what's the point? We're supposed to be looking at religion here, not science. What's the relevance of the strangeness of the universe as revealed by quantum/particle physics for our attempt to figure out how we can make sense of religion in the 21st century?

In a certain direct sense, there's no relevance at all. That is to say, the astounding weirdness of the observable universe as revealed by quantum theory does not *prove* anything about the existence of or the nature of a spiritual reality. This is an important point to acknowledge, and we need to do so in a clear and emphatic manner, since there have been many efforts to interpret quantum theory as if it functions as proof that some sort of spiritual reality does indeed exist. There is an entire genre of spiritual writings (what we will call "quantum spirituality") that attempts to establish a connection between the scientific perspective of quantum theory and the existence of a spiritual reality, usually one that is based on a non-dualist perspective such as is found in Vedantic Hinduism, Daoism, and certain schools of Buddhism. This genre began in 1975 with the publication of Fritjof Capra's classic, *The Tao of Physics*, followed shortly thereafter by Gary Zukav's *The Dancing Wu-Lei Masters*, both written by scientists who, impressed by the parallels between quantum physics and the Asian non-dualist traditions, attempted to argue that the former somehow functions as evidence for the latter. These are interesting works, and they have inspired countless similar efforts which now extend beyond books to film, websites, meditation practices, and other expressions.

To some, the quantum spirituality genre is the key to the spirituality of the future; to others, it is at best a well-meaning but misguided interpretation of the scientific evidence and at worst an irresponsible exercise in sloppy thinking that sucks people into thinking that science "proves" something (Spirit) that it does not. Quantum theory is, after all, about the *stuff* of the universe, and regardless of how strange that stuff might be (particle and wave, weirdly interconnected, etc.), *it still is only stuff*, and does not seem to have any bearing on transcendent spiritual qualities such as moral goodness and meaning.

But for our purposes, how one assesses quantum spirituality is somewhat irrelevant. Our brief look at quantum theory was intended to make a broader point, one about the false sense that adherence to a scientific worldview necessarily precludes belief in a spiritual reality. The scientific worldview has a firm hold on the contemporary psyche, and that worldview has been one that proclaims the certainty of a material universe in which there is only the realm of matter following fixed, invariable laws of physics. And as such, according to such a worldview, there is no room for a God or spiritual dimension in such a universe. Ask an intelligent, intellectually honest person today why they don't believe in God, and many will begin with some sort of assertion along the lines of, "science proves that there's nothing but the physical universe," or "believing in science is incompatible with believing in religion." This is said with considerable confidence, and rightly so if one is only considering the macro-level reality that operates according to the laws of Newtonian physics.

But the whole point of our discussion of quantum theory is *that the traditional Newtonian model is not an accurate account of what science tells us about the nature of reality.* It used to be an accurate account based on what we knew at the time, and it still is what most people firmly believe that science tells us about what exists. But that understanding of the scientific worldview is wrong. That's no longer what science says. Quantum theory has demonstrated that we live in a universe in which "reality" as understood in scientific terms is very, very strange. Indeed, so strange that it cannot be adequately described using the categories of language and logical thought that we humans have at our disposal. Quantum theory reveals that our confidence in the existence of some sort of solid, predictable, easy-to-understand universe is completely misplaced. Quite to the contrary of what the traditional scientific perspective so confidently asserted, the universe is really weird! More weird, in fact, than we can possibly imagine.

Does that "prove" anything about the existence of God or a spiritual reality? Of course not. But what it does do, or at least should do for the intellectually honest thinker, is free one from the false restrictions of the traditional scientific perspective and open up the *possibility* that reality could be far different than it appears to be to our everyday understanding of things. The traditional scientific worldview seemed to leave no room for anything other than the mechanistic world of cold, hard, deterministic matter, and in that world there was no room for Spirit. The quantum worldview demonstrates that that traditional scientific perspective is false, and consequently the post-quantum scientific perspective leaves open the *possibility* of almost anything. To the intellectually honest thinker, the insights of quantum theory can only lead to a sense that reality is something incomprehensibly mysterious and unfathomable. To the thinker familiar with quantum theory, for whom the "scientific" worldview is the quantum-informed worldview rather than the outmoded traditional Newtonian one, science does not provide the rock solid foundation for asserting that we live in a Godless universe. Rather, science (when quantum-informed) provides us with an awareness that we live in a mysterious and marvelous universe, about which it's very difficult to say anything in definitive terms. Quantum theory does not prove that the reality in which we live includes Spirit; but quantum theory does demonstrate that we live in a very strange place, such that the only reasonable perspective taken by someone who wishes to be intellectually honest is one that is open to potentially unimaginable possibilities. Science neither proves nor disproves the existence of a God, but science as properly understood in contemporary terms (i.e., in quantum terms) does not prove the existence of a matter-only universe either. To the extent that science demonstrates anything about the larger nature of reality, it's simply that what we call reality goes far beyond what was conceived of by pre-quantum traditional science.

So how do we think about the relationship between science and religion in the 21st century? The intellectually honest person does not think, "I can't believe in God because of what science proves," but rather, "I have no idea what to believe because of what science proves." And it's *through that opening that is created by an enlightened understanding of science that we begin to find a path back to Spirit.* With this understanding of the contemporary scientific worldview, fully informed by the puzzles of the quantum realm, it's OK to acknowledge that we live in a mysterious world which science has not comprehensively explained. And in that context, it's permissible to wonder: could it be the case, that in this mysterious cosmos, a spiritual dimension does exist?

Chapter 8

Basic Epistemology:
How We Know What We Know

So far we have established that the view of reality that is produced by a scientific perspective is not necessarily a threat to a spiritual worldview. Certainly the scientific perspective does not prove or confirm anything of a spiritual nature, but it does reflect the exceedingly mysterious and strange nature of the cosmos in which we find ourselves, and it leaves open the possibility of dimensions of reality other than those which we access through a scientific approach.

But there is a deeper issue here with regard to the implications of our assessment of the role of science. We've already looked at the view of the universe that we achieve through a scientific approach, and discovered that it's not the spirit-denying materialism that it is often thought to be in the popular imagination. But the deeper issue is how we achieve that view, or for that matter, any view. In other words, how is it that we come to "know" what we claim to know about anything? In daily life, this is sort of an unexamined issue: we just assume that as conscious creatures we have the capacity to "know" things, and that knowledge, while subject to evaluation and error, is, generally speaking, accurate. Philosophers, however, have called this everyday assumption into question (sometimes using the label "naïve realism"), and that leads us to the topic of epistemology.

Epistemology is the study of how we know what we know. It gets into some very complicated considerations, but we'll stick with the basics here.

Let's take something as simple as color. How do I know that the banana that I'm looking at right now is yellow? The simple answer, of course, would be that you're looking at it and seeing yellow, so of course it's yellow. And yet, when we start to break down the process through which we arrive at this knowledge of the yellowness of the banana, the certainty of that knowledge quickly becomes rather uncertain.

Consider, for instance, the process that occurs that allows us to perceive yellow (or, for that matter, any color). I look at the object (banana). Light is striking that object as I look at it. Some of that light is absorbed by the banana, and some of it is reflected. Some of that reflected light enters my eye, where it triggers a variety of electrochemical neurological events, running from the cornea through the retina and the optic nerve to, eventually, specific visual-processing areas of the brain. Only when that process has been completed do I have the experience of seeing the color yellow.

But here's the catch: does the fact that my perceptual system (eye, nerves, brain) produces a perception of yellow in my consciousness actually mean that the *object itself* is yellow? Or is it the case that the perception of yellowness is more the product of how my particular perceptual system works, and it really doesn't tell us much at all about the banana itself?

This issue has been explored for centuries by philosophers, including the 18th century British philosopher John Locke, who made a distinction between primary and secondary qualities. A primary quality is a quality that inheres in the object, and is not dependent on our perception. The shape of an object, for instance, is simply a quality of the object and is not dependent on our perception of it. Secondary qualities, however, are not part of the object itself, but rather are the result of interaction between the object and our perceptual system. "Yellow" is not in the banana – it's in our brain, or more accurately, in our consciousness. If we would break down the structure of the banana to its atomic components, would they still be yellow? No, not at all. Breaking down the banana would alter how light strikes it, which would alter what light gets absorbed and what gets reflected, which in turn would alter what happens to the human visual perception mechanisms that produce the perception of "yellow."

This clearly points to a truth that seems rather counterintuitive and contrary to our common-sense understanding of our knowledge of the world: color is not something that is "out there" (Locke's primary quality) but rather something that happens "in here" (a secondary quality). What we believe to be an obvious quality of the world that we observe is in fact an internal experience that occurs as the result of a series of complex interactions between a perceived object, our sensory apparatus, and consciousness. We don't live in a world of colors: we live in a world of internal experiences of colors.

This example illustrates the profound implications for our purported understanding of the nature of what's "out there." All of our understanding of what we call "reality" is not so much a direct knowledge of what's out there as it is a mediated experience in which what we know about what's out there is entirely dependent on the specific means that we, as human creatures, have at our disposal for interacting with what's out there. The five senses, our capacity to reason, and consciousness itself all take the raw sensory data that comes to us and process that material as best we can.

Something very crucial follows from this recognition of how perception is an interactive process dependent on the perceptual capacities of the observer. It means, quite starkly, that we never know reality as it is, but only that aspect of reality that can be known through the specific and limited sensory capacities that we possess.[33] What looks to us as yellow might look to another organism as grey or red. Which is the "correct" perception of its color? The answer, of course, is that there is no "correct" color perception, since color is in the eye of the perceiver, so to speak.

This observation radically relativizes the nature of our knowledge of the world: we can only know that slice of reality as it is processed through our senses. Not just color, but sound, touch, smell, taste, shape... indeed, everything that we know about the world is dependent on our sensory apparatus, and that sensory apparatus is a rather limited one. As humans, for instance, we can see certain colors, but that doesn't mean that those are the only colors in the light that is reflected off the objects we perceive. Ultraviolet and infrared colors also exist out there, but we don't see them (unless, of course, we are using the appropriate technology) because our sensory apparatus doesn't have the ability to do so. We look at a field on a dark night and see blackness. A lion looks at the same field and sees all sorts of living creatures, due to the capacities of the lion's sensory apparatus. We step outside on a quiet night and enjoy the silence, while the bat flying overhead "hears" (or, perhaps more correctly, in some manner "perceives") a multitude of sounds generated by movement, including our own. What we know about the nature of reality is not reality itself, but a very limited slice of reality based on our very limited sensory capacities.

This observation has some very problematic consequences for scientific knowledge. Science is based on empirical observation and rational inferences made from those empirical observations. We observe certain things about the world, put that information together, and process it in a rational, logical manner to produce various generalizations about the way things are. But if we recognize that our sensory apparatus only produces a very limited view of what's out there, the value of the empirical observation that is the root of scientific knowledge is radically diminished. Science is based on that aspect of reality that humans can perceive, what humans can perceive is based on their sensory apparatus, and that sensory apparatus is of a rather limited nature. What science can perceive is only that presumably small part of reality that is perceivable through the lens of the five senses possessed by the human species.

Unfortunately, we generally fail to acknowledge this profound limitation on our capacity to know reality, which in turn leads to a profound limitation on the role of science as the means by which we come to know the nature of what is real. In a sense, we are deeply caught up in a bad case of *epistemological parochialism*, or the mistaken belief that our very limited and localized perception of reality is equivalent to knowledge of reality as a whole. One can understand how we might get seduced by science, given the steady accumulation of knowledge and the dramatic changes to our world brought about by the technological innovations that have flowed from scientific knowledge. But when examined solely from the perspective of whether or not it produces a comprehensive understanding of what's out there, science is shown to be quite limited.

We can appreciate the depth of this epistemological parochialism when we consider that, as a species, we could have evolved in a multitude of different ways, which in turn could have led to the development of different capacities to perceive the world. Why should we assume that the specific and limited perceptual capacities evolved by this one species are the capacities necessary to gain an accurate and comprehensive understanding of the nature of all reality? Would it not be much more reasonable to suggest that what we perceive is simply the result of our specific evolved capacity to perceive, with the understanding that we could have evolved differently, developed different perceptual apparatus, and consequently come to know other aspects of reality? Indeed, it clearly is the case that other species have developed different sensory apparatus and can consequently perceive aspects of reality (infrared light, temperature changes, whatever it is that allows birds to migrate over the same course year after year, etc.) that we cannot.

When we recognize the parochial nature of the commonly held belief that through science we can come to understand the entire nature of reality, there is a certain intellectual humility that is in order. Epistemological parochialism is essentially the arrogant belief that a single species, which is simply a *single constellation of matter/energy* that has existed for a *short period* of time in a *tiny spot* in the known universe, should possess the capability to understand the nature of all of existence, throughout the entire expanse of space and time. We don't assume that an ant has the capacity to do calculus, and in the context of the vastness of all time and space, the human species is no more likely to be able to understand all of reality.

So what's the point of this discussion of the epistemological limitations of science with regard to the larger concern of this book, namely how to think about religion in the 21st century? In a certain sense there is no point: that is to say, recognition of the epistemological limitations of science does not lead to any sort of conclusion regarding the existence (or nonexistence of) a spiritual reality. But recognizing this limitation of science as a means of knowing what is real does free us from the culturally-imposed restrictions on what is considered to be an "acceptable" belief, and indeed has been increasingly considered as such for the past century and a half or so. Deconstructing the epistemological scope of the scientific way of knowing allows us to see that that way of knowing is not the only way of knowing open to someone who, here in the 21st century, wishes to maintain their intellectual honesty and self-respect. It simply is not the case that scientific knowledge is "obviously" the only respectable way to understand reality. In fact, as we've shown above, it's a rather limited and parochial approach to understanding reality as a whole. Scientific knowing (empiricism and reason) works wonderfully when applied to that domain out of which it evolved: that aspect of reality which we can perceive through our five senses is indeed knowable through science in a manner that cannot be known through other means. But that's the limit of scientific knowledge, and that limit should be clearly seen when one puts scientific knowledge in the context of its evolutionary development, as we have done above.

In a sense, then, both this chapter and the previous one simply clear the air; they free us from modern culture's mistaken acceptance of scientific knowledge as clear, comprehensive, and exclusive. As we indicated in the previous chapter, what 20th century science revealed about the world of space and time is indeed far more strange and mysterious, and in some cases seemingly irrational, than we tend to recognize. Taking that a step farther, in this chapter we have demonstrated that aside from science producing knowledge of a limited dimension of reality that is quite strange and hardly the affirmation of materialism that it is often assumed to confirm, the very enterprise of pursuing knowledge via the scientific method is itself extremely limited. In the realm of what science is capable of knowing, it has revealed a reality that is not the dead, predictable materialism that the nonbelieving advocates of science would have us accept, and the epistemological parochialism of science demonstrates that the realm of what science is capable of knowing is extraordinarily limited.

All of this "proves" nothing with reference to spirituality, *but it leaves open an enormous space of possibilities* that many in our culture have tended to close off by erroneously assigning science a role as the exclusive means of acquiring accurate and comprehensive knowledge of what's out there. Science can't do that. And that leads us to the possibility that perhaps there are other means of knowing – including spiritual means.

So with reference to thinking about religion in the 21st century, if (as we discussed in earlier chapters) there is good reason to reject much of the language and concepts of traditional religion, and if, as also covered in this and the previous chapters, there is good reason to not confine our knowledge to what can be known through science, where does that leave us, especially with reference to religion?

Here's where things get interesting – really interesting, and quite tricky, and that's where we're headed next.

Chapter 9

A State of Transition

So with regard to the question that we're looking at – how to think about religion in the 21st century – we've just spent eight chapters clarifying how *not* to think about religion in the 21st century. It's OK to reject the traditional ways of thinking about religion, or at least to reinterpret those traditional ways in fairly radical ways, and still identify oneself as a "spiritual" person. That's more or less been the background theme to what we've covered so far.

But in terms of some sort of *positive* content, how should we think about religion once we've set aside the traditional religious worldview? It's easy enough to set aside ways of thinking that are deemed no longer adequate, but replacing those discarded ideas is another matter, especially considering that intermingled with the easy-to-discard mythological elements of traditional religious belief there is a deep core of spiritual truth. It's important, and exceedingly difficult, to separate the wheat from the chaff, so to speak. We need to hang on to the deeper wisdom of traditional spirituality even while developing alternative ways to think about all things spiritual. It's toward the development of that positive content that we now, finally, turn.

Before proceeding, however, a few words of caution might be in order: in a very fundamental way, the "religion of the future" might be something quite different from religion as we know it today and have known it for the past 2000 years or so. And we're referring to a difference not in content (although that too will likely be different) but rather a much broader difference in its very nature.

More specifically, the religion of the future is not likely to be the precise, clearly defined set of beliefs and practices that are clearly laid out in doctrinal confessions and manuals of correct practice. That's how religion as we know it has always been: a specific set of beliefs and a specific set of practices, clearly identifying a religion as its own thing, and clearly separating it from other claimants to the title of the one true faith.

For a variety of reasons which we will be examining in the following chapters, it's reasonable to believe in the existence of a spiritual reality. But, again for reasons that we'll be covering throughout the following pages, perhaps it is no longer reasonable to pretend that we can articulate the nature of that spiritual reality in precise terms, and certainly not with the professed degree of specificity that one finds in the creeds of the Christian Church or in the theological and philosophical writings of Islam, Buddhism, Hinduism, etc. Christianity has its Apostles Creed with twenty explicit propositions that a Christian is expected to affirm as true. Islam is a bit more concise, but nonetheless there are the Five Pillars, which articulate the specific expectations, in both belief and practice, of a believing Muslim. Even a generally non-creedal tradition such as Judaism has the thirteen Fundamental Principles of Moses Maimonides. And then, of course, aside from the concise statements of the content of faith provided for the ordinary believer, there are the virtually endless volumes of theology that profess to lay out in great detail the nature of God, the nature of the soul, our ultimate destiny, and basically all things spiritual. Even in the Asian traditions where creedal-type statements are less prominent, we find extensive theological/philosophical works that offer remarkably detailed speculations about the nature of sacred reality – all the more remarkable in light of the prominent theme in Hinduism, Buddhism, and Daoism that the nature of spiritual reality is ineffable, or something beyond words.

If you're anticipating that the transition to a new spirituality will be accompanied by equally confident, explicit, and detailed accounts of the nature of Spirit, you're likely to be disappointed. The spirituality that is developing – and the way of looking at spirituality in the 21st century that we will be describing below – is something quite different. In a certain sense, it's a glimpse at something, and only a glimpse at something. This vagueness might be rather frustrating to some, but it exists for good reasons.

First, consider that we are in a transition phase from Axial Age spirituality to post-Axial spirituality. Considering that we've been immersed in Axial Age spirituality for over 2000 years, moving away from that will not be an easy or rapid process. We're clearly leaving behind one way of thinking about religion, but the new way which will replace it is still evolving. Evolution of human concepts, especially about something as elusive as Spirit, is a slow process, and we are in the very early stages of this spiritual evolution. The transition from pre-Axial to Axial spirituality spanned well over 1000 years, so humanity will need to be patient as we slowly wean ourselves away from some of the traditional ways of thinking about Spirit and gradually, in fits and starts, develop new alternatives. It will take time, and we've only recently (as in, the past 200 years or so – a short time in human spiritual development) begun.

But aside from the fact that we're only at an early stage of a long developmental process, it could also be the case that the spirituality of the future might never be quite like that which it replaces in the sense that, even as our understanding of Spirit detaches itself from Axial Age thought and coalesces into something with more defined content than what we have now, that new understanding of the nature of God and all things religious might always lack the level of detail and sense of certainty found in traditional religion. In a sense, humanity has developed a sense of self-awareness that is accompanied by a decreased ability to engage in self-deception. We now can introspectively reflect on our ideas about God, and recognize that they are that and only that: *our ideas* about God, which is to say, the mental content generated by tiny pieces of matter at a brief moment in time at a tiny spot in the universe, using a tiny chunk of gooey grey matter known as a brain. Given that insight into what we are and the context of how we know what we know, there will hopefully be a certain element of humility in future assertions about spiritual matters that was lacking in our predecessors. We can put our efforts at knowing God in an epistemological context that earlier humans never could have imagined, and with that distinctly modern context comes the recognition that we should maintain a certain humility in recognizing the somewhat preposterous notion that a tiny chunk of matter could grasp the essence of that which is the source, sustenance, and end of all time and space.

What's more, we now have a cross-cultural perspective that our ancestors lacked. It was probably much easier to believe that God spoke only to one ethnic group when that ethnic group was largely confined to the geographical area we now call the Middle East. And it was easier for Christians to believe that God had become incarnate once and only once in the person of Jesus of Nazareth when Christians (or at least the vast majority of Christians) had never heard of the Indian tradition of the incarnations (avatars) of Vishnu, a tradition that probably originated prior to the beginning of the Christian era. But those days of cultural isolation that allowed beliefs in one's parochial understanding of Spirit to sound convincing are long gone.[34] We are now, whether we like it or not, global citizens exposed to a wide world of spiritual ideas. We have a global consciousness, and that includes a global awareness of spirituality. We now know that there are seemingly countless ways to think about Spirit, and a seemingly endless variety of practices designed to connect us with an awareness of that Reality. And in that context of pluralistic spiritual knowledge and experience, to assert that one particular understanding of God is the only valid one is no longer an option for the honest believer.

Along these same lines of changes in the evolving human consciousness, we also need to recognize the modern insight into the nature of myth. The existing world religions all emerged at a time in the Axial Age when humanity still thought in mythical terms, which is to say they thought in terms of grand cosmic events and fantastic heroes and saviors performing supernatural deeds. Our understanding of myth today no longer makes it possible to naïvely accept these ancient stories, and more importantly for our consideration of the religion of the future, it prevents us from articulating the content of the emerging spirituality in mythical terms. This is not intended to in any way disparage the old myths ("old" in origin, but, of course, still with us in all of the surviving Axial Age religions), but it is to acknowledge that an honest, historically self-aware, self-reflective consciousness finds it difficult to accept myth on the same terms that it has been traditionally accepted. That is to say, a contemporary consciousness cannot accept myth as history, but rather acknowledges myth as myth. Again, this is not to devalue myth: to say that a myth is not an account of a historical event is not to deny that the *meaning* conveyed by the myth contains profound spiritual truth. But there is, of course, a difference between treasuring a story about, for example, a dying and rising God as a story about a historical event and treasuring a story about a dying and rising God as an expression of the spiritual vindication that comes from commitment to truth and goodness even if that commitment leads to physical death. One might even say that the latter, non-literal interpretation of the event elevates rather than denigrates the myth, in the sense that it elevates it to the status of an expression of a universal spiritual truth rather than merely an account of something that happened at a particular moment and place in space and time.

But our concern here is not to defend the modern (and post-modern) understanding of myth, but rather to simply acknowledge that mythical thinking is something that the 21st century person of faith simply cannot do, at least not in the naïve and unquestioning way of those who created myths centuries ago and those who have clung, at much sacrifice to intellectual honesty, to those same myths right up to today. In light of our increasingly "demythologized" 21st century consciousness, it is not likely that, as we see the emergence of a new spirituality (or spiritualities), it will be expressed in mythical terms. Some forward-looking thinkers such as Thomas Berry have called for the need for a "new myth" or "new story" to replace the dualistic, human-centered myth of the Western religions,[35] but no such myth has clearly emerged yet, and no such myth is likely to emerge given the nature of our consciousness. With reference to the religion of the 21st century, this means that it's unlikely that there will emerge any neat, tidy, enthralling stories (myths) that, in poetic language, express the essence of this new spirituality. It would be nice to have a new myth, *but we don't think in those terms anymore*, so it's just not likely to happen.

Of course, what the alternative to a new myth will be is open to speculation. How *will* we express our understanding of spiritual reality in light of our post-Axial, post-mythic, multicultural consciousness? The answer may be in modes of expression of which we are not yet aware, perhaps modes that somehow transcend but also include both the mythic and scientific modes of knowing. Time will tell, but in the meantime, let's proceed – finally – with what we can positively say about religion in the 21st century, given the cognitive capacities and modes of expression which we already have at hand.

Chapter 10

Perennialism: What We Already Know

And so, finally, we get to the details of the task that we set out to accomplish: identify how one can be a religious believer in the 21st century. Having in effect used the previous chapters to perform the deconstructive task of challenging much of the traditional religious worldview and dispensing with any sense of guilt over taking that step, we are now ready for the constructive step of trying to figure out what sort of spiritual perspective can replace the traditional one. If it is indeed possible for someone to be intellectually, morally and spiritually honest in the 21st century and still believe in some sort of transcendent spiritual reality, what would that belief be like?

We should begin by repeating the earlier observation that a 21st century (or what might more accurately be called post-Axial) spirituality might not be nearly as specific, detailed, and definitive as that which we find in the Axial Age religions that are still with us. Post-Axial spirituality is not likely to contain explicit statements of beliefs and practices as can be found in, for instance, the Christian Nicene Creed, the Five Pillars of Islam, the Three Jewels of Buddhism, or any of the many other confidently precise and comprehensive statements of Axial tradition faith.

In other words, the new spirituality that we are about to try to unpack is likely to be a bit fuzzy. In part, that's because it's still developing. The shift from pre-Axial to Axial spirituality took place over a span of several centuries (some might argue over a millennium), and during that long period of time the traditions that seem so clearly defined today evolved slowly and fitfully. The concept of one God or a unitary spiritual principle, for instance, does not just appear overnight. Even in the Biblical tradition, for instance, the transition from polytheism to a definitive monotheism was a long, slow process. Christians and Jews might firmly assert their belief in one God, but even in the early books of their sacred text one can clearly see that the "one God" of the Hebrews was initially a god among gods – the most powerful of all gods, but nonetheless not the only one. In other words, it took time for Abrahamic monotheism to evolve to the refined and pure form that it eventually reached in Judaism, Christianity, and Islam. All three traditions claim to a clear and emphatic allegiance to belief in one God, but that belief evolved from something quite different and had to change in many ways over a long period of time before it became the belief that we find today in those traditions.

One could cite similar examples of how beliefs and practices which are now considered definitive in other traditions are actually the product of a long developmental process (karma in Hinduism, the Bodhisattva in Buddhism, Li (Principle) in Chinese religion, etc.). Keeping that in mind, as we look in a forward direction to the content of a 21st century, post-Axial spirituality, we should recognize that it will take time – probably a very, very long time – for our spiritual consciousness to move from 2000 years of Axial spirituality to whatever it is that will succeed it. Something else is coming, but what it is and when it will reach some sort of definitive expression, is anybody's guess.

But even leaving aside the fact that the new spirituality is in a process of development and hence constantly changing, it might be the case that post-Axial spirituality never attains the degree of specificity and concreteness that we find in traditional religion. Our reason for suggesting the possibility of an always-fuzzy sort of spirituality is that, as a species, we have developed a sense of self-consciousness that did not exist on a wide scale and with such depth at the time of the emergence of the traditional religions. Personally, culturally, and historically we are more self-aware than our ancestors who lived during the formative years of the current world religions. We now recognize the extent to which culture and history influence our perceptions and cognitions. We now recognize that knowledge, whether secular or spiritual, is always to some extent conditioned and contextually limited by the personal, cultural, and historical circumstances of the knower. Consequently, we also recognize that there is no complete "truth" to which we have access, but only that part of truth that we have the capacity to perceive, based on our limited perspective.

The consequence of this self-awareness, in terms of the future development of religion, is likely to be an ongoing sensitivity to the need to remain open about spiritual "truth," recognizing that it is something that will always be open to modification. Once self-awareness reaches the point of recognizing the relativity of our epistemological positions, it becomes difficult to assert that truth as one sees it is the only and final truth.

Nonetheless, keeping these preliminary thoughts in mind, let's proceed: What will post-Axial spirituality look like (however tentative and open to change that might be)?

Paradoxically, in looking to what might be a valid spirituality for the 21st century believer, we will begin with a reassessment of those very Axial Age traditions that much of this work has suggested are becoming obsolete. This may seem somewhat contradictory: Why look for insight into the very traditions that we have just critiqued as the product of an earlier time, based on concepts no longer tenable in the 21st century, and headed to eventual demise?

The answer is that there is a distinction between the *specific* elements of the Axial traditions and the *underlying* truths that they express. The specific elements are indeed culturally and historically relative, and will slowly be replaced by concepts that are more aligned with contemporary modes of awareness. But behind those specific elements, there appears to be the broader, more fundamental truth from which those elements derive. Behind all of the specific creeds and rituals there is the awareness of the spiritual reality that transcends the specific expressions of any given tradition. The details of any Axial Age religion might be the product of a specific culture and time period, but the spiritual awareness that generated those ideas is universal. Perhaps we can look at the existing traditions in an attempt to identify the broader, non-culturally relative elements that reflect this deeper spiritual awareness, an awareness of a reality that is there all the time, and hence would be just as much a part of the spirituality of the future as it has been of the Axial Age religions.

This is hardly a new idea, and in fact has a name: *Perennialism*, or the *Perennial Philosophy*. Perennialism was quite popular in the mid- to late-20th century, and was championed by notable figures such as the celebrated literary figure, Aldous Huxley (author of *The Perennial Philosophy*) and Huston Smith, the author of what for many years was the most widely used college text on World Religions.[36]

The basic idea of Perennialism is that behind the vast diversity of beliefs and practices found in the world's many religions, there is a common core of universal spiritual truth. Perennialism argues that when one looks beyond culturally and historically conditioned surface appearances, as found in tradition-specific doctrines, creeds, rituals, ethical codes, etc., one finds a common substratum of spiritual truth. This spiritual substratum is available to be recognized by all humans, regardless of where and when they live. Once recognized, however, it tends be interpreted through and overlaid with the symbols and concepts that are part of that culture, as is the case with all human knowledge. A human being living in India in the first century will see the bright object that rises in the East in the morning, traverses the sky while providing light and warmth, and sets in the West, and refer to it with the only linguistic symbol that he/she possesses – Surya – and understand it according to his/her available repertoire of knowledge: it's a divine celestial being which provides sustenance in response to the appropriate petitionary sacrifices. By contrast, an American in the 20th century will refer to that same object as the "sun" and understand it as a ball of burning gas around which the planets of this solar system orbit, emitting heat and light according to the presently known laws of physics. Two very different descriptions, but both based on a perception of the same object, according to the categories of understanding and expression available to the first century Indian and 20th century American. There really is something out there, and each party is perceiving it (and, one could argue, perceiving it in the same way), but when it comes to using words to understand and describe what they commonly perceive, the descriptions are quite different given the different linguistic toolboxes that they possess.

Perennialists argue that a similar scenario applies to perception of spiritual reality. A spiritual reality does exist, independent of human perception of it. But when we try to understand and articulate our awareness of that spiritual reality, we employ the categories of our culturally- and historically-limited linguistic and conceptual toolboxes, and hence the different religions. Perennialists attempt to look behind those diverse expressions and identify the common object of experience and belief that has been described using the limited means available to whatever culture the particular religion emerged from. Perennialists would argue that just as "Surya" and "sun" both refer to the same real object, likewise Yahweh, Allah, Brahman, Dharmakaya, and Dao also all refer to the same reality. The challenge for the Perennialist is to dig behind the culturally-generated expressions and find the non-culturally biased reality to which the expressions refer. And when this is done, Perennialists argue, one finds a "perennial truth," or a core of assertions about the nature of Spirit that are universal and cut across cultures.

Put in terms of Axial Age spirituality, Perennialists believe that while the specific doctrines and practices found in existing religious traditions reflect the culturally and historically limited perspectives of the cultures in which those traditions emerged and evolved, one can peer behind those Axial Age cultural limitations and get a glimpse of the spiritual reality that each tradition is an expression of, however partial and inadequate that expression might be. And what one finds beneath those culturally limited expressions is a core of spiritual truths, found in all religions, that has not changed significantly over time (and, hence, is "perennial").

Of course, to demonstrate that there are commonly shared generic beliefs among the existing world religions is not to prove that those beliefs are valid. The existence of a shared package of beliefs is not equivalent to establishing a truth claim in any decisive sort of way about those beliefs. One could argue that the perennial wisdom simply reflects a universally shared wish-fulfillment for freedom from suffering and death. Or one could take sociological or psychological reductionist approaches and argue that the existence of the perennial truths can be explained away, or reduced to psychological and sociological factors that simply reflect universal human needs.

Our purpose here, however, is not to explore the validity of attempts to explain away religion via reductionist explanations. We would suggest that such explanations, while based on valid insights of limited applicability, are nonetheless unprovable explanations in the same sense that strictly spiritual explanations are for the origin of religions. Freud, Durkheim, Marx and others make valid observations about certain elements of religion, but their theories are hardly the all-encompassing explanations of religion that they claim to be. But again, for our purposes we will be leaving aside the question of reductionism.

What, then, can we learn from the Perennialist attempt to discern a common core of spiritual truths behind the specific manifestations of spiritual truth in the existing religions? Perhaps for starters, we should simply acknowledge three fundamental points: 1) a common core of spiritual belief does exist (on this, see more below); 2) the existence of that core begs for an explanation (it's not something that likely could have occurred by chance); and 3) the derivation of that common core from an actually existent spiritual reality is a reasonable (but by no means proven) explanation. In other words, it's not unreasonable to infer from the existence of a common core of religious beliefs that those beliefs have come into existence as the result of human awareness of an existing spiritual reality. This does not *prove* the existence of Spirit/God/Sacred Reality, but it certainly functions as a piece of evidence that can be woven into the broader tapestry of ideas that are reasonable and credible to the 21st century citizen and hence can contribute to the groundwork for how to think about religion in the 21st century. So let's take a look at that common core, or Perennial Truth.

Bearing in mind that Perennialism seeks to identify the generic and universal elements found in all religions, the elements of Perennialism are few and simple, and might be summarized as follows:

1. *A spiritual reality exists.*
2. *Nothing is more important than our relationship with that spiritual reality.*
3. *Virtue, or morality, is an essential element of that sacred reality.*
4. *The existence of that spiritual reality is the basis for a broad interconnectedness between all beings.*
5. *In the end, all will be well.*

Of course, what we are positing here could be broken down, expanded upon, sliced and diced, and complicated in an endless variety of ways, but what we're trying to hone in on here is the true essence of what we find when we seek to discern the commonality that exists across the wide spectrum of existing Axial Age religious traditions. These are the basics, but one should not say *only* the basics. To the contrary, it's precisely the basics that are important. It's that core kernel of universal spiritual insight that suggests that there is indeed a "perennial" spiritual truth hiding behind the confusing array of different beliefs and practices in the world's religions. So let's briefly look at each of the five components.

A spiritual reality exists

All religions assert that the totality of reality is not fully accounted for by the physical universe. However unimaginably immense the size of the universe might be, however unimaginably long the age of the universe might be, however marvelously complex and multifaceted and astounding the structures of the universe might be, *there is something more than the physical universe*. There is *something more than the totality of all time and space and matter and energy*.

In a sense, that may sound like a rather prosaic assertion, but it is perhaps the sort of assertion that one needs to step back from a bit to fully appreciate its weight and depth: there is something more than the totality of all time and space and matter and energy. All means *all*; totality means *totality*; something more means *something more*. When fully grasped, this is a quite astonishing assertion. And, indeed, one might argue, an assertion that is so radical that we can't even begin to grasp what it means (more on this important point in later chapters).

But clearly, we find this assertion in all religions, expressed in the specific symbols and cultural expressions available to the particular people who attempted to articulate and make some sort of sense of this intuited awareness of a "something more." Of course, this is not to say that all religions agree on what the specific nature of this Something More is. The Jewish understanding of Yahweh is not identical to the Christian understanding of the Triune God, which is not the same as the Muslim understanding of Allah, which is not the same as the Hindu understanding of Brahman, which is not the same as the Buddhist understanding of Shunyata or Tathata, which is not the same as the Chinese understanding of the Dao.[37] But the point is that all of the diverse cultures out of which these notions evolved asserted, in quite definitive and confident terms, that some sort of reality – some sort of Spirit – exists. Jews, Muslims, Christians, Hindus, Buddhists, Daoists, and others might differ about the precise nature of that spiritual reality. Indeed, Jews, Muslims, Christians, Hindus, (and even) Buddhists and Daoists have fought each other, not just in a theological/literary sense but in a quite literal, deadly sense, over their competing claims to possess the truth about the nature of that spiritual reality. But again, the point is not the elements of disagreement, but rather the agreement that a spiritual reality or dimension does indeed exist. *There is something more.*

The differences of opinion on the nature of that spiritual reality are easy enough to explain. As we've said before, how could one expect a tiny creature that has existed on for a brief moment in the history of the universe at a tiny pinpoint in that universe to be able to adequately understand and articulate the nature of something so radically other, mysterious, and grand as that of Spirit? What is remarkable is simply the universal assertion, cutting across cultures and time periods, that *there is something more.*

Nothing is more important than our relationship with that spiritual reality

The second insight that we find, expressed in the usual wide variety of forms in the existing religious traditions, is the assertion that nothing in life is more important than our relationship with that spiritual reality. Granted, the specific concepts of that spiritual reality vary greatly, and the specific interpretations of what our relationship with that reality should be like are equally diverse; nonetheless there is that universal sentiment that it is our relationship with that spiritual reality that takes precedence over everything else in life.

At first glance this may seem to be nothing more than an obvious truism, to which the reader responds with a, "So what?" But stepping back for a moment and looking at the human predicament from a fresh perspective, it actually is quite extraordinary that with all of the daily concerns and needs that are characteristic of human life, many of which are indeed necessary for the sheer sake of survival, humans, quite universally, should identify our relationship to the sacred as more of a priority than our very survival needs. As embodied creatures existing in space and time, as constellations of mass and energy that have become self-conscious and recognize the tenuous nature of our existence, that in such a precarious and frighteningly dependent circumstance our species should proclaim the importance, and indeed the priority, of something that exists outside the realm of space/time/matter/energy and has no immediate survival value, is quite remarkable. Of course, humans do not consistently remain true to the aspiration to put spiritual concerns first, and one might easily argue that, quite to the contrary, we often if not usually attend to immediate survival-oriented physical needs first and turn to Spirit only in times of, paradoxically, both extreme desperation and extreme security. But this reflects human frailty, not the human ideal.

That we fail to live up to the ideal not does negate the existence of the ideal itself.

The primacy of our relationship to a spiritual reality can be seen in various monumental achievements of a grand scale throughout history. Egyptian and Mesoamerican pyramids, Stonehenge, Carnac and related monolithic/menhir structures, Ethiopian rock temples, Gothic cathedrals, Persian mosques, elaborate Hindu temples, Buddhist monastic cells carved into impossible-to-reach cliffs – these and countless other examples demonstrate that even in pre-modern culture where subsistence and survival were at the forefront of human need, unimaginable effort, resources, and creativity were devoted not just to foraging for food, growing crops, finding game, building shelters, gathering fuel, and making clothing, but also to the creation of these monumental structures that reflected the importance that humans, from a very early time, assigned to establishing and maintaining a right relationship with Spirit. Of course, the construction of many of these religious structures involved horrendous hardships and even death for oppressed classes of the population and, from a modern ethical perspective, it's difficult to look at something such as the pyramids without a sense of the tragic toll that was inflicted on those who built them. But applying contemporary moral insight to past periods of human history can be a tricky matter, and in any case even the moral revulsion that we feel toward the process by which such structures were built does not change the fact that they were indeed built, and that very construction reflects the depth of the human sense of the importance of maintaining a right relationship with the sacred.

But the importance of our relationship with spiritual reality can be equally appreciated by setting aside the large-scale, historically recognized monuments and simply looking at everyday, ordinary human behavior as it has been manifested since at least the Neolithic era. Going back to at least 40,000 years ago, we see that in dealing with death early humans, even while existing in the most precarious of situations regarding their very survival, took the time and effort to bury the dead in anticipation of an existence in another world. Even in the midst of the pressing needs of food, shelter, and protection from predators, humans took time to recognize spiritual reality by burying the dead with flowers, tools, special pigments, and other non-utilitarian items.

Similarly in the Neolithic era, we find the remarkable cave paintings such as those found at Lascaux, Chauvet, and elsewhere. The precise meaning of these paintings is unclear and lost forever to the mists of history, but they clearly seem to recognize the existence of some type of spiritual relationship between the human and other transcendent realms. What is perhaps most remarkable about these paintings is the effort and time that was put into creating them. Traveling deep into a cave, bringing the necessary supplies such as paints and brushes and some sort of primitive "scaffolding," and even providing some sort of illumination must have required enormous effort and time. That such effort and time was put into the creation of these paintings again points to the recognition, as early as the Neolithic, of the importance of our relationship to a spiritual reality.

But even on a more mundane basis, we can simply look to the evidence of the universal practice of religious sacrifices, rituals, prayer, etc. On an everyday basis, human beings throughout the world, from a very early time, set aside time to cultivate and maintain a relationship with the sacred. In the midst of the daily concerns of everyday life in a physical and social environment that was often hostile and threatening, even in the awareness of the precarious nature of mere survival, humans set aside time (precious time that could have been devoted to more immediate, worldly, survival-oriented concerns) to establish and nurture a relationship with something that they could not even see, touch, or hear. That we in the modern world of urban-industrial mass production of goods, we in the era of healthcare advances that routinely lead to a life span of 80 or more years, that we who live in the relatively stable sociopolitical environment of the modern state, should set aside time for religious concerns should not be surprising – we have the security, safety, and stability that permits us to devote some time to non-survival activities, whether it be sports, literature, video games, or religion. But that humans in pre-modern cultures, going all the way back to at least the Neolithic era, should set aside time to maintain a connection to a sacred reality is indeed quite remarkable.

Looking at Christianity, we see the admonition regarding "man shall not live by bread alone." In Islam we find that the greatest of all sins is *shirk*, narrowly defined as idolatry, but in a broader sense understood as making anything more important in your life than God. In Buddhism (and other religions as well, of course), we find the widespread practice of monasticism where attachment to the usual worldly pleasures and possessions is severed on behalf of solidifying one's relationship with ultimate reality. In the Hindu tradition we find the four stages of life, in which the ideal is to reach a point where, after having completed a successful life in the everyday world of work and family, and having accrued sufficient wealth to provide for those that you leave behind, one becomes a *sannyasin*, or wandering holy person with no permanent attachments and no possessions other than the clothes on your back and a few ritual implements connected with your true purpose of remaining connected to the sacred.

Of course, like all things human, the yearning to cultivate our relationship with Spirit can be perverted in ways that are damaging to both oneself and others. Masochistically punitive asceticism, misogynistic fear and punishment of sexuality, harsh Puritanism that sees the relationship with God as incompatible with appreciation and enjoyment of the precious beauty of the world of space and time, can be found all too frequently in the world's religious traditions. But we would suggest that these are misguided understandings of our relationship with the sacred, rooted in one-sided interpretations of the nature of the relationship between the tangible world and the intangible Spirit. As important and universal as the human awareness of the relationship with the sacred might be, it is nonetheless a subtle and nuanced sensitivity that can easily become unbalanced and lead to contorted spiritualities which, while recognizing the need for the relationship, have a peculiar and often harmful understanding of its content.

The reader might object to the idea that a relationship with spiritual reality is a universal aspect of human behavior by pointing out the undeniable fact that contemporary life suggests that many human beings choose to get along with no consideration whatsoever of their relationship with the sacred. We live in a largely secular culture. Congregational membership is declining in most Christian denominations. Churches and parishes are closing and/or consolidating at an alarming rate. The shortage of professional clergy has reached a crisis point. Obviously, the proportion of our population that seems to be attentive to a relationship with a spiritual reality seems to be declining rather rapidly, at least in the dominant, mainline denominations. Or just look around at the culture in which we live: it's almost exclusively secular. Entertainment, politics, education, business, the arts: all seem to function with little or no consideration of religion. As we define our life in terms of education, career, financial success, image, social status, exotic vacations, sexual prowess, Facebook friends and Twitter followers, the role of religion appears to be (at least on the surface) virtually nonexistent. Clearly we are living in a secular culture.

And yet, the "we" of that last sentence would only apply to a rather small part of the global population, and perhaps even more importantly, to only a short slice of time in the larger context of human history. Yes, it's true that Western (American/ European) culture in the 21st century has become significantly secularized. But that secular culture is the exception, not the norm. In the broad span of human history, the importance of our relationship with the sacred has always been there, with only occasional exceptions. Even in today's world, while secularism dominates much of Europe and America, much of the rest of the world continues to manifest the traditional awareness of the need to have a connection with something spiritual, however diversely that might be understood. Christianity of the mainline variety might be shrinking, but other religious traditions (e.g., Islam and Buddhism) continue to grow. And even in America and Europe, the rise of unaffiliated spirituality and the self-identification of the "nones" as spiritual but not religious[38] suggest that even in the midst of secularized Western culture, there persists a widespread and growing awareness of the importance of our relationship with God.

Virtue, or morality, is an essential element of that sacred reality

The third insight that we can derive from the Perennialist observation of a universal ground of spirituality that exists in all religious traditions is the belief that virtue, or morality, or the Good, is an essential element of the sacred and our relationship with that sacred reality. We can see this in the simple fact that all religions include some sort of moral code: the Torah in Judaism, the Shari'a in Islam, the Laws of Manu in Hinduism, the Analects of Confucius, the Precepts of Buddhism, and more. All religions express what seems to be a universal insight that virtuous behavior is an essential element of the spiritual life.

A skeptic, of course, might question the value of this observation given the obvious differences that exist when one looks at the specifics of the moral codes in the different religions. In some traditions, meat-eating is considered morally wrong, while in others it is completely permissible. Some traditions demand severely oppressive restrictions on the role of women, while others extol the value of the feminine. Polygamy is condemned by some, permitted by others. Pacifism is demanded in some religions, while violence in the name of God is extolled by others. And on and on we could go in citing *specific* differences in the moral codes of different religions.

But there is a broader and more fundamental point, in that behind the specific moral prescriptions, there is 1) the recognition that morality is indeed an essential part of our relationship with God; and 2) an agreement on the general nature of what a moral life consists of.

Regarding the first point, the mere presence of any moral element in a religion, and the presence of such an element in all religions demonstrates our initial point, namely the intimate connection between morality and the sacred. Details regarding the nature of what it means to lead a moral life that is in synch with the divine nature may differ, but the idea that leading a moral life is an essential component of the spiritual life is agreed upon universally. As finite beings limited to the capacities made possible by our possession of a specific and very limited material existence, our ability to discern the details of what constitutes living a life consistent with our spiritual nature may be quite limited, and the moral codes of the various faiths can be seen, from a 21st century perspective, to be essentially "best guesses" or informed intuitions of what the specifics of a spiritually sound moral life should consist of. But behind those best guesses is the recognition that moral goodness, or virtue, however it is understood to be manifested in specific behaviors, is an essential component of spiritual life. We need to lead a good moral life in order to follow a spiritual path, even though we may struggle with identifying the specific do's and don'ts of that path. Morality and spirituality are inseparable.

But to get to our other point, even in the context of uncertainty regarding the *specific* elements of the moral life, there is nonetheless universal agreement regarding the *general* nature of virtue or moral goodness. All religions acknowledge that our behavior should be governed with reference to some sort of limitations on aggression and sex. The specifics may vary, from monogamy to polygamy, from cannibalism to vegetarianism; but the notion that leading a moral life involves channeling our biological drives in a manner that places limits on aggression and sex is universal. Of course, that only covers the constraining side of morality, the "thou shalt nots," so to speak. In addition, there is the converse which is implied by such restrictions, and manifested in positive expressions of virtue such as kindness, compassion, justness, generosity, patience, etc. But in either case, we see the same elements of human life channeled in a similar direction, even though the details may differ.

The existence of that spiritual reality is the basis for a broad interconnectedness between all beings

In everyday ordinary existence, we perceive ourselves as separate, discrete individuals. We define our identity as a "self" that is associated with a specific body which includes a specific brain that generates a sense of consciousness or self-awareness that is unique to that body. "I" know that I am "me" and not "you" by virtue of the fact that I have a different body from you. And consequently I have a different brain-generated sense of self-awareness. My brain generates my consciousness, and no one else possesses that consciousness, nor do I possess anyone else's consciousness.

This is a model of solitary monads, beings which exist in constant awareness of the duality of self and other: I am me, you are not me. Perhaps in a sense, there is something somewhat noble and stoically laudable about such an individualistic existence. Certainly the trend toward an increased sense of unique self-identity is one of the hallmarks of evolving human civilization, as the sense of self slowly arises from its emergence in the shared obscurity of tribal and extended kinship membership.[39]

But such an understanding of what we are can be disturbing as well. Solitary, isolated beings, consciousness-laden bodies that struggle for recognition and survival against other isolated beings, human and otherwise; an isolated consciousness trapped in a body which is slowly (and sometimes quite suddenly) headed toward lifelessness and hence the extinction of consciousness. Such is not a very appealing representation of human existence, and yet this is an accurate account of how secularized modernity, having cast off what is disparaged as the illusion of religion and the existence of Spirit, represents human existence.

In contrast, Perennialism looks at the world's religions and sees a shared sense that a human creature is not an isolated entity, but rather is connected to something bigger than itself. In Christianity we have St. Paul's vision of the mystical "body of Christ" in which all believers are united, an idea expanded in the 20th century to cosmic proportions by the scientist/priest Pierre Teilhard de Chardin, who saw the evolution of the cosmos as an evolution that is gradually uniting not just the human species but all of the universe, sentient and non-sentient. In Hinduism we have the tradition of *advaita*, or non-dualism, rooted in the experiential awareness of the inseparable nature of all that exists, both divine and human. The sense of the non-dual is equally prominent in Buddhism in the notions of Suchness (*Tathata*) and Emptiness (*Shunyata*), and is a foundational element of Buddhist schools such as Vijnanavada and Hwa-Yen.

This sense of connectedness has a twofold aspect: On the one hand, religions assert that we are connected to a spiritual entity. On the other hand, there is the recognition that within the realm of space and time, all things, sentient and non-sentient, are somehow connected.

Of course, the precise nature of these often dim intuitions of sacred connections are worked out in quite different ways in the various traditions. The Christian notion of the unity of the Body of Christ is not identical to the Hindu notion of the unity of Brahman and Atman. But as with all of the elements of Perennialism, the point is not the culturally and historically conditioned specific beliefs and doctrines, but rather the underlying spiritual insight that can be discerned at the root of these various expressions. And that underlying insight is simply that we are connected to something much larger than our individual self.

As such, there is no room for those perspectives that isolate and privilege one group over another. Racism, xenophobia, and nationalism have no place in the context of the universal connectedness of humanity. Even beyond that, cruel treatment of nonhuman species and thoughtless disregard for the impact of human behavior on the nonhuman environment have no place if we are connected in some way to not only other human beings but to *all* beings.

So the Perennialist perspective, drawing from the common thread behind the diverse expressions of connectedness in the existing religious traditions, simply reminds us that we are not alone. We are connected to Something Else: at a transcendent level, connected to Spirit by its many different names, and at an immanent level with the human and nonhuman world which surrounds us. Religion reminds us that we are not alone in what, from a perspective devoid of a sense of Spirit, might seem to be a harsh and meaningless cosmos.

In the end, all will be well

The final insight that we find by extracting the perennial core from a survey of the existing religious traditions is an insight regarding the future, which in simplest terms is the affirmation that *in the end, all will be well.*

Theologically, belief about ultimate destiny (of humanity, the Earth, the entire Cosmos) is known as eschatology. As with other insights derived from the Perennialist perspective, we need to recognize that there is tremendous diversity (and apparent disagreement) in the eschatological beliefs of the world's religions. But again, from a Perennialist perspective the details are not as important as the underlying intuitive insight behind the detailed beliefs, and that underlying insight is a sense that we live in a moral cosmos which, as such, must come to a good end. In a sense, this is simply an observation of the universality and legitimacy of hope. Despite the vastly different specific beliefs about ultimate destiny, all religious traditions affirm that, even in the context of the pain, suffering, tragedy, decay, and heartache of life as embodied human creatures, there is nonetheless reason to be hopeful that in some mysterious (and, admittedly in the face of the evidence, exceedingly improbable) way, suffering will be redeemed and goodness will be the ultimate destiny of being.

In many religions this hopefulness is expressed in some sort of heavenly afterlife. In Judaism, Christianity, and Islam, we find the concept of eternal life in Heaven in the presence of departed loved ones and, of course, God. In other traditions, however, this eschatological hope is found in ideas that are less anthropomorphized and, in the eyes of some, far less clear.

In Buddhism, for example, we have the belief in Nirvana. Nirvana is certainly not, as is sometimes misunderstood by non-Buddhist Westerners, some type of Buddhist heaven. Indeed, when asked by his followers to explain the nature of Nirvana, the Buddha firmly refused to do so on the grounds that it was indescribable, beyond affirming that it was free from all suffering and unhappiness. Nirvana represents what we might call a "non-locational" eschatological belief, as opposed to the "locational" concept of Heaven in the Abrahamic traditions (as well as many other theistic religions). In other words, Nirvana is certainly not a "place" to which one goes, but rather perhaps a state of being that, being outside the realm of temporal/ spatial existence, cannot really be described using the medium of language derived from our spatial/temporal existence. The Buddha's silence on the details of Nirvana seems to be a way of saying something to the effect of, "If I say anything about something that is beyond words, it would be misleading, so it's best to say nothing, other than to affirm that such a blessed state exists." Buddhism actually gets a bit more complicated, in that in some Buddhist traditions there is a belief in heaven, or actually multiple heavenly realms or "Buddha fields," each overseen by an enlightened heavenly Buddha (or more specifically a Bodhisattva, or being who has vowed to delay entry into the state of Nirvana until all living beings are liberated). Similar to the Western traditions, the Buddha-field is sort of a heavenly paradise into which one is reborn after leading a sufficiently good life as an embodied being on Earth. However, unlike the Western concept of eternal life in Heaven, the Buddhist heaven is only a temporary place where, free from the distractions of the pain and suffering which we find in Earthly existence, one can practice the spiritual path to the point of perfection, at which point one eventually enters into (although even the use of the phrase "enters into" is misleading to the extent that it implies a spatial/temporal context) the permanency of Nirvana (again, "permanency" is not exactly an appropriate term, since Nirvana is not in the realm of time).

In the Vedanta school of Hinduism, our ultimate destiny is described in the concept of the union of Atman and Brahman. In Vedanta, Atman is understood to be what Christians might refer to as our "soul," or that part of what we are that is not subject to the limitations of physical existence. Brahman is one of the many terms that is used to refer to what is similar to the Western notion of God, but with a significant difference. Whereas in the Western religions, God is a being who is in a sense separate from that which he creates (a scenario known theologically as dualism, given that there are two fundamentally different realities: God and God's creation), in Hindu Vedanta we find the belief that ultimately *everything is Brahman*, and hence ultimately the soul, or Atman, is also in some sense Brahman. This model of belief is known as non-dualism, or *advaita*, from the Sanskrit meaning "not two." Ultimately there are not two realities but only the one reality of Brahman/Atman. Of course, the advaita model generates all sorts of theological challenges: If everything is Brahman/Atman, then how can there be suffering? If everything is Brahman/Atman, then how can it be the case that as individual human beings we do not know that or feel that we are Brahman/Atman?

But our goal here is not to explore the theological and philosophical challenges of Hindu Vedanta,[40] but simply to point out that there are ways of thinking about our ultimate destiny that are quite different from the Western model of eternal life as an individual person in a Heavenly locale. Hinduism, in other words, despite the differences from the Christian perspective, similarly affirms that in the end, all will be well.

The skeptical reader might understandably respond with something along the lines of, "But how do you expect me to actually believe that stuff? Streets paved with gold. Pearly gates. And what about babies… if an infant dies, does it go to heaven and remain a baby forever? And this notion of eternal life – I can't even conceive of what that might be like. Wouldn't it just get, well, boring at some point? And then, depending on the religion, you have notions such as purgatory, 40 virgins for every man, and so on and so on. It's just not believable."

But in response we would say that, as we expressed in our earlier discussion of "God," the point is not to believe in the specific, culturally and historically conditioned expressions of what the human intuition of a post-spatiotemporal existence might be like, but rather to simply recognize what is behind or underneath all of those specific expressions, which in this case is a sense that the presence of consciousness in the Cosmos is a good thing and is not limited to its manifestation in a physical body of the species which we call human. Not only is there "something more" in the sense of a "God," but there is something more in the sense of consciousness. Thinking about the "afterlife" in the 21st century does not have to mean thinking about the specific expression used by other, mostly ancient cultures when they tried to imagine what an afterlife might be like. Rather, it means recognizing that existence is not confined to the realm of space and time and the constituent components of matter and energy. It is recognizing that there is something unique and extraordinary about human consciousness (and about consciousness in general, no matter in what life form it is manifested), and that the nature of that consciousness is not subject to the limitations of space and time. That's enough: there is no need to try to manufacture a more specific sense of something that we really don't and can't know much about, other than that it exists (more on this later).

Having essentially deconstructed the "traditional" way of thinking about religion in section one, we have begun to reconstruct what might be a viable alternative by examining the common beliefs underlying the surface level diversity found in the existing religious traditions. We have explored the perspective of "Perennialism," or the idea that there is a common core of spiritual thought expressed in the culturally and historically diverse expressions of those traditions. The result of this exploration is the recognition of five simple universal spiritual insights, each covered separately above.

Of course, the universality of what we might call these "deep beliefs" (as opposed to the surface manifestations in specific doctrines and practices) in no way "proves" them to be true, and such proof is not our intent in pointing them out. But on the other hand, the universality of such beliefs should at least give one pause to consider the possibility that they might indeed reflect some sort of basic human awareness of the nature of things that cannot be captured through the measurable, quantifiable, objectivist perspective of rationalism and science. Proof it is not, but grounds for taking religion seriously it should be. Perhaps stories about frogs falling from the sky and books written by divine beings might not be believable to you as a citizen of the 21st century, but hopefully the notion of some sort of transcendent reality behind those myths and symbols might begin to seem at least a possibility, something that is not offensive to the intellect or moral sensibility of the person of our times.

One might object that these five deep beliefs derived from Perennialism are terribly general and do not provide the specificity and detail that one finds in the doctrines and dogma of the existing religions. It's certainly not the Apostles Creed, with its twelve articles, to say nothing of the 95 Theses of Luther, to say nothing of the massive collections of "correct" Christian belief found in the dogma of both the Protestant and Catholic Christian traditions.

But perhaps this is simply the nature of post-Axial religion, or the religious perspective that is in the process of emerging in our own time. Perhaps the "religion of the future" will be intentionally and necessarily less specific and more general in its assertions about the spiritual dimension, and for good reason. Humanity has developed a certain self-awareness of the contextual and historical nature of human belief systems.

We now recognize that there is a universal human tendency to use symbols, metaphors, stories, etc. to articulate various aspects of how we experience the world, particularly those aspects of the world that cannot be quantified and measured, those aspects that point to an element of depth and meaning, whether religious or not, that cannot so easily be described by the scientific equations and theories, but which submit much more readily to the phrases of the poet, storyteller, etc. Perhaps we have been misled over the past three centuries of scientific and technological advances to presume that the only reality is the reality that can be precisely and comprehensively observed and described by the scientist.[41] The truth is that there are other dimensions to existence, wherein are found equally "real" things such as value, meaning, and Spirit, which cannot be so easily and precisely articulated. And knowing now that the language of symbols is a language of pointers to that reality, but not the reality itself, perhaps we can refrain from saying too much about that dimension of the Real that can be sensed and experienced, but not measured, quantified, categorized, and neatly labeled in the manner that can be done with the stuff of matter, space, and time.

Perhaps, then, the religion of the future will be characterized by what might be called a "theological minimalism," or a tendency to not say more than is necessary. At the same time, however, not saying enough can be as problematic as saying too much. The theological minimalism of post-Axial religion will have to tread a fine line between saying too much – or more than one is warranted in saying – and saying too little – which can fail to provide adequate guidance for those looking for direction and can lead to misinterpretation and manipulation. But that fine line will be something that evolves over time, with swings likely occurring to the excess in either direction, as the religion of the future slowly emerges.

Chapter 11

Consciousness

But perhaps you don't find the evidence from Perennialism very convincing. Sure, there are shared beliefs among the existing religions, but you might say, so what? The fact that multiple religious traditions share certain core beliefs does not necessarily mean that those beliefs are therefore true. Perhaps it reflects nothing more than a shared illusion, or a universal human tendency to project how we would like things to be in the universe. In other words, perhaps there are ways to explain away the universality of the core beliefs in the world religions. Or regardless of whether and how one might explain the insights of Perennialism, perhaps you just aren't willing to accept something as true unless it somehow derives from your own life experiences.

Fair enough, since much of the way that contemporary humanity comes to accept basic ideas (some correct, some not) about the way things are is based on empiricism, or knowledge derived from experience. So in terms of how we think about religion in the 21ˢᵗ century, it seems reasonable to proceed with a consideration of various aspects of our experience and their potential implications for how we think about religion. And we will begin that task with a look at what is perhaps the most fundamental aspect of human experience, the very prerequisite that makes any kind of experience possible: consciousness.

It should be noted up front that the nature of consciousness and its implications for spirituality is a very "hot" topic in current religious, philosophical, and scientific writing. Some of this speculation can at times become a bit simplistic, careless, and sensationalist. Some of it, however, is quite sophisticated and penetrating. And, of course, much is somewhere in between.[42]

In any case, one should proceed with caution when exploring the relationship between consciousness and spirituality, given that in some sense it is the latest version of what some would consider to be the discredited "God of the gaps" theology.

The "God of the gaps" refers to the tendency for theologians and defenders of (usually traditional theistic) religion to cite gaps in scientific knowledge as "proof" of the existence of God. By the time we get to the 18th century in the West, science has explained many aspects of reality that were previously attributed to the work of God. The orderly movement of the planets and sun, rain and thunderstorms, the reemergence of vegetation every spring, the growth of trees – these and countless other aspects of the natural world that were once seen as the direct result of God's control of the universe came to be explained by science, making God an unnecessary part of the explanation.[43]

Having lost the need to posit a God to explain these daily activities in nature, defenders looked to what they thought was a gap in scientific knowledge to defend the necessity of God's existence, and this gap was the very existence of a universe. How could the universe exist unless a God created it? There can't be a creation without a creator. However, this argument for the necessity of God was undermined by the development of scientific cosmology and the Big Bang theory, which claimed to offer an explanation for the emergence of a universe without the need for a God.

Other defenders of religion argued that even if one could explain the existence of a universe, the existence of *life* could not be explained without positing the action of God. Of course, this "gap" in scientific theory was partially filled by Darwin's theory of evolution, which, while not really attempting to explain how life could have emerged from inanimate matter, offered an explanation of how life might have evolved into its countless varieties and manifestations over a span of millions of years, based solely on natural selection.

With the gap of the development of life now filled, some defenders of the necessity of God argued that, even if evolution has produced the circumstances that make possible the emergence of various life forms, only God can bring into existence a human being. Again, the gap of creating humans was filled with the introduction of in vitro fertilization, where new human beings were indeed "created" in an artificial environment without any apparent divine intervention.

We could continue with additional examples, but the point is that defending the existence of God on the basis of a gap in scientific explanation is a rather dubious strategy, given that, as history has demonstrated, gaps in scientific knowledge usually get filled, thereby destroying that particular argument for the necessity of God. This is not to say that science explains everything, and in the following chapters we will repeatedly argue that it does not. But when using gaps in scientific explanation as the basis for one's belief in God, there should always be that awareness of the possibility that the gap in question might someday be filled by science. So with that caveat in mind, let's take a look at consciousness.

So what exactly is consciousness? Curiously, it seems to fall into the category of things that we know intimately but have difficulty in defining. In fact, one could argue that there is nothing that we know better than consciousness, since "knowing" anything is an act of consciousness, and nothing could be more direct or personal than consciousness. And yet, when we try to define it, things get a bit tricky. "Consciousness" is often used interchangeably with various other terms: awareness, sentience, mind, perception, etc. In our discussion we will try to stick to "consciousness," although from time to time we might use another term to reflect some of the nuances in our consideration of this phenomenon.[44]

The difficulty in defining consciousness is partly the result of it being an exclusively internal and subjective phenomenon. It seems to exist only "inside" a person, in a private space which no one else has access to. It's not the sort of thing that is available to public scrutiny and shared perception that can be the basis for analysis and definition. In a sense, nothing is more hidden than consciousness, even though, paradoxically, nothing is more directly known than consciousness.

Additionally, consciousness is difficult to define because it is multidimensional, in the sense that what we mean by the word tends to encompass a variety of similar but not quite identical mental activities. Consciousness can refer to the internal experience or awareness of various sensory experiences. When I "see" something, I am "conscious" of something. When I "see" the color red, I am "conscious" of the color red, and the same could be said about other types of visual, auditory, tactile, taste, and olfactory experiences. All of our awareness of a world outside of our own subjectivity involves awareness of, or consciousness of, some sort of sensory experience.

But things get more complicated when we consider that, for example, consciousness is not only part of my awareness of the color red, but also my awareness of that awareness. Aside from seeing red, I can also reflect, or be aware of, the fact that I am seeing red. Things get even more complicated when we consider that my reflection on the experience of seeing red (as compared to the actual seeing) can occur in different temporal dimensions. In present time, while seeing red, I can be conscious of the fact that at that moment I am seeing red. But consciousness also is involved in reflecting backwards in time, when I remember a past time when I perceived the color red. All of these cases (the perception, the awareness of the perception as it happens, and the later reflection on the perception at a future point) involve consciousness.

But consciousness is not limited to awareness of sensory experiences. At least in the human species, consciousness also involves awareness of intangibles, or content that is not the immediate product of some sort of sensory stimulation. In a sense, the example cited above of remembering the experience of seeing red is an example of consciousness operating independent of a present-time sensory stimulus. But in this case, of course, the memory of the color red ultimately can be traced back to a sensory stimulus. In other cases, however, consciousness involves awareness of something that has no comparable sensory origin. Through consciousness, for example, we are aware of "abstract" ideas which have no immediate basis in sensory stimuli, including moral and spiritual concepts such as goodness, justice, virtue, meaning, etc. Here we begin to see the peculiar and unique quality of consciousness as something that allows the human species to access awareness of something that has no external, tangible, physical reality. To the extent that human consciousness is unique, this may be a key aspect of that uniqueness. Dogs, cats, birds, fish, and insects all appear to have "awareness" of some sort, to the extent that they have the capacity to perceive various aspects of their external environment. However, the capacity to be conscious of abstract values appears to be unique to the human mode of consciousness.[45]

Yet again, the nature of consciousness becomes even more complex when we consider that consciousness involves not only the awareness of abstract concepts, but also the *awareness of being aware of* abstract concepts. By means of consciousness, I am aware of the quality of moral goodness or virtue, but by means of consciousness I also can be aware *of my awareness* of moral goodness or virtue. By means of the capacity to be conscious of abstractions, I can ponder if there is a "meaning" to existence, even though there is no external sensory reference from which the notion of "meaning" is derived. In a sense, it exists in a dimension of nonphysical reality that is only accessible to human self-consciousness.[46] But I also can be self-aware of the fact that I am reflecting on the question of meaning. Indeed, I can take it back even further (actually, many steps further), and be aware that I am being aware of the fact that I'm reflecting on the notion of meaning.

In some schools of Buddhism we find that there are even deeper modes of consciousness, found only through the practice of meditation. From this Buddhist perspective, consciousness is seen as being more fundamental than matter, and in some schools (*Vijnanavada*, or the "consciousness only" school, for example), consciousness is seen as the only reality: everything that appears to exist in an external, material state is in reality a manifestation of consciousness.

So consciousness is rather complicated, given its multidimensional nature. But for the sake of our discussion, we will focus on the simple reality that consciousness exists, and it is known by all humans in an immediate sense, more immediate than anything else that we can know. Four centuries ago, the French philosopher René Descartes engaged in a thought experiment in which he attempted to only accept as true that which he was unable to doubt. Descartes concluded that he could doubt almost everything (the existence of his body and an external world could be an illusion, created by the devil), but the one thing that he could not doubt was his own existence as a conscious being. Descartes recognized that even in the act of trying to doubt everything, he was *thinking*, and therefore he knew with certainty that he existed, as, if nothing else, a thinking or conscious being, leading to his famous dictum, *Cogito ergo sum*: I think, therefore I am.

In a certain sense, this awareness or consciousness that we all experience may seem rather mundane, precisely because of its commonness and universality. But to view consciousness as such would be an enormous mistake. When we step back and look at consciousness, we find something quite remarkable and mysterious. Consciousness, in a sense, offers us *immediate proof of the existence of something that is not material*. Consciousness demonstrates that there is indeed "something more" than the material realm of matter and form. Consciousness demonstrates that, in this universe of such unimaginably immense spatial and material vastness, there is something else, and quite remarkably, that something else is part of us, perhaps even the essence of what we are. So this thing that we take for granted as we experience it day after day, moment after moment, is actually something rare, precious, and mysterious.

All of which brings us back to our initial concern: what does consciousness have to do with how we think about religion in the 21st century? To the extent that consciousness involves a sense of self and is the faculty which allows us to access concepts of meaning and virtue, the connection with religion is obvious and always has been. In traditional religions, we find consciousness expressed in the concept of a soul. Consciousness as that which is neither physical nor spatial, as that through which we have the capacity to conceive of ideas such as God, moral right and wrong, even existence in an afterlife, is simply that which in traditional religions has been designated as the soul. Of course, over time and with the development of doctrines and dogma, the soul (at least in the Biblical traditions) came to acquire a more specific content, to the point where it eventually came to be seen as something of a ghost-like entity. As we move forward on this topic, we will set aside the notion of the soul as a Casper-the-Ghost-like entity, but retain the notion that there is indeed something associated with human beings (and perhaps other living entities) that is mysterious, remarkable, and utterly different from anything else that we have knowledge of in the known universe, and that is consciousness. Leaving aside scripture and dogma, consciousness is that which provides immediate, direct evidence of the existence of "something more" than the realm of space, matter, and time. Consciousness, in a sense, provides immediate evidence that something of the nature of the nonphysical, or "spirit," does indeed exist. This thing that we experience all the time and take for granted as nothing special, is actually an inexplicable, mysterious link to a dimension of existence that could represent the essence of religion or spirituality. All of these "mundane" things that we mistakenly take for granted – my capacity to perceive light and sound and beauty, my ability to recognize moral qualities such as kindness and compassion, my power to think of concepts such as meaning, and my ability to contemplate the idea of God and all that goes with this – all of this is made possible by consciousness, which hence can be seen as a starting point for a reconstructed view of the Cosmos in which the possibility of Spirit reemerges.

In a sense, with reference to our consideration of how to think about religion in the 21ˢᵗ century, consciousness is the starting point. Set aside the scriptures which are no longer accepted as the revealed word of God, set aside the doctrines and dogma which are no longer accepted as the product of the work of a Holy Spirit, set aside the countless teachings based on scripture and dogma, and we are still left with a foundation for a spiritual view of reality, and that foundation is consciousness. In fact, one might say that consciousness, when fully recognized as the mysterious and sublime reality that it is, provides a much firmer foundation for a 21ˢᵗ century religious perspective than do sacred texts and church doctrines, in that consciousness is something we know in an immediate and irrefutable sense, whereas sacred texts and doctrines require faith in a variety of ways. In simple and stark terms, consciousness is the 21ˢᵗ century starting point for a spiritual view of reality.

But this elevation of the status of consciousness to something that functions as a gateway to the spiritual is quickly shot down by those who suggest that consciousness is nothing more than a biochemical phenomenon, easily explained by processes that occur in the brain. Consciousness is nothing more than electrochemical activity in the brain (what we will refer to as a brain event), which is rapidly being analyzed and explained by medical science. Consciousness, in other words, is nothing special: it's just stuff happening in that gooey mass of matter in our skull. Consciousness is nothing more than rather complex physical processes happening in the brain.

This perspective has been gaining widespread acceptance as advances in the scientific study of the brain have progressed dramatically over the past few decades. While the connection between the brain and the human capacity to think, feel, perceive, and engage in other conscious activities has been recognized for centuries, advances in medical technology over the past few decades have led to an understanding of the connection between brain events and conscious activity that has far surpassed that of earlier generations. Biochemistry has advanced to the point where we now have an understanding of how specific chemical substances have an impact on human cognition and affect, leading to a whole new class of drugs that, by changing brain chemistry, can change how a person feels and thinks. But the most significant factor in the growth in our understanding of the brain has been the development of imaging devices such as CAT and PET scanners, which provide a fairly precise image of internal activity within the brain which can then be correlated with mental activity of the subject whose brain is being scanned. We can now identify changes that occur in blood flow to certain parts of the brain when, for instance, a person sees red, thinks about mathematical equations, or feels sad. Studies using scanners have even been conducted to identify what is happening in the brain when subjects are engaged in deep meditation or prayer. Through this research we have identified what are often referred to as the "neural coordinates of consciousness," or NCC. We can identify the specific neurological activities that occur in coordination with specific mental experiences.[47]

One possible implication of this research is that, since conscious activity clearly corresponds to specific events happening in the brain, conscious activity (and by implication, consciousness itself) is *nothing but* a biological phenomenon. Consciousness isn't something rare and unique and mysterious: it's just electrochemical activity happening in that gooey mass of matter that we call a brain.

In light of this, some have gone so far as to suggest that the very notion of consciousness and conscious activity is nothing but an illusion. We *seem* to have subjective experiences (perceptions, thoughts, feelings) and we *seem* to have this subjective awareness of being a self (consciousness), but it's all an illusion, created by incredibly complex electrochemical activity in the brain.[48] Matter is real, and is all that there is. Mind, consciousness, and, of course, soul or spirit, are all fictions.

And yet, when we look at the literature, both scientific and philosophical, that has emerged over the past few decades, we find a shockingly different conclusion. Indeed, more recently there has been a reevaluation of the once-confident and unchallenged scientific assertion that consciousness can and has been comprehensively explained as nothing more than electrochemical activity occurring in the brain. The notion that consciousness is nothing more than a physical phenomenon has been challenged by scientists and secular philosophers alike, leading to a surprising return to the earlier notion that consciousness is indeed something special, and perhaps even something inexplicable in purely materialist, scientific terms. Let's take a look at these diverse but related observations that have led to this revaluation of the nature of consciousness.

To begin with, there's a blatantly logical flaw in the argument that reduces consciousness to nothing more than matter by arguing that the neural coordinates of consciousness, or electrochemical events in the brain, completely explain consciousness as nothing more than brain activity. The flaw in this argument is not the identification of brain events that occur simultaneously with various types of conscious activity: neuroscience has made remarkable progress in identifying what happens in our brain when we think, feel, perceive, etc., and it's almost certain that progress in this area will continue at a rapid pace as brain imaging devices become more accurate and sophisticated, and can be integrated with computer models that can identify algorithms corresponding to brain activity. The existence of the NCCs is a fact: the problem is in the inference that is made from the existence of the NCCs.

To say that there is a brain event that corresponds to every act of consciousness (thought, feeling, perception, etc.) is actually an acknowledgement that we're looking at two different things. *In order for a correspondence to be identified between two things, those two things must in some sense be different,* since if there was no difference there could be no correspondence. Science has identified various NCCs, and in doing so has demonstrated that, somehow or other, consciousness is related to electrochemical activity in the brain. However, identifying those NCCs does not *reduce* consciousness to *nothing but* brain activity. Quite to the contrary, the recognition that there is a correspondence between brain activity and conscious events implies that the brain events and consciousness *are not the same thing*. When a consciousness event happens, a brain event happens. Perhaps it is even the case that the consciousness event is in some sense caused or generated by the brain event (although, as we will see shortly, that clearly is not always the case), but it still remains the case that two distinct kinds of things are being acknowledged: the physical event in the brain, and the experiential event of consciousness. In a somewhat ironic sense, those who have attempted to reduce consciousness to nothing more than a brain event have actually contributed to the recognition that consciousness is indeed something unique, something that happens simultaneously with electrochemical activity in the brain, but which is not identical to that electrochemical activity in the brain.

Another way to look at this is to consider what you would observe if you examined the specific area in the brain that was associated with a specific type of conscious experience. For an easy example, let's look at sensory perception, or more specifically, the conscious perception of the color red. Scientists have identified the part of the brain where visual activity occurs, and let's say that we can identify the precise location in the brain where electrochemical activity occurs when the subject perceives redness. Let's take it a step further, and open up the skull and look at that specific location in the brain at the precise moment when the subject perceives red. Will the party observing the brain see red? Of course not. And yet, if conscious experience is nothing more than brain activity, what is that "something else" that is and never can be observed in the brain that constitutes an actual conscious experience of the color red? Clearly it is more than just what's happening in the brain, since we've just observed the brain event. We could do an MRI, we could look at the brain through a powerful microscope, we could measure the precise electrical activity happening in the brain at the very moment when the subject perceives red, and yet, we will not perceive what the subject perceives. We will perceive a gelatinous greyish substance, while the subject will perceive the color red. If you pause to think about it, that's quite peculiar! We know precisely what happens in the brain when red is perceived, we observe what's happening in the brain when red is perceived, and yet – we don't perceive red. All of which suggests that the identification of conscious activity as nothing more than physical events in the brain is flawed and inadequate. There's something going on here, even in the simple experience of a color, that is quite strange, something that seems to involve something that is more than physical. It might be dependent on a physical event, it might be initiated by a physical event, but it's more than just that physical event. Something exists – consciousness – that is not physical.[49]

Things become much more perplexing when we consider non-sensory conscious activity. Consider, for instance, the feeling of anger. Again, let's grant that we know precisely what happens at a specific point in the brain when a subject experiences anger. And again, let's open up the skull and observe that spot on the brain when the subject is experiencing anger. Will we see anger? Not only will we not see anger, the very question is absurd. Anger is an internal conscious state, which, unlike the color red, does not necessarily have any external objective counterpart. So once again, a conscious experience seems to be something that is radically different from what's happening in the brain when that conscious experience occurs.

We could continue with even more examples of how conscious activity is different from the activity that occurs in the brain simultaneous with that conscious activity. We could consider the conscious perception of an abstract thought such as space or time; or the conscious perception of a mathematical entity, such as the number 4; or, to carry things about as far as possible into the realm of the abstract, the conscious perception of the idea of "God." In each case, it can be acknowledged that brain activity occurs in conjunction with the abstract thought, but in each case the thought is clearly something other than the brain activity itself.

This peculiar characteristic of consciousness that seems to suggest that it is something different from activity in the brain has led contemporary philosopher David Chalmers to speak of the "hard problem" of consciousness, a concept that has been hotly debated in philosophical circles since Chalmers first articulated the issue in 1995. Chalmers refers to the ongoing task of correlating conscious activity with brain events as the "soft problem" of consciousness. It's a problem, in the sense that we're still working on developing a full understanding of the neural correlates of consciousness, but it's a "soft" problem in the sense that, in theory at least, it would seem to be the case that given sufficiently sophisticated scanning and similar medical devices and given sufficient time to continue the research, there is good reason to believe that we will eventually be able to comprehensively understand the correlation between specific acts of consciousness and specific physical events in the brain. Granted, our understanding of this correlation is still rather limited, but the field is in its infancy and with adequate time it's reasonable to project that our knowledge of the NCC will continue to grow.

And yet, no matter how accurately and comprehensively we map out the NCC, we still have not explained consciousness itself. As we explained earlier, establishing that something happens in the brain at the precise moment that specific conscious activity occurs demonstrates a correlation, but it does not in any way explain *what consciousness is*. Again, reflecting the points made above, the nature of consciousness is so radically different than the material substance that we observe in the brain that, as Chalmers suggests, bridging the gap between brain event and consciousness event may be an impossible task, and hence the "hard problem," in the sense of a problem that might never be solved.

Put differently, the actual nature of consciousness is an experience of *what it is like* to be a knowing subject. We might be able to identify what's happening in a brain when that conscious experience occurs, but in doing so we are not in any way describing the actual subjective experience itself. We are not experiencing or in even a remote way providing insight into the nature of what it is like to have that experience. This again illustrates the peculiar character of consciousness, in that not only is it the case that we at present cannot describe in scientific terms what it is like to have a conscious experience, it would seem to be the case that the very question of describing what it is like to have a conscious experience is non-sensory. Objective realities – including activity in the brain – can be described, explained, measured, etc. by an outside observer. The actual experience of consciousness cannot be described: it can only be experienced. The one thing which we know most immediately and intimately is the one thing that completely eludes scientific explanation.

It's significant that a philosopher such as Chalmers should suggest that consciousness is so radically different from material reality that its nature can perhaps never be explained by science, given that Chalmers is not writing as a religious person, but rather as an agnostic or atheist. There are no references to scripture, dogma, or theology in Chalmers' analysis of consciousness: he is writing as a strictly rationalist philosopher, and writing as such, he comes to the conclusion that consciousness may well be inexplicable.

And David Chalmers is not alone: the reader might be inclined to suspect that this interpretation of the radical uniqueness of consciousness and the inadequacy of a materialist model of reality for explaining it as the position of religious-minded apologists, seeking to insert their biased view of consciousness as a means to support their religious belief. But the recognition of the unique nature of consciousness and the failure of the current materialist scientific paradigm to explain it has been expressed by a variety of important nonreligious figures and a school of thought sometimes referred to as the "new mysterianism," reflecting the notion that consciousness not only is but likely will always remain a mystery with regard to scientific explanation.[50]

As a case in point, consider the philosopher Thomas Nagel. As a prominent figure in American philosophy for over four decades, Nagel has authored over a dozen books and countless articles, many of which are standard fare in undergraduate and graduate curricula in Philosophy. Nagel identifies himself as an atheist, so there is no concern that his thought is a subterfuge for undermining science and reestablishing the dominance of a religious worldview. Nonetheless, writing in his recent book, *Mind and Cosmos*, Nagel argues that the nature of consciousness is so radically different from the nature of matter that it is difficult to accept the position that consciousness is nothing more than an emergent property of matter, or something that emerges as matter reaches a certain level of complexity. The radically different nature of consciousness from matter is such that Nagel questions how one can believe that the former emerges from the latter. Granted, increased levels of complexity in matter can lead to the emergence of new manifestations and functions of that matter, but consciousness is not matter. How can something of one kind emerge from something of an entirely different kind? A tree leaf emerges from the branch of a tree, but a leaf does not emerge from a rock or a trumpet: there needs to be some element of similarity between that which emerges and that from which it emerges, and no such similarity seems to exist in the case of a material brain and immaterial consciousness.[51]

But the unique nature of consciousness is known not only through philosophical reasoning but also through everyday experience if we only pause to step back a moment from what only seems to be "ordinary" because of our constant exposure to it. When we step back and look at certain aspects of ordinary, everyday experience, we see confirmation that consciousness is indeed something quite extraordinary.

Take, for example, any of the various human emotional responses that result in a physical manifestation, of which there are many: anger, jealousy, fear, embarrassment, grief, joy, and so on. As a test case, let's look at embarrassment. When a person feels embarrassed, it often is manifested in such physical symptoms as increased heartbeat, red cheeks (increased blood flow), sweaty palms, etc. What exactly happens when the physical manifestation of an emotional experience occurs, and how does that demonstrate anything special about consciousness?

Consider the example of a musician who is playing a solo performance in front of an audience of peers. In fact, let's say that you are an aspiring cellist playing a solo Bach piece (just you, no accompaniment) in an intimate setting of 20 or so peers who have gathered in great anticipation of hearing your performance. It's a very important performance, since it will determine whether or not you are admitted to the exclusive music academy which you hope to attend. Everything is going well, your performance has been flawless, and then... at the point where the piece directs you to play a sustained C, you have an inexplicable mental lapse and instead play a C sharp – which, of course, sounds *terrible*. You've committed a musical faux pas of enormous magnitude, as is immediately apparent by the reaction of the audience, which ranges from gasps of shock to poorly suppressed snickers. Instantaneously, you're humiliated. Never in your life have you felt such embarrassment. As often happens when you feel embarrassed, you can feel your face getting warmer and you know that if you could look in a mirror, you would see your cheeks turning red.

So what's happening here? If your cheeks are turning red, that means that there is increased blood flow to that area of your face. And in order for there to be increased blood flow to your face, various synapses in your brain have to be firing as the result of electrochemical activity (we're simplifying things here: obviously, the specifics of the physiological reaction of red cheeks involve multiple intermediary steps). So in a certain sense, you could say that your cheeks are turning red because of activity taking place in your brain. But taking that one step back, there's the question of what caused that activity to occur in your brain. It wasn't just hearing that you were playing the wrong note and it wasn't just the reaction that you were observing and hearing in the audience. In itself playing a wrong note or observing gasps and snickers does not necessarily involve any specific emotional reaction, or any emotional reaction at all. Perhaps prior to the performance you had decided that you really didn't give a damn about getting into the school, in which case playing a wrong note and observing the audience reaction would not have been accompanied by the feeling of embarrassment. Rather, the embarrassment only comes in to play as the result of how you are *thinking about* what is happening. It's not the note itself that causes embarrassment, but your *thought* that you've just done something that you didn't want to do. It's not the gasps and snickering that cause embarrassment, but your *thought* that people are expressing disapproval and harsh judgment over what you've just done.

But taking this even a step further, if it is the case that red cheeks are the result of physiological activity associated with the thought that you have done something embarrassing, that means that a thought has caused activity in your brain. It's the thought of "I've really screwed up in front of all these people" that precedes the activity in the brain that leads to the increased blood flow to the cheeks that leads to the red cheeks. This may initially sound quite mundane, but it's actually quite astounding, since it demonstrates that thought or consciousness, something that is purely immaterial, can somehow cause physical changes in the brain. Mind can indeed exercise control over matter. This is quite remarkable, and illustrates the peculiarly inexplicable character of consciousness. How can something immaterial cause changes in something material? That is not something science can presently explain, and it confirms our earlier philosophical analysis of the unique nature of consciousness: it really is a mysterious and inexplicable phenomenon.

Further evidence of the unique nature of consciousness that requires no special scientific or philosophical background to appreciate is the well-known placebo effect. In this phenomenon, an inert substance, such as a sugar pill, produces a change in the subjective state of a patient who believes that he is receiving a medication with an active ingredient. When a placebo is administered to patients experiencing conditions such as depression and neuropathic pain, with the (false) belief that they are receiving an active medication, a certain percentage of these patients report alleviated symptoms. Since the experience of depressive feelings and neuropathic pain are generated by brain activity, the reduction of these symptoms must be generated by a corresponding reduction in that brain activity. But what is causing the reduction in that brain activity? Not the ingested medication, since it has no therapeutic content. Rather, the patient's *belief or thought* that they are ingesting a therapeutic substance must somehow cause a change in brain activity, which in turn leads to the diminished symptoms. Once again, at first glance this might not seem to reflect anything unusual, but when we consider what is happening in the brain, we again see evidence that mind, or consciousness, can actually cause physical changes in the material substance of the brain. Somehow that which is immaterial (consciousness) causes activity to occur in the synapses of brain matter, leading in turn to changes in the electrical stimulation happening in the central nervous system. As we saw in our examination of emotional reactions, here too it appears to be the case that mind has a causal impact on matter.

The strange and unique character of consciousness is also demonstrated in what, in a certain sense at least, is a peculiarly human quality: *will*, or the ability to make choices.[52] At this very moment, I can exercise my will by, for instance, choosing to raise my left hand above my head – an action which I am actually doing as I type with my right hand. So what is so unusual about choosing to raise one's arm? Once again, we see mind moving matter. The skeptic might point out that my arm rises only because of an electrical signal sent through my nervous system from my brain to the muscles that are associated with such movement. But that signal originated in the grey matter of my brain, amidst an incredibly complex combination of chemical and electrical activity, only as the result of my *willing* to raise my hand. I think, "I'm going to raise my hand," at which point activity occurs in my brain matter, leading to the required neural activity that results in my hand rising. The precise way in which this happens is not completely understood, but that's beside the point. What seems to be quite clear is that a thought, or consciousness, is having a causal impact on matter in my brain. Once again, the peculiar quality of consciousness is demonstrated.

Lastly, no discussion of consciousness would be complete without some reference to quantum physics. Our discussion of the relationship between quantum physics and consciousness will, however, be relatively brief, despite the fact that that relationship is a widely discussed issue that has produced something of a publishing subculture of speculation about the strange findings of quantum theory and the equally inconceivable implications for our understanding of consciousness.[53] In addition, there is yet another publishing subculture that has taken the quantum physics-consciousness connections a step further and attempts to demonstrate that there are *spiritual* implications for what quantum theory tells about the nature of reality and, in particular, the nature of consciousness. This gets into some very controversial (but fascinating) issues, but it's not something that we have the space to delve into here. Quantum theory itself is incredibly complex; the relationship between quantum theory and consciousness only adds to that complexity; and the alleged spiritual implications of the relationship between quantum theory and consciousness lead to yet another level of complexity. We'll only touch on the most basic point, but works with fuller treatments are referenced in the endnotes.[54] What's more, our larger point about the spiritual relevance of the unique nature of consciousness is not dependent on information from quantum physics. The nature of consciousness and the spiritual implications of the nature of consciousness can be demonstrated without any reference to the findings of quantum physics. It may indeed be the case, as argued by many, that quantum theory appears to offer science-based reasons for concluding that consciousness is indeed a unique phenomenon, but the spiritual relevance of consciousness can clearly be seen without any reference to quantum physics.

Quantum physics is the study of the nature of matter at the atomic and subatomic levels. It's the physics of matter at the level of the very, very small. Right away, the trickiness of this topic is manifest, in that the very notion of "matter" as a solid, discrete substance comes into doubt at the quantum level, where it's more accurate to speak of matter/energy in describing atomic particles. We can't possibly do justice to the strangeness of how matter/energy acts at the quantum level,[55] but we can briefly touch on a few noteworthy observations.

First, as mentioned above, at the quantum level there is no solid "matter" in the sense that we understand matter at the macro-level. An electron is not a solid particle with a consistent and enduring size and location. Sometimes it appears to be that, and sometimes it appears to be quite different. In fact, perhaps the most fundamental peculiarity about the quantum level is that particles appear to be both particles and waves. Of course, this would appear to be nonsense. How can something be both a particle, which has a specific location and a specific dimension, and a wave, which is spread out in an indefinite manner? And yet, this is precisely what is the case at the quantum level. Sometimes an electron or photon acts like a particle, and sometimes it acts like a wave. What's relevant to our consideration of consciousness is that *being observed* is what determines whether the electron acts like a particle or a wave. Strange as this may seem, it appears to be the case that, in some sense, if we observe an electron it acts like a particle; if we don't observe it, it acts like a wave. But how can this be the case? How can observation (which, of course, includes consciousness) have an influence on something that is "physical"? Physicists have recognized this for decades, and it can be demonstrated through the simple "double-slit" experiment, but no one can really explain it!

But things get even stranger in quantum theory. The act of observation appears to be able to affect particles in a manner that is retroactive, which is to say my present observation of a particle determines whether or not the particle collapsed from its wave state at some past moment. And then there's the odd phenomenon of quantum entanglement, where two particles have an instantaneous effect on each other regardless of how far apart they are and with no known connection of any sorts – what Einstein (who mistakenly refused to believe that such a thing could happen) derisively referred to as "spooky action at a distance."

Again, we're only briefly mentioning some of the peculiar aspects of quantum theory without going into detail, and, understandably, skeptical readers should refer to the sources listed in the endnotes for a fuller account of these remarkable phenomena. For our purposes, we simply wish to point out that, in addition to the various types of evidence discussed earlier in this chapter, even in a hardcore science such as physics, the peculiar nature of consciousness is affirmed. Consciousness appears to have a role in *everything*, even in the very nature of the "material" world.

But given the purpose of this book (how to think about religion in the 21st century), one might still ask: *So what?*

It's here where we get into controversial territory, or at least controversial in the eyes of some. Beginning with Fritjof Capra in 1975, there has been a steady stream of writings suggesting that quantum theory provides evidence in support of various spiritual worldviews, usually those reflecting the non-dualist perspective found in certain branches of Buddhism, the Vedanta tradition in Hinduism, Daoism, and various non-dual mystical traditions. While these speculations are often quite interesting in pointing out the curious parallels between some aspects of quantum physics and non-dual spiritualities, there also has been ample criticism of this perspective as grossly exaggerating what can be reasonably inferred about spiritual matters from our understanding of what happens to physical matters at the quantum level. For our purposes, we'll set aside these arguments for a strong connection between quantum theory and any spiritual perspective, and simply argue that quantum theory offers two insights with reference to contemporary thinking about religion.

First, quantum theory clearly suggests that materialism, or the belief that reality consists of nothing but the material or physical world is false. Observations at the quantum level suggest that "reality" is more than just material "stuff." And, secondly, quantum theory appears to affirm that consciousness has a fundamental place in the nature of reality. Consciousness is not just a minor by-product of matter being organized in specific complex ways, but rather an ontological something that seems to exist in its own right, in a relationship to "matter" that is really not fully understood. Indeed, the role of consciousness at the quantum level is so pervasive that even some physicists have suggested what previously had only been offered by spiritual teachers and philosophers: perhaps consciousness is primary, and matter secondary. Perhaps, in some sense, consciousness is the fundamental basis for that which we call reality.[56]

We've spent a lot of time talking about consciousness, far more time than we've spent on any other topic. We've touched on a number of unique aspects of consciousness, such as:

- The existence of consciousness confirms the presence of a nonphysical element in reality.
- Consciousness presently cannot be adequately explained by science.
- Consciousness allows humans to have access to the realm of moral value.
- Consciousness allows humans to have access to the realm of meaning.
- Consciousness, at least in humans, makes possible the exercise of will.

But this prolonged exploration of consciousness is justified, given the importance of acquiring a full appreciation of what consciousness is and its relevance for a contemporary religious perspective. Actually, one could look at this as a *recovery* of our appreciation of the specialness of consciousness, given that in traditional religions we find the same insight expressed in the notion of a soul or supreme Self. Recognizing the mysterious and unique nature of consciousness is simply recognizing what human cultures have recognized for thousands of years and expressed in the symbols and myths of their religious traditions. We have perhaps been lulled into a false sense of complacency about the remarkable thing that is present with us every moment: mind, awareness, consciousness. We have become accustomed to accept the notion that scientific explanation explains everything, and hence nothing is really that remarkable, as if we simply live in a universe of stuff, following mechanistic and deterministic natural laws.

And yet that's simply not the case. Science cannot explain everything, and the one thing that it has not and perhaps will not explain, is right under our nose, so to speak. The most mysterious and unique aspect of reality is something that we carry around with us all of the time, and we need to step back a moment from the false sense of scientific casualness to fully appreciate this miraculous, strange thing that is our sense of awareness or consciousness. In traditional religion, this was clearly understood and expressed in teachings and doctrines about an "immortal soul" or "supreme Self." We're not suggesting the need to return to those specific past labels, categories, or perspectives on consciousness (where there is often something of a "Casper the Ghost" way of thinking about these matters), but we are suggesting that a contemporary perspective about religion is fully justified, independent of any sacred text or church doctrine, in reasserting that there is something remarkable, mysterious, and spiritually significant about consciousness. Consciousness provides a gateway to the recognition that there really is a "Something More," beyond the deterministic realm of material reality described by science. Consciousness provides confirmation that, independent of sacred text or church doctrine, there is good reason to believe that there is a "spiritual" element to reality. So simply recognize what's right there with you at this and every moment, set aside the misguided perspective of scientific reductionism that sees it as nothing special, and let yourself fully embrace the miraculous, mysterious, awesome nature of being a living entity with consciousness. One might object that what we're asserting here is rather vague, and others might be inclined to draw far more numerous and detailed inferences about spiritual matters from the nature of consciousness, but recall our discussion earlier in this book about the tendency of traditional religions to claim to know more than they really do. That's a practice that we will avoid, here and throughout the book, sticking to a practice of "spiritual minimalism," which is likely to be the norm for the religion of our future.

So what does consciousness tell us with regard to how to think about religion in the 21st century?

Stepping back from traditional religious dogma and flawed scientific materialism, we can recognize that a gateway to recognition that there is "Something More," as in a spiritual dimension to reality, is right there in front of us, right there with us, all of the time. The presence of consciousness re enchants the world, providing a dogma-free affirmation that there is more to reality than cold, hard matter. And from that initial step into a new, dogma-free, empirically grounded faith in "Something More," we can proceed further.

Chapter 12

The Sense of Moral Goodness

In the last chapter we looked at an aspect of ordinary, everyday life, something experienced by everyone all the time, and saw that it had important implications for how to think about religion in a post-Axial world where the old gods, old scriptures, old doctrines, and old sources of authority are no longer convincing to many sincere, informed, well-meaning, good-hearted human beings. We saw that this aspect of everyday experience – consciousness – provides good reason for believing that there is indeed a spiritual dimension to reality. Let's take that same approach and look at another aspect of ordinary life: *the sense of moral goodness*.

We could use the term "morality" to identify what we're talking about, but "morality" has taken on some connotations that just don't apply to what we're going to be looking at. Morality, in the minds of most people, is associated with rule-following, obedience to authority, compliance with external demands, limit-setting, control, restriction, and so forth. Rules and laws are important, of course, a necessary part of human civilization. But we're looking at something much deeper than moral rules per se: we're looking at what one might argue is the *basis* for morality, or the underlying quality that makes morality meaningful. We're talking about the *human sense of moral goodness*, the notion that there is a "right" way to act, the intuitive sense that there is a "should" to things, not simply because somebody has set a rule, but because moral rightness or moral goodness is an actual aspect of reality. Specific, widely varying, and unique rules are set by all human communities, but the sense that there is a moral rightness is universal and, one might argue, is both the basis for those rules and the motivation for following them (when they are followed for the right reason). In ancient thought, the sense of moral goodness was sometimes referred to as "virtue," so we will use "moral goodness" interchangeably with "virtue" (even though the meaning of "virtue" has also been lost in contemporary times, such that it is mistakenly equated with rule-following morality, sometimes associated specifically with rule following in the area of sexuality).

We've already covered the fact that moral goodness is a universal aspect of religion. Wherever you find religion, you will find the idea that there is something good about following a certain way of life according to a prescribed set of moral rules, and, again as we've covered earlier, despite differences in specific ethical teachings, in a broader sense there tends to be a consensus about moral goodness among the world's religions. Traditionally, moral goodness has also been associated with religious founders who, among other things, function as figures who teach these prescriptions for good moral behavior Moses, Jesus, Mohammed, Buddha, Confucius all of them are connected to ethical teachings about how we should live.

But, of course, we're looking at religion from the point of view of the 21st century citizen who is no longer likely to uncritically accept in a literal way the historical validity of those founders and the sacred texts which purport to represent their teachings. So if we set aside those religious figures and their teachings, and if rather than looking at a specific set of ethical teachings we look at the general sense of moral goodness, what can we discern about spirituality? Even if, for the sake of argument, we begin with the position that those religious founders and their teachings are the semi-mythic product of stories modified and amplified from one generation to the next – even if, in other words, we begin with the position that there is no direct divine revelation of moral law that occurred thousands of years ago, whether in Israel, Arabia, China, or India – is there anything that we can conclude from the existence of a universal human sense of moral goodness that is relevant to how we think about religion? If we simply look at the empirically verifiable evidence, namely the fact that the human species displays this peculiar sense of moral goodness, something apparently not found in any other species, what, if anything, does that say about religion in a more general sense?

In answering this question, we should consider *why* we act morally, or more precisely (since we often do not act morally even though we think we should), why do we have this sense that we *should* act morally? We're not talking about a sense of should do *this* or shouldn't do *that*, but rather the more fundamental notion that we even have a sense that we "should" do anything at all. Where does that sense of "shouldness" come from, and what does it say about spirituality? Not unlike consciousness, our sense of shouldness is such a fundamental aspect of who and what we are that we tend to not even be aware of it, and to the extent that we are aware of it we tend to take it for granted. But step back a second and consider what a peculiar thing this sense of moral shouldness is. In some cases we have a sense that we should act in a certain way because it's in our own self-interest. We don't assault other humans in public because we know that doing so could result in harmful consequences to ourselves if we should do so. Sometimes we have a sense of "shouldness" that is linked with tradition, family, social pressure, etc., where we know that acting in a certain way will result in negative consequences, whether they be internal (guilt, shame) or external (criticism and sanctions from family, friends, etc.). In either case and in many similar cases where there is a known consequence that is likely to follow from an action, we feel that we "should" act in a certain way because, ultimately, it's in our self-interest to do so.

But that's not true moral activity, or action motivated primarily by the sense of moral goodness. Acting in a moral manner, acting out of a sense of moral goodness, means choosing to act (or not act) in a certain way simply because we believe that or feel a sense that we *should* do so – regardless of consequences. Of course, our motivation for doing what we do is almost always quite complicated, and can be a mixture of all sorts of different combinations of motives. But I'm suggesting that if the reader reflects on the motivation for why she does what she does, it's pretty clear that while sometimes we do what we do because of a calculation of consequences, sometimes we do what we do because – well, simply because we think that it's the right thing to do, and because it's the right thing to do, we have a sense that we *should* do it.

Parents have this sort of experience all the time: you treat your child in a certain way, not because of any anticipated consequence for yourself, but simply because you feel that you should take care of your child. Your child might respond positively or negatively, but because you believe that it is in your child's welfare, you have a sense that it's what you should do.

We have a similar experience in all sorts of situations where we make moral choices outside the public view. Opening the door for an elderly person when no one is watching, smiling and saying hello to a stranger that you pass out of sight of others, picking up a piece of litter in a secluded area, putting the expensive watch that you find on a hiking trail in an easy-to-see spot rather than keeping it for yourself... we could go on and on with countless examples of making choices not because of anticipated consequences for ourselves but simply out of a sense that we should do the right thing.

And here's the point: that's quite unique and strange – doing something simply out of a sense that we should do it, regardless of consequences and regardless of traditions, rules, laws, etc. Humans appear to have developed an *innate sense of shouldness*, or what one might call a *moral sentiment*, and like consciousness, this sense of shouldness is quite remarkable and unique. And like consciousness, perhaps it points to the possibility that there is something going on with humans that is difficult to explain without reference to a "Something Else" that is the source of that sense of shouldness.

But the similarity to consciousness goes even further: precisely because we experience consciousness all the time, we become used to it, we take it for granted, we fail to recognize what a remarkable and mysterious thing it is. Likewise, we experience a sense of moral rightness all the time; we swim in the water of a sense of "shouldness" and all of the internal experiences that go with it: empathy, duty, compassion, moral guilt, shame, etc. But precisely because we as human creatures are immersed in the awareness of the sense of moral goodness, we fail to appreciate how remarkable it is. As with consciousness, we can scan the immense space of our galaxy, and indeed the entirety of the heavenly realm as far as we (and the high tech instruments that we use) can see, and we find no evidence of consciousness and no evidence of the sense of moral goodness. Images of faraway planets might amaze us with their beauty, but on the surface of Saturn, one will find no sense of kindness. Faraway stars revealed by the Hubble and Webb telescopes might astound us with their majestic appearance, but there is no love or compassion or justness or fairness to be found in any of those immense and beautiful galaxies. The universe (or at least what we can see of it) is an incomprehensibly vast and beautiful place, but it is also a cold and barren place, morally speaking.

Only here, in this peculiar arrangement of material particles that has evolved into this odd entity which we call a human being, do we find the presence of those moral qualities which are absent in the rest of the vast universe that we can observe. That's odd. How could something so fundamentally different than what we find in the vast expanse of the universe have emerged on this tiny planet, and what might we reasonably infer from this unique moral sensibility about the existence of "Something Else"?

Some would argue that on the basis of the existence of the moral sentiment we can't infer anything whatsoever about the existence of a spiritual or transcendent reality. Morality, they would argue, is explainable in entirely naturalistic terms. More specifically, morality can be explained as the product of the human need to maintain order in a social setting. As humans evolved into ever larger social groupings, from family to clan to tribe to state to nation to empire and beyond, there emerged a concomitant need to insure that human behavior remained within the bounds that are necessary for any particular form of civilization to be maintained and prosper. People cannot live together without rules, and morality is simply the humanly-invented set of rules that have been created to insure the level of order necessary for life in a complex society. Morality, in other words, is a human construct reflecting a sociological necessity – and it's nothing more than that. All that is needed to explain morality is sociology and evolution.

Well, yes and no. Of course specific moral codes are the product of specific cultures that develop those codes over time in response to the need to maintain social order. That can't be denied. But we're talking about something deeper than the moral codes per se, something deeper than the specific laws, the do's and don'ts which comprise moral codes and are indeed socially constructed on the basis of social necessity. We're talking about the moral sentiment which *underlies* those moral codes, which sometimes exists outside and against moral codes, and which is the precondition that makes moral codes functional.

A group of people living together creates certain rules to live by, and sometimes imbues those rules with greater force by associating them with a divine origin, all in the interest of insuring compliance within the parameters of human behaviors necessary for the group to survive. But the very existence of the rules and the tendency to project their origin onto a divine being suggest that there is something innately moral about the human species. We create moral codes because we have a moral sentiment, a sense that we live in a universe in which there is a sense of *shouldness*. Without this sense of shouldness, the existence of a moral code would be useless. We follow moral laws not merely out of a sense of obedience, and not merely out of a sense of a need to preserve social order, but out of a much deeper awareness that moral goodness, or virtue, is something that has existence and value for its own sake. We follow moral codes because it is a good thing to do so, and that sense of the goodness of following a moral law is not the same thing as the moral law itself or the subject's awareness of the law as a law. There would be no compliance with moral laws without the deeper presence of the moral sentiment that generates the sense of a transcendentally-originated shouldness.

That that deeper moral sentiment is different from the moral law per se and different from the evolutionary impetus to preserve social order is seen in the fact that the moral sentiment often leads to defiance of moral laws and disruption of the social order. The moral reformer and the revolutionary are driven to act counter to the approved moral code of a society in a manner that creates social disruption rather than order. The historical examples are, of course, innumerable, from the prophets of the Old Testament to the Buddha in 6th century BCE India to Gandhi in the 20th century. And such cases are not always overtly religious in nature. The Russian Revolution was carried out by secularists who felt a moral obligation to defy and destroy the existing social order of the czarist culture in order to bring about a state that was in accord with their sense of what was a more virtuous and morally justified way of ordering society. They were motivated by a moral sentiment, or a sense that there was a right way for things to be, and they devoted their lives to acting on that moral sentiment. So yes, moral laws are a socially constructed product and they do function to maintain social order, but moral laws are not the same thing as the moral sentiment, which runs deeper than, and in some cases counter to, human-generated moral laws.

To counter the argument that there is a universal moral sentiment, it is sometimes argued that moral values differ greatly from one society to another, thus demonstrating that there is no universal moral absolute. This position is known as moral or cultural relativism. Proponents point out that in practically any area of human life, different cultures display different ideas about what is and is not morally right. In some cultures, polygamy is considered morally wrong while in others it is considered morally permissible. Meat-eating is considered morally acceptable in most Western countries, but is seen as morally repugnant in the Jain communities of India. Most cultures condemn the eating of human flesh in the strongest possible terms, and yet in some subsistence cultures cannibalism was not only morally permissible but was considered to be an honorable way to treat a corpse. We could go on and on with numerous examples of how different cultures have different moral standards. Moral standards, in other words, appear to be relative to the culture in which they exist, and one seemingly reasonable way to explain this fact is that cultures create moral standards, and in turn, if this is the case, there is no spiritual source or principle that needs to be invoked to explain the human moral sentiment.

This is an argument that has a strong initial appeal, but upon closer examination it is seriously flawed. First of all, it does not necessarily logically follow from the fact that different cultures have different moral standards that therefore there is no universal right and wrong, or no universal moral sentiment. The fact that people in a given culture *believe* something to be the case (as in something to be morally right or wrong) neither proves nor disproves that it *is* indeed the case. The fact that two different cultures have different beliefs about x does not mean that there is no independent objective truth about x – alternatively, a culture can simply be wrong. Consider, for example, that if we go back a few centuries, we would find some cultures that believed that the Earth was flat and others that believed that the Earth was round. Would it be reasonable to conclude that because cultures held different beliefs about the shape of the Earth therefore the Earth was neither flat nor round, that beliefs about the shape of the Earth had no relationship to a trans-human objective truth, that beliefs about the shape of the Earth are merely the product of the myth-making capacity of a given culture? Of course not. There is a true shape of the Earth, and the disagreement about this shape between different cultures is a reflection of that fact that some cultures *hold the wrong belief*.

The same logic can be applied to the existence of different beliefs about what is morally right. There could indeed be an objective, trans-human, spiritual moral rightness, but no guarantee that all cultures are equally tuned in to that moral rightness. Some cultures could simply be mistaken in their moral beliefs, and hence the disagreement between cultures. The moral sentiment could indeed be a reflection of the presence of a spiritual dimension to the Cosmos, but different cultures could apprehend or sense that moral sentiment with varying degrees of fullness and accuracy, thus accounting for the disagreement about moral standards from one culture to another.

But one could also argue that the disagreements between cultures regarding what is morally right and wrong is not nearly as pronounced as the advocates of cultural relativism would suggest. Yes, it is the case that some cultures consider polygamy to be morally wrong and others consider it to be morally acceptable. But all cultures consider some sort of lasting bond between adults who engage in sexual activity – "marriage" in some form or another – to be morally good. Cultures may differ as to at what age and with whom and under what circumstances two humans can morally engage in sex, but no culture advocates the moral rightness of unlimited sexual activity with any person of any age in any situation at any time in any place. Limitations on sexual behavior are universal, even though the specific rules in a culture that define the precise circumstances under which sexual behavior is considered morally permissible may vary. Or going back to our earlier example, even though some cultures might consider it morally wrong to consume a corpse while others consider such cannibalism to be morally acceptable, all cultures exhibit a sense of the need to treat a dead body with a sense of respect and dignity... even if, in some cases, that means ritually preparing and eating that dead body. No culture, in other words, teaches that desecration of a corpse is a morally good course of action.

In fact, taking this line of thought a bit further, we can see that even though there is much disagreement in different cultures when it comes to specific rules about morality, behind that disagreement over specifics is a remarkably consistent agreement over broader moral principles. Truth-telling, kindness, fidelity, courage, honesty, limits on sexual behavior, limits on aggressive behavior – these are areas that all cultures agree are morally desirable, reflecting the presence of a consensus on broad moral principles underlying differences about the specific ways in which those principles get translated into specific moral rules.

So in a sense we are back to where we started, namely with a recognition that there exists a universal moral sentiment in the human species. And as we have also suggested earlier, the presence of this moral sentiment, this sense that there is a shouldness to things, is something that, like consciousness, can be seen as an intimation of the presence of a spiritual dimension to reality. Does the presence of this moral sentiment "prove" the existence of "God"? Certainly not, despite what many theologians and philosophers have attempted to demonstrate.[57] But it certainly strongly suggests that there might be more to reality that the valueless world of cold, hard matter. With reference to moral goodness, the fundamental affirmation of a 21st century spirituality – an affirmation that can be made without reference to a commitment to belief in anything from the mythic, anthropomorphized Axial Age religions – is simply the belief that *we live in a morally meaningful Cosmos*. Reality, in its fullest dimension (meaning not just the physical dimension, even in the immense size of the material universe, but *all* reality in the sense of the physical *and* spiritual dimensions) has a moral quality. Moral goodness is part of the very fabric of Reality. Moral goodness is not just something that human beings create for the sake of being able to maintain the social order and social stability that is necessary for human civilization to be perpetuated. Moral goodness is part of that "Something Else" that exists independent of (but at the same time in constant relationship with) the human and material realm. Moral goodness actually is a reality that exists "out there," or more precisely to avoid the misleading spatial metaphor, just *exists* as a part of the *spiritual dimension of the Cosmos*. This affirmation does not require accepting a literal understanding of any of the stories, doctrines, traditions, etc. from the existing religions. One can reject the idea that a God in Heaven or a mysterious divine power somehow handed down or communicated specific rules about morality to an actual person at some specific place and time in the distant past. One can interpret such stories as sacred legend or myth (no revelation to Moses on Sinai of the Ten Commandments, no teachings conveyed to Muhammed by Allah, no moment when the ancient Indian sage Manu received the dharma from the gods), and yet one can still firmly believe that we live in a moral Cosmos, recognizing that the specific moral codes of the various existing religions are the remnants of our ancestors' attempts to articulate in somewhat precise but necessarily inadequate terms what it means for a human to live a life in a manner that is consistent with that Moral Goodness that exists as a transcendent reality. Different cultures develop different sets of rules, just as different cultures develop different descriptions of the nature of Spirit, as each culture's sense of the Transcendent is influenced by that culture's existing traditions, symbols, language, and countless other factors that mean that any attempt to clarify an aspect of the spiritual dimension will always be a partial one. But behind those culturally limited specific sets of moral laws is the deeper sense that moral goodness is a real thing, something that is ontologically distinct. And as such, moral goodness, like consciousness, points us in the direction of recognizing the existence of a Something Else.

So with reference to how we think about religion in the 21st century, setting aside the sacred texts, dogmas, and religious authorities of the past, we can simply observe – as in the case of consciousness – what is right in front of us, accessible to all of us all of the time, and recognize the existence of the moral sentiment as yet another indicator that reality cannot be adequately accounted for in terms of mechanistic, deterministic, material descriptions, but rather must also include a recognition of a "Something More," a spiritual dimension that is manifested, however obscurely and intermittently, in our sense of moral goodness.

Chapter 13

Religious Experience

In preparation for proceeding to take a look at yet another aspect of what religion might be like in the 21st century, we need to first recall our examination of epistemology in an earlier chapter where we looked at the question of how we know what we know, or how do we know anything at all. As we saw, the question of how we know what we know, and whether what we know can be considered valid, is a frustratingly complex issue. Differences between primary and secondary knowledge, subjective and objective knowledge, public versus private verifiability, species-dependent (and hence limited) sensory capacities, and other factors make it clear that valid knowledge about the way things really are is far from a certainty. This in turn led to a consideration of the limits of scientific knowledge. Science does indeed provide humans with a certain type of knowledge, and that knowledge has been incredibly useful in terms of enhancing the human capacity to manipulate the natural world (technology). However, scientific knowledge is one kind of knowledge, but not the only type of knowledge. There are many aspects of reality that we can come to know through science, but there are also aspects of reality that we come to know through other means. In this chapter, we will be arguing that spiritual reality is an aspect of reality that we can experience and hence acquire knowledge of in a direct sense, but in a direct sense that is quite different from the scientific approach to knowing.

Religion is a multifaceted phenomenon, and especially when we think about religion in the West, we tend to think about elements other than religious experience. All religions involve some element of belief, as found in doctrines, dogmas, creeds, theologies, etc. All religions include elements of ritual in which various sorts of prescribed, repetitive behaviors are used for the purpose of communicating with and influencing the sacred through liturgy, worship, private devotion, meditations, etc. All religions (as we've covered above) have an ethical element as found in a moral code. All religions have various sorts of spiritual practices, including prayer, pilgrimage, tithing, meditation, etc. These four elements (beliefs, ritual, morality, and spiritual practices) are found in all religions, and the reader can easily look at her religious background and identify the specific manifestations of each element in her tradition, be it Judaism, Islam, Christianity, Hinduism, Buddhism, Daoism, Jainism, etc.

But in addition to these four universal elements of all religions, there is a fifth element, and that is the subject of our discussion in this chapter: religious experience. Just as talking or reading about the taste of an apple is one thing and actually experiencing the taste of an apple is quite another, so with religious experience we see the difference between talking and reading about God or the sacred (in doctrines, dogma, sacred texts, etc.) and actually having a direct experiential encounter with God or the sacred. Indeed, some would argue that religious experience is the very foundation of religion, with doctrines and texts representing inadequate attempts to put into words an actual experience of sacred reality, an experience which – not unlike the taste of salt, but magnified infinitely – can never be adequately put into words since what one is encountering – Spirit, God, the sacred – is so infinitely different than anything else that we experience as human creatures.[58]

Religious experience, like the other elements of religion that we have covered, is universal, and we find it in various expressions in all traditions in all time periods. Moses experiencing the presence of God on Sinai; Jesus' experience at the Transfiguration; Muhammed hearing the voice of God through the intermediary of the angel Gabriel; in the Pentecostal tradition, we find the believer overwhelmed by an experience of the Holy Spirit; in Islamic Sufism, the whirling dervishes cultivate an altered mode of consciousness in which their sense of self is annihilated by the experience of the presence of Allah. In the Asian traditions, where we find a greater emphasis on the role of meditation in which an experience of the sacred is intentionally cultivated through a disciplined course of spiritual practices, we find the indescribable peace of the experience of Nirvana and the Hindu experience of union of the individual self (Atman) with the divine (Brahman). In indigenous American traditions we find an experience of the sacred in nature, sometimes by a spiritual specialist, or shaman, sometimes by an "ordinary" person who embarks on a vision quest or consumes a natural substance such as peyote. We could, of course, add countless examples of direct experience of the sacred as found in the various world religions, demonstrating that religious experience is not an anomaly, but rather a universal, always-present element of religion.

Unfortunately, in many branches of Western Christianity and mainstream secular culture, religious experience has often been looked at with skepticism if not outright hostility, and this has been the case for several reasons, some coming out of the religions themselves and some coming from the secular scientific perspective. We'll take a look at the scientific skepticism about religious experience later, but for now let's consider the religious skepticism. Or more specifically, given that most readers are likely to have come out of the Western Biblical tradition, and even more specifically out of the mainline Christian denominations, let's consider why those denominations (Catholic, Lutheran, Presbyterian, Methodist, Episcopalian, etc.) have tended to downplay the importance of religious experience. After all, one might intuitively think that, if direct experiential knowledge of something (like the taste of an apple) is in a sense the most immediate and irrefutable evidence of something, all religions and denominations might embrace religious experience and extol it as the key element of leading a spiritual life. But that hasn't been the case in Christianity (or, although it's not our primary focus here, Judaism or Islam), so why not?

The answer is multifaceted and certainly varies with historical and cultural factors, but there is one common theme running through the entire history of the Christian mainline churches, and that is that faith is a matter of *belief*, and more specifically, a matter of belief in a series of propositions. Being a Christian is usually understood as essentially a cognitive act of asserting to the acceptance of certain propositions, as laid out in doctrines and creeds. In most Christian churches, for instance, confirmation as a full member of the church includes affirmation of the Apostles Creed, a document which contains 22 explicit propositions. Being a Christian is thus defined in terms of believing in the truth of a set of propositions. It is a cognitive act, not an experiential act. A Christian identifies him/herself as a "believer," not an "experiencer." Of course, in the life of the believer various affective or experiential consequences may flow from that cognitive affirmation, but it is the cognitive act of belief rather than the secondary experiential consequences that is primary and essential. Christian faith is about believing something to be the case, not experiencing it to be the case. Reverting to our earlier example, Christian faith could be said to be comparable to *believing* that an apple tastes good rather than actually experiencing the pleasantly sweet taste of the apple.[59]

But the distancing of faith from experience in Christianity goes even further: the essential propositions to which one must give cognitive assent have to do with past historical events which, as past events, one cannot experientially verify. To some extent "faith" by definition always involves belief in something that is partially removed from or transcendent to daily human experience, as in faith in moral goodness and faith in meaning. But Christianity makes the object of faith even more distant and unexperienceable, by requiring not only belief in values and meaning, but also faith in a historical event. While one can assert that belief in this event, as an act of cognitive affirmation, as an event that happened over 2000 years ago, we cannot *experience* the truth of that event.

If faith is primarily a matter of affirming belief in a historical event, then the value of experience by definition is radically diluted. The essence of Christian faith is seen as the truth of something that cannot be known by experience, and consequently the role of experience in the spiritual life is substantially diminished.

One does need to look far in the history of Christianity to find examples of what happens to those who affirmed that they had a direct experience of the Christian deity. In Puritan New England, for example, Anne Hutchinson claimed that God directly spoke to her. Rather than embracing her as a vessel through which God was speaking, Hutchinson was imprisoned, tried, and literally expelled from the Massachusetts Bay Colony. Her subsequent suffering (including painful miscarriages) and life in harsh conditions were celebrated by the pious Puritan leaders as signs of the judgment of God, and her eventual death at the hands of an Native American attack were praised as evidence of divine justice.

Our focus here is on Christianity, but similar treatment of those who see faith as a matter of experience rather than propositional belief can be found in Judaism and Islam. In Judaism, we see the historical persecution of the Hasidic movement by the mainstream rabbinical institutional authorities during the early years of Hasidism in Europe. In Islam, we see the persecution, and in some cases execution, of members of the Sufi brotherhoods who believed that one could experience the presence of Allah through techniques such as breathing exercises and ecstatic dancing.

To some extent, this rejection of religious experience can be seen as the direct result of the conflict between faith rooted in experience and faith rooted in cognitive belief. Again, believing what someone says about the taste of an apple is entirely different from believing that an apple tastes a certain way because one has actually tasted an apple. But another issue can be identified as the source of such extreme resistance to the role of religious experience, and that is the challenge that religious experience presents to institutional authority. In the mainstream Christian denominations, leaders in the church hierarchy define the content of creeds and doctrines, and these are enforced by the church hierarchy via admission and exclusion from the church (and consequently, by salvation and damnation). Religious experience radically undermines the authority of the church hierarchy and the institutional structures that empower, support, and protect that hierarchy. The person who has had a religious experience is asserting that she has directly known the sacred, and consequently the need to rely on other parties (church officials) to define the content of faith is diminished. A priest or pastor is no longer needed to explain to me what I should believe about God if I have experientially encountered God myself and derived the content of my faith from that immediate personal experience. In this sense religious experience can be radially subversive, and at times it has been dealt with as such over the centuries by the religious institutions that sought to contain faith to the realm of cognitive affirmations that the church could identify and maintain control over. No wonder that the history of religious experience has often been the history of religious persecution, by religious authorities themselves.

What's more, religious experience challenges not only the religious authorities and institutional structures that they control, but it also presents a challenge to the sacred texts that are often cited by religious authorities as the basis for the authority. Religious authorities often identify themselves and their institution as both legitimized by a sacred text and as the sole competent interpreter of that text, and as such their power is quite substantial. This was acutely the case in earlier centuries when the majority of the population was illiterate and hence completely dependent on a literate clergy to explain the content of the Bible and its teachings on avoiding damnation and achieving salvation. But even in contemporary times, the trained clergy retains a position of power as the interpreters of the Bible, a text that is long and often confusing, and hence not the sort of book that the typical parishioner, caught up in the business of the daily tasks of raising a family, holding a job, etc., is likely to have the time or inclination to read in a careful and exhaustive manner.

Religious experience undercuts the authority of the clergy as needed interpreters of the path to salvation, since he who has experienced God directly has less need to refer to a book and/or a professional theologian or pastor to accurately interpret it. Religious experience can be a direct path to knowledge of God, thereby diminishing the need for both a sacred text and the professional religious authorities who claim to have the exclusive interpretation of that book for the keys to salvation.

For these and other reasons, then, religious experience has not played a prominent role in Western religion for most of the history of Judaism, Christianity, and Islam. Religious experience is seen as something granted to historical founders in long ago times, but not something that remains an option to present-day believers, who instead must rely on the sacred texts and their professional interpreters.

But thankfully, over the past three centuries, religious experience has made something of a comeback in Western religions. This is a complicated and multifaceted development, so for the sake of brevity we will only look briefly at three figures: Friedrich Schleiermacher, Rudolf Otto, and William James.

Friedrich Schleiermacher was a Protestant pastor and theologian who wrote in the late 18th and early 19th centuries.[60] This was a time when some Christian theologians were beginning to break away from the belief that the Bible needed to be interpreted in a literal sense, church doctrine was beyond questioning, and the Christian faith was the only path to salvation. This movement was the result of a number of factors, including the German Romantic movement which valued human experience and feelings, the application of a scientific, critical approach to ancient writings (including the Bible), and a broader appreciation of the presence in other religions of ideas and practices which were comparable to what was found in the Christian tradition. Schleiermacher was convinced that the essence of religion was not doctrine and dogma, nor even an ancient text believed to be revealed by God, but rather a certain feeling, or experience, from which doctrines and practices subsequently derived. The essence of religion was seen as a direct awareness of God, and the doctrines of the Church, as found in creeds and elsewhere, were seen as somewhat secondary elements that described or pointed to that primal experiential encounter with the divine. Schleiermacher initially described this essential religious experience as one of unity with the divine or Infinite, and later as an overwhelming sense of absolute dependence on a transcendent Power.

Two points should be noted: first, Schleiermacher usually described this experience in largely nonsectarian terms. That is, he did not describe the experience as exclusively Christian, and by implication seemed to suggest that this experience was universal, available to people of faith in all religions. Secondly, he saw this experience as occurring outside the context of church dogma, ritual, institutional practices, etc. For Schleiermacher, the essence of being religious was an experience, not a belief or adherence to a ritual or participation in a religious institution.

The modern recovery of the value of religious experience was advanced further by the German theologian and philosopher, Rudolf Otto, in his classic 1917 work, *The Idea of the Holy*.[61] Like Schleiermacher, Otto sought the essence of religion, and found it in religious experience. Otto saw religious experience as entailing an overwhelming sense of awe and majesty at the awareness of something (the "holy") so majestic, powerful, overwhelming, and mysterious that he coined a new word for it: the *numinous*. To Otto, the experience of the numinous, or the experience of a sacred reality that was beyond description, was the basis for all religions, regardless of where it might be found. To illustrate his point that the experience of the numinous is a universal type of religious experience, he wrote *Mysticism East and West*, one of the first comparative works on religious experience, in which he points out, often using passages from sacred texts and other religious writings, the remarkable similarities found in the religious experiences of Christians and Hindus, drawing especially from the Christian mystic Meister Eckhart and the Hindu sage Shankara.

But while Schleiermacher, Otto, and others did much to rehabilitate the importance of religious experience in the 19th and early 20th centuries, no one contributed to this project more than the America psychologist/philosopher, William James. In 1902, James delivered the Gifford Lectures at the University of Edinburgh in Scotland, and these lectures were subsequently published in a work that became (and remains to this day) a classic work in the field of religious studies, *The Varieties of Religious Experience*.[62]

William James worked in many fields, but above all he considered himself a psychologist, and is considered the founder of American psychology, having written the first authoritative college text and opened the first psychology lab in America (at Harvard). In *Varieties*, James attempts to examine religious experience as a psychological phenomenon, without necessarily passing judgment on the material that he is examining. James thus begins with a simple but significant phenomenological observation: religious experience happens. In other words, it is a psychological fact, regardless of what its theological, philosophical, neurological, or scientific status might be. James acknowledged that religious experiences really do happen, and hence can be studied in the same sense that one can study any other aspect of human psychology. James' approach was important, since it lent a certain legitimacy to religious experience, which could now be looked at by a modern, scientifically-informed, myth-liberated population of scholars, researchers, and thinkers as something both real and deserving of serious study.

In *Varieties*, James examines a wide range of different types of religious experiences: visions, voices, conversions, apparitions, saintliness, and more. But for our purposes (and finally leading us to the whole point of our discussion of religious experience), the most significant chapter in *Varieties* deals with James' discussion of a particular type of religious experience known as *mysticism*.

Unfortunately, the word "mysticism" is a poorly chosen word to describe this type of experience, given its multiple meanings, many of which bear little resemblance to the specific experiential state which James and other scholars mean when they use the word. In everyday usage, mysticism can refer to experiences of ghosts and other paranormal phenomena; muddled, fuzzy thinking; irrational superstition; and all sorts of other types of experiences, usually in a critical, negative context. None of this is what William James meant by mysticism, nor is it what is meant by the word in the field of religious studies today or the meaning that we will ascribe to it.

Rather, following James, what we mean by mysticism is a very particular type of religious experience that is characterized by a sense of *unity* or oneness with a larger reality, sometimes in the sense of loss of self and sometimes in the sense of an expansion of one's sense of self. Mystical experience involves a strong sense that one is connected to a larger whole, and that whole is the Supreme Good, however it might be labeled as God, Spirit, or even no label at all. More suitable terms have been proposed to describe this type of experience: unitive, non-dual, transpersonal (in the sense that one experiences a sense of being more than an isolated egoic self), cosmic consciousness (in the sense that one feels a connection with the entire universe), but "mysticism" has remained the commonly used term, so that is what we will employ as well.

There are several interesting characteristics of mystical experience that we will briefly examine: the similarity of the experience in diverse traditions; the nondenominational character of the experience; the common observation that the content of the experience is indescribable; the related and almost contradictory assertion that the experience conveys wisdom about the true nature of reality; the spontaneous nature of the experience; and the frequency with which the experience occurs.

One of the most notable aspects of mystical experience is how similar descriptions of it are across different traditions and time periods. Theologically speaking, for instance, Judaism and Hinduism appear to be worlds apart, and yet one can find descriptions of religious experiences in both traditions that are so close that they are virtually interchangeable. Many anthologies of mystical writings similarly offer numerous descriptions of the experience which, though produced by followers of different traditions, sound remarkably similar. Rudolf Otto's classic work *Mysticism East and West*, while acknowledging that differences exist, nonetheless offers numerous passages which illustrate the universal aspects of the mystical experience, and D.T. Suzuki does the same in *Mysticism: Christian and Buddhist*. In these various accounts, the common element is an immediate, experiential sense of the unitive nature of reality, a sense of the "oneness" or connectedness of things, along with a sense of one's intimate connection to that oneness.

Not surprisingly, what is usually absent in these cross-traditional accounts of mystical experience is any reference to denominational particularities which set the experience apart as consistent with one religion or denomination but not with another. Indeed, we find surprisingly few attempts to connect the experience to the specific theological concepts of any given tradition. In this sense, mystical experience is the ecumenical experience par excellence, seemingly shared by members of all religious traditions. Christian mystics, for example, often tend not to describe their experience as an experience of Jesus or the Trinity or any other specifically Christian theological concept. In a sense, mystics seem to have an experience which supersedes the understanding of the sacred that comes from their own culturally and historically defined and limited tradition. The mystical experience is portrayed as something that cannot be restricted by the limiting language and concepts of any one tradition.

This in turns leads to another hallmark of mystical experience: the assertion that it is an experience that is *ineffable* (one of the four essential characteristics of mysticism described by James in the *Varieties*),[63] or unable to be described using human words. There are countless examples which we can't take time to recount here, of mystics declaring that that which they have experienced is something indescribable, and that any words that they use to describe what they have experienced will necessarily be inadequate and hence somewhat misleading. For readers who want to go straight to the sources, check out the Christian mystic Meister Eckhart or the anonymous 12th century

Christian classic, *The Cloud of Unknowing*; in Hinduism, the teaching on *"neti neti"* found in the Upanishads; in Buddhism, the teachings on Shunyata or Emptiness, found in texts such as the *Diamond Sutra* and other Mahayana and Zen texts; in Judaism, the teachings of the Kabbalah masters, where one can say nothing about the supreme nature of God, other than that it is *Ayin*, or Nothingness. Of course, there is a bit of a paradox here, in that we have a voluminous corpus of writings by individuals who claim to have had experiences about which one cannot say anything, or at least not say anything with much precision! But many mystics openly acknowledge that their written accounts of their experiences are nothing more than pointers or guides to give the seeker a slight, and admittedly imperfect, taste of something that can only be fully known in a direct experiential sense.

Furthering the paradox of mystical experience is the curious, yet commonplace, sense that this experience which is fundamentally indescribable nonetheless is an experience which conveys a profound sense of meaning and truth (what James refers to as the *noetic* quality of mysticism). Individuals who have had a mystical experience commonly report that the experience leaves them with a knowledge that they did not previously have, and this knowledge is of a very profound, deep, life-altering nature. In general terms, this "knowledge" acquired in the mystical experience is confirmation that there is indeed a spiritual reality, or "Something More" besides the realm of matter. What's more, this awareness of a Something More conveys a sense that, however things may appear to the contrary through our ordinary experiences, we live in a universe that is meaningful and good, where Spirit/God is the ultimate reality, and where all things share in a common bond of spiritual interconnectedness. Those who have had a mystical experience often say something to the effect that their spiritual belief no longer is based on faith, but rather is rooted in the much more secure ground of direct, undeniable, powerful experience. In the same way that we acquire knowledge that an apple is red or sugar tastes sweet through our ordinary five senses, we have a similarly direct, immediate, irrefutable experience of Spirit through the opening up of our spiritual sense, thereby making belief in a proposition or in a past event a less significant aspect of one's faith.

The skeptic might say, "So what?" Even if mystical experiences do occur, they occur with such infrequency that their relevance for a broader understanding of the nature of religion and their relevance to religion in the 21st century is negligible. And yet there is ample evidence to suggest that such experiences are not so rare at all. This is particularly the case if we recognize that mystical experiences exist in various degrees. A full-scale mystical experience in which there is a complete loss of the sense of isolated individuality and a complete sense of union with Spirit may indeed be quite rare, but partial mystical experiences, often quite brief and spontaneous, characterized by some small but undeniable sense of being part of a larger whole and some sense that there exists a unitary reality with which one is connected, appear to be quite common. In a widely publicized 2009 poll by the highly reputable Pew Research Center, for instance, 49% of the respondents indicated that they had had a "religious or mystical experience." A 2006 poll by Pew had produced almost identical results (47%).[64] It should also be noted that many of the examples of accounts of mystical experiences contained in James' *Varieties* were collected from friends, colleagues, and ordinary individuals who had no professional or strong personal relationship to a church or other religious body. There is reason to believe, in other words, that humans have developed an innate capacity for mystical experience, or *an innate capacity to experience their connectedness to part of something larger than their individual embodied self.* Some have suggested that this spiritual capacity is an evolving aspect of human perception, such that just as humans have slowly evolved the capacity to engage in increasingly complex rational calculations, so they also have slowly evolved the capacity to directly experience the spiritual nature of the unitive reality that is the essence of mystical experience. If this is the case, one could postulate that religious experience of this sort will continue to become more and more common in the coming centuries.[65]

But the skeptic could further argue that, even if it is the case that mystical experiences do indeed occur, and occur with some frequency, these experiences reveal nothing about the nature of reality, since they are simply delusions. People have internal experiences all the time which are "real" in the sense that an internal experience is happening to the person, but the experience has no connection to a reality outside the experiencing subject. The experiences are nothing more than delusions.

But two responses can be made to this argument:

First, there is the *compelling quality* of the accounts of mystical experiences. Individuals who have had such experiences consistently maintain that they retain full consciousness, including their critical intellectual faculties, throughout the course of the experience. We are not talking about a circumstance in which the subject enters into a highly emotionally charged state with diminished objectivity and capacity for self-reflection or a hypnotic state in which clarity of thought is diminished. This may happen in some types of religious experiences, but not in the experiences referred to as mystical. In fact, quite to the contrary, the person who has experienced a mystical state often describes it as a heightened sense of awareness and objectivity, in which there is a certain detachment from the biases of one's own ego and the emergence of a broader epistemological perspective. The reader who is suspicious of the validity of mystical experiences is advised to simply read the accounts (in, for instance, James' *Varieties* or any of the numerous anthologies of mystical experiences). These accounts are quite compelling in their lucid, clear-minded quality. They are also frequently written by individuals with sufficient intellectual and introspective sophistication to recognize the difference between experiencing a delusion and experiencing an aspect of reality, and their accounts confidently assert that they have experienced the latter and not the former.

But aside from the compelling quality of the descriptions of mystical experiences, there are legitimate epistemological considerations that argue for taking mystical experience seriously and not brushing it off as nothing more than an illusion. We take for granted that our five senses allow us to have certain kinds of perceptions and experiences that produce valid knowledge of the nature of reality. Through those five senses, operating as part of a neurological system which includes the brain, we have access to a certain dimension of reality, namely that dimension which is comprised of time, space, and physical matter. This is all part of everyday, ordinary experience, which is accepted as the basis of valid knowledge.

The epistemology of mysticism is based on the notion that, in addition to these five senses, humans have access to additional sensory capacities, capacities which are normally inactive but which are nonetheless latent in the perceptual capabilities of a healthily functioning brain and mind. In a sense, we have a "sixth sense" or "third eye" which, while usually dormant, has the capacity to become activated (sometimes through intentional cultivation, sometimes spontaneously), and once activated this additional perceptual capacity makes possible an awareness of aspects of reality that are not perceived through the ordinary five senses. The five senses generate perceptions of the objects of ordinary, everyday consciousness, while the sixth sense generates a non-ordinary or altered mode of consciousness in which aspects of reality are perceived that are not available through the ordinary five senses. It's this additional sense and the mode of consciousness that is made possible through its activation that is the basis of mystical experience. The person having a mystical experience, such as the overwhelming sense of the unitary nature of all things, is simply perceiving what's out there through the use of an additional sense, or a part of the brain that is not activated in most everyday conscious perception and experience. Through the activation of this usually latent part of the brain and the non-ordinary mode of consciousness that ensues and the non-ordinary type of perception that is thereby made possible, one experiences aspects of the sacred, or Spirit.

Note that this understanding of the epistemology of mystical experience does not require any sort of divine revelation from a heavenly being or miraculous intervention from without. In a sense, mystical experience can be explained in fairly naturalistic terms, as long as one is open to the notion that "natural" extends far beyond its usual sense. This understanding of mystical experience recognizes that our perceptions and the knowledge that we derive from our perceptions are dependent on the processes that occur in the human brain. But it also suggests that the processes that occur in the human brain are not limited to those that generate the five ordinary senses, but rather include additional processes – usually latent but activated at the time of a mystical experience – and these non-ordinary brain processes make possible non-ordinary perceptions and the non-ordinary knowledge that ensues. Mystical experience, or a direct experiential awareness of the sacred dimension of reality, is known through a fuller use of the perceptual capacities of the human brain.

Having spent so much time on the topic of religious experience, it might be appropriate to wrap up this chapter by asking, "What's the point... why spend so much time on this topic?

What does religious experience have to do with thinking about religion today, in the 21st century?"

The answer is that, in an era when many of the traditional bases for religious faith are no longer credible to much of the educated population that thinks in 21st century terms, religious experience stands out as perhaps the most reliable, substantial, unassailable basis for belief in a spiritual reality.

For many, faith as belief in a literal interpretation of whatever is found in an ancient text is no longer tenable; faith as belief in explicit propositions (dogma) is no longer tenable; faith as belief in mythological beings with anthropomorphic characteristics (often including very human flaws) is no longer tenable; faith as belief which is dependent on a historical event (a resurrection, a revelation on a mountain, a levitating teacher) which one cannot confirm as factual is no longer tenable; faith as unwavering acceptance of the authority of pronouncements of church leaders is no longer tenable. And faith as the product of rational philosophical "proofs" of God's existence is no longer tenable.

In other words, and to the dismay of believers, the traditional justifications for holding to a religious worldview have all been radically undermined. Not surprisingly, then, we see the churches which rely on such justifications continue to lose members as a larger percentage of the American (and European) population becomes de-Christianized.

But it is precisely in this context of the loss of traditional reasons for believing that the important role of religious experience comes to the fore. Religious experience is not dependent on belief in an ancient text, loyalty to a church hierarchy's doctrine, acceptance of a mythological portrayal of the sacred, or anything other than what one directly experiences. Just as I can come to know about the existence of a structure known as the Eiffel Tower in Paris by testimony of friends or pictures in a book or a documentary film, I can also set aside all of these secondary sources on the existence and location of the Eiffel Tower and simply travel to Paris and experience it for myself. I can have a direct experience of the Tower, and in doing so I am freed from any dependence on sources outside of my direct personal experience to confirm the Tower's existence.

Religious experience allows us to acquire a taste of the nature of the sacred (with vastly different degrees of intensity, depending on the nature of the experience) without any dependence on scriptures, church dogma, myths, etc. Religious experience provides us with knowledge of God that is immediate and powerful, just as seeing the Eiffel Tower is a far more meaningful confirmation of its existence than is reading and viewing secondary accounts of it. So in times when the Church, its scriptures, its mythologies, and its doctrines no longer seem believable to a substantial part of 21st century humanity, religious experience is still available as a point of contact with that transcendent realm of Spirit that can be known in no better way than through direct experience.

Of course, one might point out that this only applies to those who have had such an experience, and that leaves out a substantial part of the population. That's true: those who have had the good fortune of having a religious experience possess a basis for their faith that the non-experiencer does not. But nonetheless, we would suggest that the widespread presence of religious experiences, and the frequently lucid, compelling accounts of those experiences, can be a valuable path to faith even for the person who has not had such an experience. We say this in the sense that while accounts of religious experiences certainly cannot be accepted as "proof" of a spiritual dimension by those who have not had such an experience, it is not unreasonable to suggest that such experiences should function as *evidence* for the existence of that spiritual dimension or transcendent realm.

What's more, we would argue that accounts of religious experiences function as very *compelling* evidence of the existence of Spirit. Accounts of religious experiences are rarely of the nonsensical, raving, mad sort, but quite to the contrary seem to be the product of a mode of cognition that is well-grounded, rational, sensible, and capable of distinguishing reality from illusion and delusion. As we've suggested above in discussing James' *Varieties*, it's difficult to read the many selections in his chapter on mysticism without coming away with the impression that these are intelligent, emotionally sound, sane people describing actual experiences that they have encountered.[66] Hence, even the person who has not had any sort of religious experience, after reading the accounts found in James' and countless other books, will hopefully at least open himself or herself up to the possibility of an experience of the sacred.

We should also add in closing that being open to spiritual experience does not have to mean being open only to a full-scale mystical experience as described in this chapter. Certainly such experiences are intense, profoundly moving, and deservedly cherished. But we should also put a word in for what might be called the *spiritual quality of the everyday*. That is to say, to those who are open to it, everyday experiences which we encounter in ordinary, unaltered states of consciousness can be faith-affirming in the same sense – although less dramatically so – as can a full-blown mystical state of altered consciousness. And the kinds of subtle, precious, and quite ordinary moments when such experiences occur, when that fleeting sense that "there's something more" flashes briefly but deeply in the depths of one's awareness, are many and varied. The birth of a child. An act of great compassion. An unexpected gesture of generosity or forgiveness. The beauty of a sunset or ice glistening on the tips of tree branches. The peaceful death of a loved one... whether human or animal. In these and countless other everyday moments, we can be momentarily transformed into a subtle but undeniable awareness that there's something going on in existence other than particles moving through time and space. There really is a Something More, even though we can't define it, and even though we know that it is not identical to, and in some ways dramatically different from, the concept of God that we were taught in Sunday School and church. The old God may be gone, but when the old gods die (to paraphrase Ralph Waldo Emerson), that's when the new God can arrive – a new sense of the sacred and transcendent, a sense of Spirit that is "believable" in the context of all that we know in the 21st century.[67]

So with reference to how we *think* about religion in the 21st century, consider that the question should be expanded to how should we *experience* religion in the 21st century. And the simple answer is to open up your consciousness to the reception of the full range of experience that is available to you – not just the narrow band of experiences that derive from the interaction of our ordinary five senses with the physical world, but the full spectrum of vast, mysterious, awe-inspiring awareness that is available to each of us in the 21st century, even to those of us who have rejected the traditional image of God, sacred text, church, and doctrine.

Chapter 14

Making Sense of Suffering

So far we have argued that even if one sets aside many of the elements traditionally seen as the basis of religion – ancient sacred texts, church doctrines, creeds, the anthropomorphic depiction of "God," the authority of church officials – there are still ample reasons for an intelligent, reasonable, good-hearted person in the 21st century to have faith in the existence of a spiritual dimension of reality. The nature of consciousness, our moral sensibility, and the nature of religious experience provide sufficient grounds for an intelligent contemporary thinker to have faith in the existence of a spiritual dimension.

But now we have to take a step back and recognize that there also is a significant impediment to faith, and this impediment has been vexing people of faith from all cultures and all religions in all time periods, going back to the very origins of the existing world religions. And that impediment, as challenging today as it was 3000 years ago, is the problem of suffering.

More specifically, it's the question of how can one believe in God or any sort of spiritual dimension when the world in which we find ourselves is so full of suffering, pain, and evil. The breadth and depth of suffering is particularly acute when we fully and honestly acknowledge the extent to which pain and suffering are prominent, unavoidable aspects of human life, and not just occasional, anomalous interruptions of an otherwise blissfully serene and pleasant existence. Illness, injury, pain, and death are happening all of the time, if not directly to us at this moment, to others who surround us. If not to us today, then certainly to us at some later point. All people experience pain and suffering, and often in rather intense and intolerable ways. And even those few who manage to have the good fortune of going through an entire life with good health, adequate food and shelter, freedom from accidents and violence, and a relatively happy life, nonetheless will eventually be confronted with what many would consider to be the most profound of all of life's dark sides: the annihilation of one's entire existence in the finality of death.

Some believers attempt to deflect the awfulness of existence on the grounds that so much of the suffering in the world is caused by humans, and that slowly but surely, humans are evolving into more morally sensitive beings, such that eventually human-generated suffering will be eliminated or at least drastically minimized. Perhaps, but even so we still have, in the meantime, the countless acts of incomprehensible cruelty: assaults, torture, rape, murder, and the countless more subtle daily acts of evil perpetrated on an everyday basis that bring pain and suffering to each and every one of us.

But one can leave aside the evil caused by humans and we still find a world full of pain and suffering. Famine, drought, floods, fires, catastrophic storms, infectious diseases – this is all part of the natural world that surrounds us, a world that is also populated by living creatures that seek to devour and destroy, from the tiniest microorganism to venomous snakes to beasts that tear apart a human, casually and with apparent relish, and consume it.

The challenge of defending religious belief in the context of widespread suffering is perhaps even greater in contemporary times, where we have to confront not only the suffering that besets individuals and local communities, but also a uniquely modern fear of catastrophic suffering on a scale that could encompass not just individuals and communities, but the entire human species and potentially the entire planet. The vast scale of destruction that could result from various weapons of mass destruction such as a nuclear holocaust, or the disastrous consequences of climate change that could radically change the

Earth's natural environment into one that can no longer support the delicate balance of forces and resources necessary to sustain life, both pose a real threat of suffering on an unimaginably enormous scale. Reconciling religious faith with the suffering of individual persons is a challenge; how much more so is the challenge of reconciling belief in the existence of God with the vast scale of misery that would result from such global catastrophic events?

So put bluntly, we live in a world in which suffering and pain are everywhere. And the problem posed by the omnipresence of this suffering and pain is this: How to reconcile it with the belief in the existence of a spiritual reality?

This is hardly a new dilemma, but one that is attributed to thinkers at least as far back as the Greek philosopher Epicurus in the 4th century BCE.[68] Beginning with the understanding of God as a being who is both all-powerful (omnipotent) and supremely good (omnibenevolent), and assuming that as an omnipotent being God has created and sustains the world, how do we explain the existence of evil? If God is indeed omnipotent, it would follow that he can control everything, including whether or not suffering exists in the world. Hence, the presence of suffering in the context of an omnipotent deity would seem to suggest that God can control suffering but chooses not to. But this would suggest that God is not omnibenevolent, which is the other essential attribute of God. On the other hand, if we begin with the assumption that of course God is omnibenevolent, then the presence of suffering would seem to suggest that God, as a benevolent being, wishes to eradicate suffering but cannot do so, thereby denying God's essential attribute of omnipotence.

As the 19th century Scottish philosopher David Hume put it, "Is He willing to prevent evil, but not able? Then he is impotent. Is he able, but not willing? Then he is malevolent. Is he both able and willing? Whence then evil?"[69]

This nicely describes the apparent logical conflict between the existence of God as an omnipotent and benevolent Being, and the presence of suffering – endless suffering, unspeakably horrible suffering, senseless and gratuitous suffering – in the world.

But the real challenge that the omnipresence of suffering poses for religious belief is not just a rational one but also an *existential* one. Yes, there seems to be an irresolvable logical contradiction between a good and all-powerful God and the existence of suffering, but the depth of the challenge of suffering for religious belief is not found so much in rational concepts but rather in the lived experience of suffering in all of its endless manifestations. A debilitating illness, a tragic accident, a brutal natural catastrophe; a stillborn child, a woman in the prime of her life tortured by untreatable cancer, the agonizing daily decline of a once bright and insightful man reduced to gibberish by Alzheimer's; starvation from famine, electrocution and burning from a lightning strike, the torture of freezing to death. There is no point in cataloguing the countless daily ways in which human beings are subjected to not just suffering, but suffering of an agonizing and horrific sort, through no fault of their own. And it's this recognition of the pervasive reality of intense human pain and suffering that leaves the thoughtful mind asking, how could there be a God in a universe in which the innocent suffer so?

And yet, despite the problem posed by the challenge of suffering, our species has persisted in believing in God or some sort of spiritual reality for over two millennia. How can that be the case? In part, it's the result of the remarkable human capacity to develop creative ways to explain away unpleasant and contradictory aspects of life. In this case, we are talking about the creation of what philosophers and theologians call *theodicies*, or attempts to explain how it could be the case that a good and all-powerful God could exist simultaneously with a world (created by that God) full of immense suffering by conscious beings.[70] The ingenuity of humans in developing explanations for this apparent contradiction is quite remarkable and has resulted in pages upon pages of sophisticated philosophizing and theologizing, producing an output of theodicies far beyond what we have time to cover here. However, let's take a brief look at a sampling of the major theodicies that have been used in the Christian tradition (and, to some extent, in Judaism and Islam as well) over the past 2000 years.

One popular theodicy is the free will explanation, which argues that evil is simply the by-product of God having created humans with free will. While this might be a possible explanation for the suffering caused by humans (although we would suggest that it doesn't even succeed in this limited task),[71] it completely fails to address the problem of *natural* evil. The existence of free will in humans might indeed require the possibility of choosing evil over good, since otherwise the notion of making a free choice is meaningless, but still this theodicy says nothing about the immense suffering that humans experience at the hands of not other free-willed humans, but the impersonal, but presumably God-created, forces of nature. From the victims of mass natural disasters to the heartbreaking fetal genetic abnormality that guarantees a life of chronic pain, the world is full of suffering which is not the product of human choices, and an explanation of this type of suffering is left unaccounted for by the free will theodicy, and hence its usefulness as a convincing theodicy is quite limited.

The "soul-making" theodicy argues that evil exists for the sake of giving us something to struggle against, and only through such struggle do we develop the most unique and treasured human qualities such as courage, patience, compassion, faith, etc. This is a version of the "no pain, no gain" mentality, suggesting that God has actually done us a favor by providing something to struggle against. While there may indeed be considerable psychological validity to the "no pain, no gain" concept, this hardly offers an adequate account of how a good and benevolent God could allow *so much* suffering in the world, and suffering that is sometimes so overwhelming that there is no opportunity to use it for edifying purposes of spiritual growth. The bolt of lightning or the massive tidal wave causes instant death, leaving no opportunity for soul-building of any sort.

Sometimes theodicies are couched in historical terms. One version attributes the presence of suffering in the world to the Fall of Adam and Eve as found in the Biblical book of Genesis. To the modern reader, however, this explanation is not likely to carry much weight in terms of explaining why countless humans living today should experience suffering because of something that might have been done by another party many years ago. And, of course, even many Christians no longer interpret the story of the Fall as an account of an actual event, so again, its usefulness as a convincing theodicy to a modern reader is fairly limited.

Along somewhat similar lines in terms of incorporating a historical element in trying to explain evil, the "Divine Plan" theodicy suggests that even though we cannot currently understand how it is the case, nonetheless suffering is part of God's larger plan, and at some point in the future of humanity or at some point in our individual afterlife, we will recognize that all things happen for good, even if it didn't seem to be so at the time that the suffering occurred. But this theodicy also comes with multiple challenges: *Why* did God create a plan for the universe which required suffering, and *so much* suffering, and why suffering *of such a horrible nature*? Would a truly benevolent God devise a Master Plan for his creation which would involve so much suffering?

And lastly, there is the "afterlife" theodicy, which argues that we shall be compensated in an afterlife for whatever suffering we have experienced in this life. In other words, God will make up for the pain that we have experienced, and in the end it will all balance out. Of course, as in the previous theodicy, one might ask how a benevolent and all-powerful God would come up with such a seemingly callous if not sadistic idea of allowing creatures to intensely suffer now in return for rewarding them at a later point. Fyodor Dostoevsky offers a moving and penetrating critique of this theodicy in *The Brothers Karamazov*, where the character Ivan Karamazov declares that he will never believe in a God that allows a small child to suffer, since that suffering can never be undone despite whatever wonderful rewards the child experiences in heaven. A good and all-powerful God would not let the innocent child suffer in the first place![72]

There are many other attempts at constructing a convincing theodicy, some quite subtle and philosophically sophisticated, but we would suggest that none have any more credibility to the contemporary reader than do the theodicies described above. But if that is the case, then what are the implications for the viability of religion in the 21st century? If there is no satisfactory way to reconcile the presence of suffering in the world with the existence of a good and all-powerful God, then how can the thoughtful person possibly subscribe to religious belief, regardless of the specific faith or denomination?

It makes no difference if we replace the traditional understanding of the transcendent as anthropomorphic deity with the contemporary model of the sacred as part of the evolutionary process. Indeed, the persistence of the problem of theodicy cannot be overestimated and does not go away even in the most nontraditional, contemporary models of spiritual thought. In many of the more creative contemporary spiritualities, the traditional model of the anthropomorphic deity is often replaced by an evolutionary model of an unfolding cosmos that has an innate spiritual element. Often, as is the case, for instance, in such diverse figures as Aurobindo, Teilhard de

Chardin, and Ken Wilber, the evolutionary process is portrayed as movement toward increasing awareness of and presence of Spirit in the material Cosmos. This model is quite appealing to the contemporary mentality and it does solve a number of the roadblocks to faith that are found in traditional spiritual perspectives. But evolutionary spirituality does *not* solve the problem of suffering, since the process of evolution itself is one that proceeds, at least in large part (although perhaps not exclusively), via natural selection, or "survival of the fittest." The evolutionary process is one which crushes and annihilates the countless beings which are less successful in adapting to their environment. The evolutionary process appears to be a heartless, amoral, indifferent process, of which pain and suffering are an innate part. The problem that this poses for a theodicy is quite obvious and stark: how can the process that is identified as the vehicle by which Spirit enters into and saturates the Cosmos be a process in which unlimited and unimaginable suffering and death are an innate part? If the evolutionary process is an expression of Spirit, then Spirit lacks the same quality of moral goodness that we find lacking in the criticism of the theodicies associated with the more traditional model of God.

So whether we are dealing with the traditional model of the anthropomorphic deity or the nontraditional contemporary model of evolving Spirit, in both cases we are left without a convincingly comprehensive and adequate account of evil, and hence in both cases we are left with the need for an element of *faith*.

This is not to say, however, that since an element of faith is needed in both models, the models are on equal footing. Quite to the contrary, the type of faith required by the traditional model is quite different than the type of faith required by the contemporary model that we are presenting. The traditional model requires faith in historical events and dogmatic assertions that reflect ideas that are often not very credible from a contemporary perspective. By contrast, an evolutionary nontraditional contemporary spirituality requires faith in an idea about the nature of reality, namely the idea that there is meaning and goodness behind the vast mystery (including its evil) of the Cosmos. This is indeed faith, to the extent that it is not "provable," but it is a type of faith that is likely to seem more justifiable to the 21st century citizen.

So getting back to the key question: if there is no satisfactory way to reconcile the presence of suffering in the world with the existence of a good and all-powerful God, then how can the thoughtful person possibly subscribe to religious belief, regardless of the specific faith or denomination?

We should reply by first of all fully accepting the profound extent and depth of suffering that exists in the world, and acknowledging that such suffering cannot be neatly explained away by any theodicy, however cleverly worded and however philosophically and theologically complex. The honest thinker must begin by fully recognizing the pervasiveness of suffering and fully affirming how its presence cannot be logically reconciled with the existence of an all-powerful and omnibenevolent deity. Honesty about the fact of suffering must be the starting point.

But we would suggest that acknowledging the pervasive nature of evil does not necessarily negate the reasonableness and legitimacy of religious faith, especially if that faith is of the sort that is reflected in what we have presented in previous chapters. Yes, it is undeniably the case that the reality in which we exist is full of unimaginable suffering, and if that suffering was the only thing that existed, if that suffering was the only attribute of reality that we are aware of, then that indeed would be grounds for denying the viability of any sort of belief in a spiritual reality. But, of course, suffering is not the only thing that we perceive and experience in the world. Alongside that suffering there is also much that is good, beautiful, creative, sublime, meaningful, expansive, virtuous, and all of those many other qualities that offer us tastes of a spiritual, transcendent, Something More. Yes, there are many terrible moments in the life of a human being that are full of pain, torment, harm, deceit, etc. As Soren Kierkegaard was fond of saying, death and destruction are always potentially just around the corner.[73] *But that's not all that there is.* The presence of the negative elements of reality exists side by side with those elements that abound with life, beauty, and love. Just as it is naïve and inauthentic to hold a simplistic faith that denies the reality of the dark side of reality, so it is equally inauthentic to hold a simplistic form of disbelief that denies the sublime and beautiful side of reality. The various reasons for the type of contemporary faith that we've covered in the previous chapters of this book are not negated by the presence of suffering.

What, then, does this mean for religion in the 21st century? Caught between the poles of the recognition of the sublime mystery of the numinous quality of existence and the awareness of the crushing reality of omnipresent, unrelenting pain and suffering, how can the sincere and serious inquirer come down on the side of religion?

The answer, we would suggest, is that the thoughtful and open-minded seeker can indeed maintain confidence in the existence of a transcendent, spiritual dimension, and that this confidence must be grounded in faith. But, as indicated previously, we're talking about a very different kind of faith than that which is extolled by and practiced in Christianity and the other Abrahamic religions (as well as, to various degrees, some non-Abrahamic traditions). We are suggesting that, in the end, faith is needed, but it is not faith in a historical event which we cannot verify, nor is it faith in a doctrine or dogma consisting of abstract concepts not susceptible to confirmation, nor is it faith in the authority of religious leaders, or even faith in the wisdom of an ancient text.

Rather, we are talking about an existential faith, born out of the experience of opening oneself up to the fullness of the Cosmos, fulling embracing the mystery of the reality of Spirit, even though the nature of that Reality cannot be captured in words, no matter how much complicated philosophizing and theologizing might be put into the effort. We are talking about an existential faith that is *rooted in one's own experience*, not rooted in the experience of historical personages from centuries ago, not rooted in confidence in church leaders who are no more omniscient about such matters than each of us, not rooted in ancient doctrines written in language and symbol that perhaps made sense to the authors but which say little to us now, not rooted in old texts which sometimes seem to express wisdom but sometimes seem to be archaic and even offensive. In a sense, to use a currently popular (and often misused) term, we are talking about an "evidence-based" type of faith, one that is based on our open and honest experience of the Cosmos rather than on blind acceptance of a past event or abstract doctrine.

Yes, faith is necessary, given that the spiritual dimension and its interaction with the physical universe is an elusive, mysterious, bewildering, and at times seemingly contradictory thing. But it is a reasonable faith, a faith that the thoughtful seeker in the 21st century can affirm without any reservation or embarrassment It is a faith in the innately self-validating nature of our experience of consciousness, Goodness, meaning, and the other dimensions of spiritual reality which, indefinable and elusive as they might be, are always right there in front of us awaiting our embrace.

Of course, one could object that it's rather arbitrary to elevate those experiences that evoke cosmic optimism over those that evoke a sense of despair, hopelessness, and meaninglessness. Both kinds of experiences happen, but on what grounds can we justify the step of subordinating experiences of pain and suffering to experiences of spiritual awe, mystery, meaning, etc.? Looked at with the detached objectivity of the distant observer, there is no logical reason to elevate one type of experience over the other. But when we take into account the experience itself, things look quite different. There is a *quality* to moments of experience of the sacred that is absent in moments of experience of evil. The experiences are radically different in a qualitative manner. On the one hand we have experiences which innately communicate the notion that "This is the way things should be/are," as compared to experiences of pain and suffering which innately communicate a sense that "There's something wrong here," or "This is not the way things are supposed to be," or "This is an aberration." In a sense, when we experience a taste of Spirit or the sacred, we intuitively sense its ontological primacy, or the sense that the Good, however it might be characterized by the multiplicity of religious traditions, is superior to and ultimately ascendant over the evil. The faith that is born out of this experience of Spirit does not in any sense deny the existence of pain and suffering, nor does it pretend that there is some sort of tidy rational way to reconcile it with Spirit. Rather, this faith is simply a confident sense – despite the evidence to the contrary as found in the manifest suffering in existence – that in the end, all will be well, the Good will triumph, Spirit will be all.

Again, this sort of faith is certainly not a theodicy, but we would do well to again ask on what basis we should presume that there should exist a successful theodicy, or that humans should be able to rationally explain all aspects of the Cosmos. As we have previously suggested in various contexts, why should it be the case that a species that has existed at a tiny point in the vast universe for the span of a brief second in the vast expanse of time and which has developed a three pound organ, known as a brain, which has a limited capacity to manipulate and correlate abstract ideas – why should we think that such a creature of limited scope and limited means would have the capacity to fathom the entirety of the Cosmos, including not only all of the material world but also the nature of the spiritual realm as well? At face value, this would seem to be a somewhat preposterous and arrogant assumption! We don't assume that ants, given the nature of their perceptual apparatus, are capable of doing calculus, so why should we presume that humans can fathom such ultimate questions? The gap between an ant's perceptual apparatus and calculus is almost certainly far less than the gap between the human perceptual apparatus and knowledge of all things (including Spirit), so perhaps we should just humbly acknowledge the limits of reason and accept the possibility that the truth of some aspects of reality can be experientially sensed but never adequately articulated. We should, in other words, recognize that in the domain of spiritual matters, faith is necessary, but it is a faith rooted in something that we can and do directly experience or sense. So put aside the notion that being a person of faith means having to believe in things that you have no means of confirming. Faith is simple acceptance of the reality of Spirit that is confirmed (though never explained, categorized, rationalized, etc.) by our own immediate experience of the nature of the Cosmos in which we reside.

So with reference to suffering, how should we think about religion in the 21st century? First, we should not look to inadequate rational theodicies that presume an ability to fathom decidedly unfathomable cosmic spiritual questions. Rational explanations of suffering simply don't work. And in the absence of those rational theodicies, then secondly, we should simply acknowledge that the presence of suffering is one of the many aspects of the Cosmos that we, as tiny human creatures, are unable to rationally reconcile with the existence of God or Spirit. But finally, we should also recognize that amidst that suffering we also find, *as equally real*, goodness, kindness, love, beauty, and countless other qualities that point to the presence of a transcendent spiritual dimension, a dimension that we might not be able to rationally prove, but in which we can have faith, even in the presence of suffering.

Chapter 15

The Question of Meaning

So far we have explored how, from a perspective that is fully informed by a 21st century consciousness, one might be able to reassess several aspects of religion in order to make it more "credible" in today's world. However, we still have to examine what some might consider to be the most important, essential, and universal element of religion: providing a sense of meaning in human life.

The question of meaning is, of course, universal, and found in religious and philosophical traditions from across the globe and dating back over two millennia. Religion, in its many manifestations, has been the primary source of providing humans with a sense that there is some sort of meaning or purpose – however dim and vague it might be – in their lives.

And yet, the very notion of "meaning" becomes rather elusive when we try to identify exactly what is meant when someone asserts that religion makes life meaningful. What does it mean to say that there is meaning to life? Is meaning gauged by each individual's existence, and if so, what is it about a single person's life that makes it meaningful? In order for a human life to be meaningful, does there need to be some sort of continuation of that life after the death of the body, or is it sufficient to label a life meaningful if it is "well-lived" in some (again, hard to define) sense, even if that life is terminated upon bodily death? Some would argue that meaning in life must include some sort of afterlife, but that in turn raises the question of why must it be included and what type of afterlife would it have to be. Yet again, some would argue that the question of meaning has to be understood in cosmic and historical terms: not only must each individual life be meaningful, but there must be meaning to the existence of the universe as a whole, including the direction of the universe, which must culminate in some sort of positive fruition rather than cooling down into lifeless nothingness. Some would argue that if the cosmos as a whole is meaningful, individual entities within the historical span of the cosmos do not need to be meaningful per se: the Universe displays some sort of meaningful Grand Design, even though individual entities, including humans, make their contribution toward that design and then are set aside or annihilated in the universe's march to Cosmic Completion.

If we look at the existing religious traditions, we can discern two basic models of meaning in life. In the Western/Abrahamic tradition (Judaism, Christianity, and Islam), there has been a tendency to view meaning in terms of the full scope of history, from a divine creation through God's providential guidance of human history, to an ultimate eschaton in which God's purpose is fulfilled in human and cosmic history. From this perspective, the meaning of an individual existence must be understood in the context of this larger plan of historical salvation. Curiously, this historical model of meaning has even been appropriated by some who offer both spiritual and secular interpretations of the meaning of life. Hegel, for instance, sees meaning manifested in the orderly and predictable evolution of the human species and human society as Spirit becomes increasingly manifested in both the individual and social realms. In the mid-20th century, Teilhard de Chardin attempted to reconcile religion and evolution by producing a model in which meaning is understood in the context of ever-increasing levels of complexity and consciousness as the universe, guided by a divine spirit, evolves from matter to mind to spirit, culminating in the pinnacle of meaning which Teilhard referred to (but perhaps never clearly described) as the Omega Point.[74]

Even the explicitly atheist and secular philosophy of Karl Marx can be seen as derivative of the very Christian doctrine of meaning in history that Marx was quick to condemn. For Marx, human life was meaningful in the context of an inevitable, progressive transformation of society and the individuals in those societies, leading eventually to the utopian ideal of the pure communist society. In a sense, Marx kept the Christian doctrine of meaning in history while dispensing with God and replacing him with a natural socioeconomic evolutionary process.

And yet, despite its popularity, this historical model of meaning has some significant limitations. In particular, it makes meaning dependent on something that is far away, abstract, highly speculative, and unknowable. If the meaning of my life is dependent on a historical process and its culmination at some indefinite point in the future, then that meaning is something that, in a sense, remains experientially far removed from my own life. How can I know that there is meaning to existence if that meaning will not be apparent until some point far into the future?

From a traditional religious point of view, this dilemma is resolved by inserting the need for faith: by having faith that history will develop according to the trajectory described in the Bible, Qur'an, or other sacred text or teaching, we can be assured of the meaningfulness of life even though it is not apparent in our own existence. But from the viewpoint of a 21st century perspective on religion as outlined above, where we are no longer dependent on old texts and rest our faith on experience that is available to us in the present, this solution is simply not tenable.

But the historical model of meaning is not the only one. The notion of meaning as something that unfolds in and can only be discovered in the context of history, which is to say, over time in the light of changes that take place, is a particularly Western notion, found in the tradition of the Abrahamic religions and the cultures – even secular ones – that grew out of them. By contrast, in non-Biblical traditions and in many Asian religious traditions, meaning is usually understood as an innate, immediately present aspect of experience, and is not dependent on any sort of historical narrative. This perspective on meaning is the one that is dominant in Hinduism, Buddhism, Jainism, Daoism, and Confucianism, as well as ancient Greek philosophy. Of course, there are exceptions, especially where Asian traditions have been influenced by contact with Western religions (for instance, in the incorporation of the concept of a future savior being, as found in the Buddha Maitreya), but for the most part the historical sense of meaning is not a significant element in Asian religions.

In Greek thought, a meaningful life is discovered through one's experience of the Good, the True, and the Beautiful, or in other words, through a direct awareness of the transcendent spiritual values that inherently make life meaningful. Leading a meaningful life from this ancient Greek perspective is a matter of conducting oneself in accordance with these spiritual realities, just as leading a meaningful life in a Daoist, Confucian, or Chinese Buddhist sense consists of conducting one's life in accordance with the Dao. In this ahistorical model of meaning, there is no need to place meaning in the context of a sense of history and some future eschaton. Perhaps there is meaning to the course of history and perhaps the evolution of the Cosmos does lead to some final grand Teilhardian culmination, but in the ahistorical model the meaningfulness of an individual human existence is not dependent on this historical narrative. Maybe history has meaningful direction, and maybe it does not. But in either case, a life lived in accordance with Spirit carries with it an awareness of the inherent meaningfulness of such a life. To live in accordance with the Good, True, and Beautiful, to live in accordance with the Dao, is inherently meaningful without reference to any larger historical narrative, even if such a narrative is indeed slowly and imperceptibly unfolding. In order for life to be meaningful, no larger historical narrative is necessary. Meaning can be found through everyday experiences and interactions which establish meaningfulness, regardless of the context of larger historical events.

Put differently, from this position a spiritually meaningful life is simply a life lived in accordance with spiritual reality. That simple. There is that Something Else. Our life takes on a sense that it matters, that it's meaningful, to the degree that we live our life with primary reference to that Something Else (with Goodness, Truth, Beauty, etc. or Dao/Li), rather than with reference to values, beliefs, wants, etc. that run counter to that Something Else. And when we live a life in such a manner, what happens externally cannot negate the meaningfulness of our life. What happens externally can of course cause great pain, suffering, anxiety, disruption, heartache, destruction, etc., but it cannot negate the sense that we are leading a meaningful life. As long as we are hanging on to the Good, our life has meaning; as soon as we let it go – no matter what is happening historically and externally – that meaning is gone.

By now it is probably obvious to the reader that it is this ahistorical model of meaning that we are suggesting can be readily adopted by the 21st century person who wants to embrace spirituality without sacrificing his reason, historical perspective, or other aspects of a 21st century sensibility. As we have suggested above, accepting the legitimacy of religion in the 21st century means dispensing with belief in an anthropomorphic sky God who is providentially guiding history, setting aside a literal interpretation of old sacred texts (including those that offer a narrative of history made meaningful by fulfilling a divine purpose), and stepping back from a blanket adherence to church doctrines and dogmas. All of this can be done while still retaining a sense of the meaningfulness of life, since the ahistorical understanding of meaning is not dependent on any of those elements of traditional religion which we are suggesting can be set aside. Thinking about religion in the 21st century depends only on an openness to the intuitive sense that there is a Something Else, that that Something Else is the Supreme Good, and living with a sense that one's life is meaningful involves nothing more than living one's life in accordance with that Something Else.

And yes, that may sound rather vague, and yes, that certainly doesn't offer the same security as finding meaning through following the rules and plans of a personal God who has delivered a specific set of rules and a detailed account of the course of history, all written down in a book of unquestionable authority and confirmed by a body of (usually male) religious authorities in precise doctrinal statements. But that sort of spiritual security simply isn't available to us anymore, or rather that sort of spiritual security is not available to us if we want to be honest about our religious beliefs. The spirituality of the 21st century is indeed likely to be something of a less defined and fuzzy sort, but that vagueness and fuzziness is a small price to pay for spiritual honesty. What's more, there is a sense in which grounding our spirituality in our own direct experience or awareness of that Something More provides a far more preferable kind of spiritual security, to the extent that we know what we believe and we know why we believe it, something which often cannot be said by those who attempt to convince themselves to believe in ideas and practices that they have acquired through inheritance rather than through genuine experience.

But there is another crucial element in how many people think about what constitutes a meaningful life. The question of meaning in life is often paired with the notion of some sort of preservation of the individual self after death. If we look for the meaning of life in the context of individual, rather than historical, terms, a perennial question immediately emerges: in order for life to be meaningful in a religious sense, does life have to continue after death of the physical body, and, carrying that even a step further, does that post-mortem existence have to be eternal? Put a bit differently: In a universe governed by a good God or, to say essentially the same thing in less theistic terms, in a cosmos in which Spirit is the ultimate reality, does it necessarily follow that souls or individual human consciousnesses cannot be forever annihilated and doomed to extinction upon death of the body, but rather, as a logical and necessary expression of the fundamental Goodness of God/ Spirit, each soul/consciousness must be preserved in some dimension of existence beyond that of the material realm which we now inhabit? From this perspective, if the fate of a human being is utter annihilation upon the death of the physical body, life would be a meaningless and absurd cruelty and nothing more. Meaning in life is dependent on some sort of afterlife, and by providing belief in an afterlife, religion thereby provides a sense of meaning.

Traditionally, of course, the notion of an afterlife and an eternal soul have been part of most religions, especially but not limited to the Abrahamic traditions. But in some Asian traditions, things get a bit more complicated, especially in those traditions grounded in non-dualism, or the belief that ultimately there is some type of identity between Spirit and the Cosmos, God and the world, the divine and the human, etc. In some of those traditions it can be said that the *individual* soul is not eternal, but such an assertion is made only in the context of that individual soul becoming something much greater than itself after death, or even *presently* being much greater than itself but lacking in such awareness of its divine nature. Rather than being annihilated, the individual soul *expands* to assume (or, as some would say, re-assume) its true identity as Spirit itself. The classic expression of this is in Vedantic Hinduism, where the Atman (self) is declared to be identical with Brahman, or the Supreme spiritual being (comparable to the Western notion of

God, but usually conceived of in impersonal terms, and often understood as encompassing the entire Cosmos, rather than as a Being that resides in a heavenly realm that is separate and different from the created realm). Nonetheless, since we are writing primarily to a Western audience, we should spend some time examining the implications of the Abrahamic (Jewish/Christian/Muslim) perspective on the afterlife and its role as a necessary component of a meaningful universe.

While the notion of personal immortality in a heavenly realm has become commonplace in these traditions, it should be noted that there are some rather perplexing questions raised by this model which the 21st century would-be believer might struggle with. If the individual soul exists after death of the body, what form does it take, and if the afterlife is an embodied afterlife as suggested in many Christian traditions, what would that embodiment be like? First, there is the age question and accompanying identity question: If someone dies, for instance, as an infant, would they be resurrected in the afterlife as an infant, leading to the peculiar scenario of an eternal life as a baby? Or would such a person be resurrected in the afterlife as an adult, thereby raising the question of identity: how would someone recognize this adult person who never existed in an adult body in their earthly life?

A similar dilemma derives from the notion of an individual soul living an eternal existence. What exactly would it be like to live *forever*, as the same person, day after day? And is there a sense in which the consciousness of a truly never-ending existence as an unchanging identity would at some point become – well, boring? And do we even have the capacity to conceive, even in vague terms, what an immortal existence would be like? As human beings with the capacity to think of time in a sense that perhaps no other species does, we conceptualize time in the context of beginnings, continuations and endings. Do we even have the capacity, using the cognitive abilities of that three pound gelatinous organ called a brain, to even remotely imagine what eternity might be like?

But the difficulty of imagining in a detailed way what a post-mortem survival of consciousness would be like is not necessarily that important. In fact, we would argue that our perspective on existence after death of the physical body should be viewed in terms somewhat similar to the manner in which we described the 21st century perspective on God. The perpetuation of consciousness, like the existence of Spirit, is something that can be rather clearly and firmly intuited, despite the fact that, like the existence of God, it can only be intuited in a very vague sense, and hence, perhaps the less said the better. We run into problems when we start to pretend that we know more than we really do about the existence and nature of God or whatever we choose to call that transcendent reality. And similarly, we run into problems when we start to pretend that we know more than we do about an afterlife and the ultimate status of the personal identity which we currently experience while attached to a physical body.

So perhaps all that can be said on the topic is something like this: the sense or sentiment or intuition that we do live in a meaningful universe, however poorly and vaguely that sentiment might be articulated, is accompanied by a similarly vague and poorly defined, *but adamantly convincing*, sense that there is some kind of preservation of individual identity or consciousness after death of the physical body which we presently inhabit on this plane of existence. How that can be the case remains unanswered and perhaps is unanswerable given the epistemological limitations of our current capacity to understand reality via the limitations of the human brain. And yet, to the person who experiences that sentiment, that uncertainty seems rather irrelevant. There is a direct experience of the sense that we live in a meaningful universe in which individual consciousness, or personal identity, is a precious and valuable thing, and in order for that universe to be meaningful, that consciousness must somehow be preserved.

There is a line in a song by the Australian singer Nick Cave, written after the tragic accidental death of one of his teenage sons, in which he simply but movingly states with reference to his dead son, "I am here, and you are where you are."[75] In a sense, in all its beautiful simplicity, perhaps that's as much as should be said.

Chapter 16

Putting It All Together

So finally, after covering much ground, we have reached the point where we can summarize the basic arguments that have been presented in this short work – bearing in mind, however, that the nature of the task that we set out to accomplish is such that far more words will need to be written and many more books published in order to even begin to present an adequate account of what we are trying to convey here. This book is, in a sense, simply an introduction to an issue that will be struggled with by minds far sharper than mine over the coming years, decades, and generations. This is, in a sense, a taste of what is likely to come in the ongoing effort to clarify and crystallize the understanding of Spirit that human consciousness is perhaps on the brink of entering into on a broader scale than ever before. Some of what we have proposed will hopefully come to be seen as accurate predictions of where the human sense of the spiritual is headed; in other ways, no doubt, some of our strongest hunches about the nature of religion in the future will prove to be quite misguided. Nonetheless, even if we are approaching the future development of human spirituality as though (to use the Apostle Paul's oft-cited phrase) "looking through a glass darkly," we hope that the reflections in this book do indeed offer at least a glimpse of what that other side is like, and encourage others to similarly pursue the task of making that glimpse into future spirituality one which is made through a glass that is less and less dark and eventually transparent.

We began by asking a fairly simple and straightforward question: how can one think about religion in the 21st century without sacrificing one's moral or intellectual integrity? Implicit in the question is the assumption that the question alludes to a task that is attainable. That is to say, we are assuming that it actually *is* possible to identify as a religious or spiritual person while still being true to the full range of knowledge that is available to 21st century humans. One can indeed confidently affirm belief in a spiritual dimension without sacrificing one's intellectual or moral integrity.

To do so, however, requires a significant adjustment to how we think about "religion," and much of the book has been devoted to the details of how we need to think differently about religion so that we can identify as religious persons without making that intellectual and moral sacrifice.

Of course, we've only covered the basic, broad elements of what such a 21st century religion might look like, and there are many areas that we haven't touched upon: worship, ritual, institutional structures, etc.

Similarly, while we have attempted to argue that it makes sense to adopt a religious position even in light of the full range of human knowledge as it exists at the beginning of the 21st century, we have not suggested that this provides "proof" that God or Spirit exists. Rather, we have simply attempted to demonstrate that it is legitimate for a fully informed 21st century citizen to believe in the existence of a spiritual reality or dimension. By "fully informed" we simply mean taking into account the full range of human knowledge and awareness, including scientific understanding of the nature of the physical universe; social scientific insights into the functioning of the human mind; historical knowledge and the perspective that it provides on the origins and evolution of all human activities, including religion; knowledge of the full range of religious beliefs, practices, sacred texts, religious experiences, etc.; recognition of the evolution of human moral awareness (including, when necessary, acknowledging the moral brutality displayed by divine beings in traditional religions, including the Abrahamic ones); and the full multitude of insights and perspectives that are available to a knowledgeable 21st century citizen, providing a degree of self-awareness that is unique in the long history of our species.

But we also have emphasized that in order to retain a spiritual perspective in the context of being a fully informed 21st century believer, a radical shift is required in how we think about religion. As Daniel Matt has said, "We can begin to know God by unlearning what we think about God,"[76] and we are suggesting that there is indeed much that we need to unlearn. Consequently, we spent the entire first half of the book "deconstructing" the basic elements of religion as it has been traditionally understood in the West, suggesting that it is OK – indeed, it is necessary to retain one's intellectual and moral integrity – to think differently about such key aspects of traditional religion as basic concepts of spirit, sacred texts, ritual, doctrine, the relationship with other religions, and the relationship between religious belief and science.

Having argued for a fairly radical revision of how we think about religion, we then attempted to "reconstruct" what a viable religious perspective of the 21st century might look like, examining alternative ways to think about God or Spirit, the role of consciousness, the significance of the human sense of moral goodness, the role of religious experience, the challenge to religious belief posed by suffering, and the question of meaning – all of these topics explored in the context of thinking about religion in a way that is freed from the constraints of traditional dogma and fully informed by the intellectual and moral insights of 21st century humans.

So in essence we are suggesting that on the one hand, the answer to the question, "Is it reasonable to believe in traditional religion in the 21st century?" is "No" (although with significant qualifications, as discussed below). But, on the other hand, we are also suggesting that a "no" answer to that question does not lead to the conclusion that the 21st century person should completely reject religion. Quite to the contrary, we argue that there are ample grounds for the fully informed 21st century citizen to believe in religion, but in a significantly different way than has traditionally been the case. Setting aside traditional (largely, but not exclusively, Western) religion does not mean abandoning religion completely. Rather, for those who are open to the possibility, it can mean being liberated from a constellation of beliefs and practices which may have seemed to make sense at an earlier point in human history but no longer seem to be credible, and opening up to new ways of thinking about, experiencing, and living in accordance with, the very real Spirit that permeates the Cosmos. As Steve Taylor has said, the alternatives are not existing religion or no religion at all, but rather a religion that makes sense to humanity today, and that is the understanding of religion that we have attempted to outline in this work.[77]

Some (many, perhaps) will be resistant to this proposal for a new type of spirituality, and even offended at the suggestion that the religious traditions of the past 2000 years need to be reinterpreted in some fairly radical ways. And yet, such resistance is rooted in the questionable belief that religion consists of a set of eternal propositions that never change. Pre-Enlightenment and pre-modern believers might have been justified in their confident belief that their religion was such a set of eternal truths. But the historical and analytical consciousness that is part of any honest 21st century thinker's psyche clearly reveals that, like every other aspect of human culture, religion changes over time. Humans in Europe in the 10th century BCE were religious, but they did not ascribe to the same sort of religious beliefs and practices as did humans in Europe in the Christianized Europe of the 10th century CE. But Christians in Europe in the 20th century do not ascribe to the same beliefs and practices as did those 10th century Christians.

The same could be said about all of the major world religions: they change over time.

As we have examined earlier, a significant change in human spirituality occurred roughly in the period from 1000 BCE to the beginning of the Common Era, a period known as the Axial Age in recognition of the sense in which humans seemed to make a rather sudden (in historical terms) shift from one type of spirituality to another. After roughly 2000 years, we have perhaps reached a moment where humanity is poised to enter into a second Axial Age, in which just as the tribal, animistic, power and survival-oriented religion of pre-Axial humanity was superseded by a religion that was more focused on universality and the essentially moral nature of Spirit, we are now seeing the first signs of that Axial Age religion getting superseded by something else. In recognition of that evolving change in human spirituality, this work has argued that it is permissible to think differently about religion but still be religious. It's OK to think differently about, and in many cases to outright reject, various aspects of traditional religion that simply are no longer credible to the honest 21st century thinker. Indeed, we would take that a step further and argue that, not only is it permissible to think differently about religion, but we have a moral and spiritual duty to think differently about religion when traditional beliefs and practices are no longer credible when examined in the light on an intellectually and morally honest 21st century consciousness. It's simply wrong to pretend to believe things that one no longer finds credible. It's simply wrong to continue to engage in practices, whether ritualistic or ethical, that no longer seem to make sense.

This all would suggest that, for many humans who are fully informed by a 21st century awareness, traditional theism is no longer credible. Describing Ultimate Reality or Spirit as a being with human-like qualities, often prone to outbursts of jealousy and rage, functioning as a King who sits on a throne, located quite literally up in the sky, ruling over subjects in a harsh and punitive manner, is no longer tenable. Humans at any given historical moment are necessarily stuck with using the categories at their disposal as symbols to try to understand and describe that which is indescribable. For pre-modern humanity living at a stage of development in which power, authority, and the source of order were often known through the person of a king, where civil order was maintained through rigid enforcement of harshly punitive laws, where scientific astronomical knowledge of what was up in the sky was absent, categories of kingship and a heaven "up there" were reasonable and meaningful concepts by which to express spiritual truths. It made sense to try to comprehend the incomprehensible through those symbols.

But those symbols do not make sense to many people today. Cultures change, and with them, the range of symbols that are available to humans in their attempt to portray the Sacred. Much of the world continues to try to make sense of the Sacred by clinging to symbols that are over 2000 years old, and those symbols are no longer working for increasingly large numbers of people. Sadly, many of those who cannot accept those outmoded symbols resort to disbelief, under the mistaken impression that a religious perspective employing 2000-year-old symbols from a very different period of human cultural development is the only option available for a believer. The gist of our argument is simply the assertion that that is not the case: *there are other options*. There are ways of thinking about, relating to, and experiencing the Sacred that are not dependent on concepts that come from previous stages of cultural development and no longer function effectively for 21st century humans.

Of course, some will be quite offended by the suggestion that traditional ways of thinking about the Sacred, and the religions built around those beliefs, need to be set aside and replaced by new symbols, beliefs, practices, etc. For some, the traditional religions are still considered to be just fine. Of course, it's unlikely that those readers have made it this far in the book, since they probably find the basic arguments laid out here to be quite objectionable, misguided, offensive, and perhaps even the work of malevolent forces, and they feel no need to set aside the centuries-old religious traditions that they follow. To those readers, we should say that it is not our intent to deny the value and (relative) truth of traditional religions, nor would we suggest that those who remain committed to such traditions should consider changing their allegiance. Quite to the contrary, if you practice a traditional religion and still find it credible and meaningful, then by all means stick with it and throw away this book. Traditional Christianity, for instance, provides a wealth of spiritual goods: a set of beliefs that present our life in the context of a larger meaning, guidelines for leading a just and moral life, a sense of community, consolation during times of grief, and many other functions that are provided by most, if not all, religions. If traditional Christianity (or Judaism or Islam, etc.) remains a credible source for providing those spiritual goods, then why should one abandon it, especially in light of the as yet undeveloped nature of the new, emerging, alternative spirituality that we have described in this work?

But the target audience for what we present in this book is not the traditional believer, but rather the contemporary men and women who sense that there is a larger, spiritual dimension to the universe, but who, if they are to be intellectually honest with themselves and true to their sense of moral goodness, simply cannot accept the content of traditional religions. We are writing for an admittedly small but rapidly growing population of individuals who have a sense that atheistic materialism is an inadequate account of reality, and that there is indeed a spiritual dimension to the universe, but not one that can be described in the language, doctrines, and practices of the existing religions. We are writing for those who believe that we are in need of a new spirituality, one grounded in a full awareness of what it means to be a 21st century human.

Much of what we have covered with reference to that newly emerging spirituality has been rather vague and nebulous, but necessarily so given that we are still at an early stage in this process of the emergence of a 21st century religious sensibility. But recognizing that any predictions are necessarily not much more than best guesses, and in the spirit of trying to bring together the various ideas that we have covered over the pages of this work, let's finish by offering some very tentative and still vague suggestions at what this religion of the future might look like:

A Different Concept of God

A persistent theme throughout this book has been the recognition that religion changes as human consciousness and human culture change. So it shouldn't come as a surprise that we would expect that the way humans conceive of that which we currently refer to by the word "God" will change as we move into the 21st century and beyond. This is not to suggest that belief in God will disappear: quite to the contrary, it's an affirmation that such belief certainly will continue, but the precise nature of how we think about "God" is likely to change significantly. This is a difficult topic, given that the word "God" is in itself a rather elusive term with multiple meanings, often quite nuanced, for different believers. But for our purposes, if we consider a broad definition of God, compatible with most theistic religions and even some non-theisms, as simply a belief in a spiritual entity or dimension that is the ultimate source of being and goodness, transcending but also penetrating the realm of the physical universe, then by all means "God" will continue to be the basis for the religion of the future.

However, there will likely be significant alterations to that concept of God, such that some might even advocate the use of a different word, such as Spirit or the Sacred, to replace the word "God." The problem with the word "God" is that it carries with it associations that, in some cases, just don't make sense to contemporary believers. Conceiving the Sacred as God as understood by traditional religions means conceiving the Sacred as a male king, ruler, lawgiver, punisher, father figure, etc. For some, the use of such symbols from everyday life are still meaningful, but for increasing numbers of believers these symbols seem antiquated and, perhaps most importantly, limiting and restricting ways of referencing the Sacred. The new emerging spirituality sees Spirit as so much *more* than that which can be described using these personal descriptors or indeed any words that create the inaccurate impression that the Entity that is the ground of all being can be comprehended in terms that derive from this single species. This is not to deny that in a certain sense it is meaningful to refer to the Sacred as "Father," but it is to say that using such person-based language *limits* our sense of Spirit in a way that can no longer be justified. Similarly, to describe Spirit as a human-like being which displays human-like qualities such as rage and jealousy is to both limit and tarnish our sense of the Sacred. This is not to say that Spirit is not "personal" in the sense of manifesting those human qualities such as moral goodness, compassion, truth, beauty, etc. – God *is* personal in that sense. But God is not personal in the sense of also manifesting those many other human qualities which the 21st century believer recognizes as qualities that even decent humans can transcend. So we are left with the option of either continuing to refer to the spiritual dimension as "God" with a radically different understanding of what that word means, or simply moving on to a word – such as Spirit or the Sacred, that carries less baggage. Or perhaps, as the new spirituality emerges over the coming centuries, a new language will develop to help humans express that which is beyond language. The "God" of the 21st century and beyond will be a much bigger sense of "God" than we currently find in the existing traditional religions, and a language to adequately refer to that "God" is perhaps yet to be developed.

Spiritual Minimalism

Existing major religions all have extensive doctrines and dogma, supplemented by even more lengthy and exhaustively detailed orthodox theologies. Christianity has its creeds (Apostles, Nicene, and Athanasian) and a vast theological tradition that dates back to the earliest decades of the Church and proceeds through the philosophically sophisticated works of the Catholic scholastic theologians such as Thomas Aquinas and continues right up to the present day, with each of Christianity's many denominations offering fairly detailed accounts of how, as a Christian, one should think about God. Similar traditions are found in every major religion. Even in Buddhism, which is often misunderstood by non-Buddhist Westerners to be a religion that sets aside discursive reasoning and theological quibbling for direct spiritual experience through meditation, doctrine and rational theology abound, and Buddhist schools sometimes quarrel over points of doctrinal subtlety in a manner similar to that in which competing Christian denominations bicker.

The spirituality of the future, however, is likely to be quite different. The strong emphasis on doctrine and dogma found in existing religions presumes a certain confidence about the human capacity to know and talk about God or Spirit, but, as we have previously suggested, a 21st century understanding of the position of humans in the context of the vastness of the Universe, to say nothing of the mystery of a nonphysical spiritual realm, is seen by many contemporary believers to call for a certain spiritual humility with regard to what we say about that which so radically transcends the human realm of the physical universe in which we reside. Doctrine-heavy religions are tainted by a certain epistemological parochialism, which presumes that what can be known by the perceptual apparatus of a tiny species, using a gooey three pound organ, existing at a small point in the Universe, during a brief moment in that Universe's history, should somehow correspond to universal truth. This arrogant overestimation of the human capacity to know is reinforced by the notion that this particular species also has access to books (sacred texts), derived from a divine source, that similarly provide access to sacred truth. Thus an inflated capacity to reason is combined with an entitled sense of being the recipient of divine truth to produce the dogmas, doctrines, and theologies that form the intellectual foundation of the existing religions.

But we are suggesting that such epistemological certainty is no longer credible, and hence the dogmatic certainty that derives from it similarly loses its credibility. The religion of the future will likely be grounded in an epistemological realism and humility that deters us from generating detailed accounts of ultimate truths disguised as statements of certainty when they are really nothing more than best guesses. A statement of dogma may have some value when it is recognized for what it is: namely a well-intentioned but decidedly limited and fallible attempt by a tiny creature to make a declarative statement about something that is far beyond that creature's capacity to see clearly. Twenty-first century religious thought will hopefully recover a sense of the humility that was present at the outset of the Christian tradition (but subsequently lost as the Church developed a false confidence in its own authority) when the apostle Paul remarked that, with reference to understanding spiritual truth, we "see through a glass darkly," which is to say that we do not see clearly or accurately. Religions of the future will hopefully reclaim that sense of always "seeing through a glass darkly," and hence refrain from the detailed creeds, doctrines, dogmas, and theologies that have been generated by all of the existing world religions.

This sense that the religion of the 21st century will be theologically minimalist is shared by many who are exploring the possible contours of the future of religion. As Sean Kelly has put it, the spirituality of the future is likely to be characterized by a "renunciation of certainty" that stands in marked contrast to the detailed doctrinal positions of existing religions.[78] Similarly, Ervin Laszlo, in exploring the religious implications for the evolving global quality of human consciousness, suggests that we should attempt no more than a "minimally speculative theology."[79] And J.L. Schellenberg argues that with reference to religion, "We simply need to start thinking more generally than we are accustomed to doing."[80]

Putting this into broader evolutionary terms, on the one hand the human species is quite unique in that, unlike any other species on this planet (and, as far as we can tell, in this galaxy), our consciousness has evolved to the point where humans can sense the existence of a spiritual quality to the Cosmos, a Something More that exists in addition to the physical universe, and from that unique perceptive capacity we have the emergence and development of religion. But on the other hand, we now recognize that that spiritual reality is a vast mystery which we have only limited ability to describe. We also recognize the human origin of what believers in the past interpreted as divine revelation. In a sense, the more we know, the more we realize how little we know. Hence, as we move forward into the 21st century and beyond, religion will persist (the evolved human capacity to sense the Sacred will remain), but it will be grounded in a minimalist doctrinal and theological base that is the product of the epistemological humility that comes with our 21st century consciousness. We will recognize that Spirit exists, and that Spirit is the ground of everything, and that living in accordance with Spirit is the most important thing in a human life.

And maybe that's enough. Maybe we do not need the detailed creeds, the official doctrines, the extensive theologies.

But some will argue that such spiritual minimalism can't work: there needs to be specific and comprehensive content to religious beliefs or the world of religion will descend into chaos. Without creeds, doctrines, and theologies, believers will have no direction, no structure, no guideposts for navigating the mysterious realm of Spirit.

It may be true that the early stages of the next step in human spirituality (which may last for decades or even centuries) will be challenging due to the abandonment of old ways of thinking about Spirit and the absence of clear replacements, and yet this has been the case throughout human history when a shift is made to a new mode of spiritual awareness. Consider the case of Christianity, where it took over four centuries after the life of Jesus for Christians to develop a set of clear and specific statements regarding the content of their faith. During those first four centuries, there were multiple and vastly different interpretations of what it meant to be a Christian,[01] both with regard to the beliefs about God that one should hold and the way of life that a Christian should follow. Christians today tend to forget that the concepts of the Incarnation, Trinity, and Atonement, which are almost universally held by Christians of all denominations today, were largely absent in the earliest Christian communities, hotly debated over the first few Christian centuries, and only became part of a clearly established "orthodoxy" after the political power of Constantine and the Roman government declared in the 4th century that these beliefs (and not the many, many others that still circulated in the Mediterranean world among communities that identified as Christian) would be the *only* beliefs permitted for churches that considered themselves to be Christian.

Similarly, we need to recognize that we are only at the beginning of the emergence of a post-Axial spirituality, and hence there will likely be a similar period of creative theologizing in which new words, symbols, concepts, etc. are offered up as the best ways to express the Sacred, and over time, as in the case of Christianity and every other major religion, preferred expressions will emerge. Even then, however, we are suggesting that spiritual minimalism will always be present, since we have acquired an epistemological humility and a historical consciousness which, once attained, will not go away.

Empirical Religion

If future religion is not grounded in doctrine, dogma, and reliance on divinely revealed sacred texts, then what will it be based on? What's left as the basis for religious faith once these traditional, Axial Age elements are found to be no longer credible?

We've already looked at the answer to that question in chapter thirteen: religious experience. The religion of the future will likely be less rooted in declarative statements, theological arguments, and stories from ancient texts, and more grounded in the everyday awareness of the sacred quality of reality that remains available to people of faith even after the legitimacy of the past's doctrines and texts have lost much of their credibility.

In a sense, this will simply be a return to a meaning of "faith" that brings us back to the origins of religion and that from which the verbal expressions of faith (doctrine, dogma, texts) derive. This is especially the case with the Western, Abrahamic religions, where the meaning of "faith" has been transformed over centuries into a set of beliefs not about the nature of Spirit per se but about specific historical events to which the believer no longer has access. Belief in a proposition about a historical event whose veracity must be accepted without evidence, or in "blind faith," is quite different from belief in a statement about the nature of reality that can be confirmed by one's own immediate awareness, or experiential faith. In the present era when many of the traditional bases for religious faith are no longer credible to much of the educated population that thinks in 21st century terms, religious experience stands out as the most reliable, substantial, unassailable basis for belief in a spiritual reality.

This doesn't mean that future believers will all be full-blown mystics who walk around in altered states of consciousness while having had intense, prolonged non-dual experiences of the Sacred. As we described in the chapter on religious experience, the overwhelming, rapturous nature of a mystical experience is just one type of spiritual experience. Equally valid and compelling is the everyday, ordinary sense of a spiritual dimension to the Cosmos, a vague but confident sense that there really is Something More than a Universe of time, space, matter, and energy. This perception of a Spiritual dimension does not require intensive and difficult spiritual practices leading to a clearly identifiable moment of overwhelming spiritual illumination. Certainly such experiences happen, and they are profoundly meaningful in the spiritual lives of those who have them. But for the everyday person of faith who has neither the opportunity nor the interest to pursue the rigorous practices that lead to such experiences, there is the simple, humble, easily acquired sense of Something – a Something which is supremely Good and which confers meaning to the Cosmos, even in spite of the daily messes, challenges, and tragedies of normal, everyday human existence. Leaving doctrines and sacred texts aside, each person still has access to those subtle, quiet, yet powerfully meaningful moments when one senses the presence of Spirit, the presence of the indefinable Something More that has never been adequately captured in doctrinal statements or pronouncements in sacred texts.

To some extent, this movement toward a more experiential-based spirituality will likely be more of a challenge for the Abrahamic religions than for Asian traditions. Making broad comparisons between "Western" or Abrahamic religions and "Eastern" or Asian religions is, of course, fraught with problems given the complexity of every religious tradition and the danger of oversimplifying for the sake of making comparisons. Nonetheless, it is not unreasonable to argue that, at least at the popular level, the Western religions have tended to understand faith as intimately and necessarily including a strong element of faith in past events: Jewish faith in God speaking to Abraham, Moses, and other historical figures during the days of the prophets; Christian faith in the crucifixion and resurrection of Jesus; Muslim faith in God speaking to the person of Muhammed, delivering what would eventually become the content of the Qur'an. By contrast, in Buddhism, most branches of Hinduism (especially the Upanishads-based Vedanta tradition), Daoism, and Confucianism, faith is understood as a particular sense of the nature of reality. While the teachings of past figures such as Buddha, Upanishadic sages, Laozi, Confucius, and others are held in high esteem, it is *what the teachings point to* rather than the teacher himself that is the object of one's faith. For all of these religions, the content of their spiritual faith is not dependent on the truthfulness of the tradition's accounts of the lives of their founders. Their founders are honored, and in some cases even worshipped as divine beings, but it is the experiential awareness of Spirit to which their teachings point that is given the highest value, not the historical existence and deeds of the founders.

We can already see the emergence of this more experientially-oriented approach to religion in the growth of the "spiritual but not religious" population. Numerous polls have consistently found a steady growth in the number of believers who, on the one hand, do not consider themselves to be "religious," as in the sense of formally belonging to an existing tradition or accepting the doctrines of a given faith, while on the other hand identifying as "believers" in the sense of affirming the existence of a spiritual reality. In a sense, this trend is the leading edge of what might likely continue to evolve from a fringe movement to the most common expression of religion in the future.

Of course, this does not mean that there will not be *any* sort of doctrinal statements in the religion of the future. After all, *something* has to be said about the nature of the perceived, experiential presence of Spirit. Even if experience of the Sacred is primary, that's not to say that, over time, doctrines won't evolve that derive from and attempt to articulate that experience – we need words to communicate – but the words will be secondary, always referring back to the experience. At the present moment we are in the early stages of the transition to post-Axial spirituality, so understandably little has been accomplished in terms of the development of a language to describe the experiential and perceptual basis of that spirituality. But in all likelihood, as the centuries proceed, and not unlike the first several centuries of the Christian Church where a constant and robust debate played out among competing versions of what it meant to have Christian faith, a similar process will gradually emerge in post-Axial religion, eventually leading to some semblance of "doctrines" that allow believers to communicate with each other, but always referring back to the experiential grounding of that post-Axial faith.

Trans-human Morality

In chapter twelve we explored how the sense of moral goodness is a universal element of religion, so consequently we should expect morality to continue to be an essential part of religion in the 21st century and beyond. The more specific nature of that religiously-grounded future morality is, however, likely to differ from much of current religious moral teachings in two significant ways.

First, our sense of spiritually-grounded moral obligation will extend to the entire human species, not just to one's "own" group, whether that be a church, nation, ethnic group, or whatever. If we look at the evolution of human morality, we see a gradual expansion of our sense of moral obligation, from family to tribe to village to larger political units such as states and nations. For many contemporary believers, that sense of moral obligation has long been extended to its maximum breadth within the human community in a sense of moral obligation to all humans, regardless of religion, ethnicity, race, gender, nationality, etc. The notion of a "brotherhood (or sisterhood) of man (or humanity)" is hardly a new idea, and its origins can be seen even in the teachings of Axial traditions, with, for instance, Jesus extending the sense of moral obligation beyond his Jewish followers to the Gentiles as well, or the Buddha teaching the importance of extending compassion and other moral virtues to people of all castes. In real life, of course, this sense of a moral commitment to the entire species is often forgotten and sullied by its confused connection with various forms of religious exclusivism (moral obligations only to fellow true believers), nationalism (moral obligation only to God's chosen nation), and similar limiting perspectives. Nonetheless, over the course of the 20th century, and especially among the post-Baby Boomer generation that has grown up with a previously unknown ecological awareness and recognition of the global consequences of many aspects of modern human technologies, we find the sense of community with the entire human species to be more and more the norm rather than the exception. Such a trend is likely to continue, and the moral teachings of the religion of the future will reflect this sense of the need to treat *all* of humanity in a virtuous manner.

But we would suggest that there are also signs that this sense of expanding our sense of moral responsibility is already extending even beyond the human species and on to the realm of all living beings. The ethicist Peter Singer has coined the term "speciesism" to describe the traditional approach to morality in which we treat one species (human) as more deserving of moral consideration than other species, whether plant or animal. Again, we already see the early signs of the emergence of what might be called a "trans-human" morality in the growth of vegetarianism and veganism (growing to the point that even fast-food restaurant chains now offer plant-based alternatives to beef and chicken) and the growing popularity of organizations and movements devoted to natural conservation and environmental protection. One might speculate that given these trends, just as today's believers look back critically at earlier religious moralities that were confined to one's own tribe, believers in the future might look at today's nationalist and speciesist morality as similarly primitive and brutal.

Of course, this will present a challenge to those existing Axial Age religions which contain a humans-only morality. The Ten Commandments, for instance, certainly make no reference to our moral obligations to the nonhuman world, and as Lynn White pointed out three decades ago, the God of the Abrahamic traditions actually commands humans to adopt an exploitative relationship with the natural world when he declares that the Earth has been created for human use and commands that humans "fill the Earth and subdue it."[82] Clearly, significant changes will need to be made in the moral teachings of these Western faiths if they are going to continue to be relevant to a population that increasingly has a trans-human, multi-species, global sensibility.

This challenge is a bit less severe in Asian traditions where a sense of the Sacred as immanent in the natural world is often accompanied by a sense of moral obligation to the natural world, as seen from the Buddhist teachings of Shantideva[83] to the Neo-Confucian writings of Wang Yang-Ming and others.[84]

This movement toward a trans-human global ethics is also explored by Ervin Laszlo, who sees the evolutionary development of the human species as heading into a post-Axial Age in which human consciousness will become more attuned to our trans-human connections and consequently a similarly expanded ethic will eventually develop. As our concept of God/Spirit/the Sacred expands, so will our sense of ethical responsibility:

"When people evolve transpersonal consciousness they become aware of their deep ties to each other, to the biosphere, and to the cosmos. They develop greater empathy with people and cultures near and far and greater sensitivity to animals, plants, and the entire biosphere."[85]

Again, this will be problematic for those who cling to Axial religions and their less expansive moral teachings, and as with basic beliefs as discussed above, it will take time to develop a more detailed set of post-Axial moral principles. But whatever form those principles take is sure to be one which is certain to reflect a moral commitment on a global scale, covering all humans and all sentient beings.

Religious Pluralism

While we can only make vague guesses about what the many dimensions of the post-Axial religion of the 21st century and beyond will look like, we can probably assert with considerable confidence, as already has been done in chapter six, that the future religion will be one characterized by an embrace of religious pluralism and a rejection of exclusivism. The notion that there is only one true religion and that religions can be neatly categorized into "true" and "false" is already rapidly disappearing among many populations, and the pluralistic appreciation of a multiplicity of spiritual beliefs and practices will undoubtedly become the new norm. The exclusivist assertion that there is only one true religion, one true revelation, and one true path to salvation is simply not credible to people whose perspective is fully informed by study of the history of religions, which exposes the sociopolitical factors that influence the formation of each religion, and the study of World Religions, which demonstrates the multiple commonalities between traditions.

We already see a movement away from the traditional exclusivist norm as, for instance, the traditional boundaries between various branches of Christianity are dissolving, with practicing Lutherans being quite comfortable attending a Presbyterian service or even a Catholic Mass, and indeed with many Protestants not even familiar with the theological differences that once created a sharp and often acrimonious wall between different denominations. Today many Protestant Christians would be hard-pressed to describe the theological differences between, for instance, Lutheranism, Methodism, and Presbyterianism, and many mainline Protestant congregations are populated by members simply by virtue of family tradition rather than theological choice. This openness to other traditions also extends beyond the different branches of one's own faith and into completely different traditions, as we see Christians and Jews practicing Buddhist meditation and participating in Hindu religious festivals.

We appear to be heading for what Duane Bidwell has referred to as believers who are "spiritually fluid."[86] Rather than feeling a need to be confined to one tradition, the spiritually fluid believers (which appear to be rapidly increasing in numbers) do not identify with any one tradition, but feel comfortable drawing different elements of their spiritual life from different religions. The spiritually fluid believer might, for instance, participate in a Christian Mass, practice Buddhist meditation, hold a worldview derived from Hindu Vedanta, and read Confucius for ethical guidance, all the while seeing no conflict in the blending of various traditions and not exclusively identifying with any one of them. To the spiritually fluid believer, being religious does not require identification with a specific historical tradition, but rather consists of an acceptance of and commitment to spiritual reality that transcends association with any particular expression of faith.

This embrace of pluralism and movement toward spiritual fluidity doesn't mean that we are necessarily headed toward some sort of universal, global One Religion. Spiritual beliefs and practices are influenced by many variables, some reflecting differences in personality and taste, some reflecting local traditions, and countless other subtle differences in human personality that lead to a preference for one rather than another mode of spirituality. These factors will likely insure that, as the religion of the future slowly evolves, it will develop along branches that reflect these many differences in preference, but the new normal in which such variations exist will almost certainly be one which strongly affirms religious pluralism.

Religion and Science at Peace

There is no need to recapitulate the observations about the relationship between science and religion that we covered earlier, but that relationship, or more importantly, the evolution of that relationship as we move into the age of a post-Axial spirituality, is so important that we need to highlight it as a key element of the future religion that we are envisioning.

Granted that for the past four centuries the relationship between religion and science has been a conflictual one in the West, there is good reason to believe that such conflict will diminish and even disappear in the coming years as we evolve further and further away from the limiting parameters of the Axial-based model of religious faith that has dominated Western culture for over 2000 years. That model was based on an a priori acceptance of a sacred text – the Bible for Christians – as the mandatory starting point for valid knowledge of the nature of reality. If one starts from that position, a conflict with science is inevitable, given both the methodology of science and the content of scientific knowledge. If you start out with Biblical literalism as a prerequisite, you're going to have a difficult time coming to terms with a scientific understanding of the nature of the Cosmos.

But that simply will not be a problem in the religion of the future if that religion is no longer dependent on ancient texts for a starting point. If the spirituality of the 21st century and beyond is grounded in empirical experience, or our capacity to sense the Sacred or Spirit, then we are not locked in to concepts of the nature of the world that were developed over two millennia ago. A contemporary, post-Axial spirituality, in which a believer need not make any intellectual or moral sacrifices in order to believe, is one which almost by definition will be open to incorporating whatever the scientific worldview has to offer. If the 21st century spirituality is rooted in a simple awareness of the existence of a transcendent Meaning and Goodness in the Cosmos, unattached to any specific culturally-limited and parochial myths and legends, then the opportunity for a religion versus science conflict does not arise. The new religion of the post-Axial Age is one which finds no basis to challenge science

At the same time, however, we should recognize that science also is likely to make certain adjustments that will further facilitate a reconciliation with religion. As we have indicated earlier, many in the scientific community already recognize that the scientific dogmatism that sees reality in strictly materialist and mechanistic terms is no longer credible in light of the findings of how the quantum world functions.

So neither religion nor science is going away, but both are changing, and changing in rather dramatic and significant ways such that the centuries-old conflict between them will continue to diminish. Early in the 20th century, the philosopher Alfred North Whitehead spoke of the need for a "deeper religion and more subtle science,"[87] and that appears to be what is slowly emerging. The spirituality of the 21st century will be "deeper" in the sense that it will be free from adherence to ancient texts and the parochial mythological worldviews found in those texts, and rooted in a spiritually open empiricism. Science of the 21st century will be more subtle in the sense that it will be freed from a reductionist, deterministic, simplistic materialism and liberated from the hubris of 20th century science's parochial notion that science alone provides a true and comprehensive explanation of the nature of reality. Science will be open to the existence of Mystery, and religion will be open to the experience of Mystery, in all of its glorious multiplicity of manifestations.

And What We Don't and Can't Yet Know

While we have speculated on many of the ways in which religion will change as we move further into the 21st century and beyond, there are many aspects of the religion of the future that we have not explored. How will worship change? What will the rituals, liturgy, music, and art of a new spirituality be like? Will new sacred texts emerge, and if so, how will their authority be perceived? Will the social dimension of religion continue to be shared in a building like a church/mosque/synagogue/temple, or will 21st century religion find communal expression in a different setting, perhaps closer to a "spiritual wellness" center? What role will electronic communications and virtual reality play in 21st century spirituality? How will the institutional aspects of religion change? What sort of authority structures will emerge to define and order future religion?

We have refrained from speculating about these issues in recognition that we are in the early stages of a state of transition that will likely branch off in multiple directions that we cannot at this time even come close to predicting. Just as the transition from pre-Axial to Axial religions led to the emergence of multiple religious traditions that all grew out of the Axial spiritual perspective, just as the ministry of the Buddha led to multiple interpretations of his teachings and a parallel diversification into dozens of schools of Buddhism, just as the 16th century Protestant Reformation within Christianity gradually, over the subsequent four centuries, led to a proliferation of Protestant denominations far beyond what Luther likely envisioned, so too the emergence of a new post-Axial spirituality in the 21st century and beyond will inevitably produce a diversification of beliefs, practices, moral codes, and experiences that will result in a rich array of religious traditions that reflect the unique elements of specific teachers, local traditions and preferences, cultural differences, etc. The new spirituality will certainly be pluralistic in its openness to a more expansive relationship to Spirit, but that doesn't mean that religion of the future will suddenly become a uniform, undifferentiated, global tradition with no sensitivity to local difference. Movement toward pluralism and simultaneous appreciation of diversity are not conflictual developments. Both will occur, slowly, over a span of centuries, producing a new spirituality which in many ways will reflect what we have discussed in this book, and in some, more specific ways, will likely head in directions that we, at the beginning of this century, have not even dreamed of.

In fact, looking forward over the span of not years or decades, but rather centuries and even millennia, the potential for meta-developments that will radically change the nature of the world that we live in, and perhaps radically change the nature of what we are as a species, makes predictions about the future manifestations of spirituality even more tenuous. The era in which we live, as one of independent, sovereign nation states, often with varying degrees of ethnic identity, will not last indefinitely. With the decline of nationalism, the end of parochial differences between "East" and "West," and the emergence of a more global culture in which humans perceive their identity as citizens of the Earth rather than citizens of a specific ethnicity or nation, would seem to be a distinct possibility when seen from the perspective of the long time scale and direction of human evolution. As we develop that less nationalistic and more global culture, our basic modes of thinking, our basic assumptions about the world will likely change in dramatic ways, and our institutions, including religion, will change as well. In this context of the emergence of a globally-oriented species, the implications for the kinds of religious beliefs, practices, moral teachings, and institutional structures that will emerge are probably beyond our current limited capacity to imagine.

Even more fascinating is the prospect that aside from human society changing to a more global identify, *the human species itself might change into something which is radically different from what exists today*. Much has been written on the possible emergence of a "post-human" or "trans-human" species which would be the product of the merger of carbon-based biological humans with information technology, resulting in what would in essence be a hybrid part-human/part-machine species with capabilities that dwarf those of today's purely biological humans.[88] The extension of life span into hundreds of years, control over the creation of new post-humans, information-processing abilities that exceed the fastest of today's computers, the ability to virtually eliminate disease: if such a species does indeed evolve over the coming centuries or millennia, what will the religion of that species look like? Religion will persist, as we have affirmed above, but in the eyes of that future hybrid species will the religious traditions of today appear to be quaint and old-fashioned, or perhaps brutal and primitive in the same sense that we look back on the human sacrifices and superstitions of our ancient ancestors? In a sense, the religion of the future that we are exploring in this book is the religion of the *near* term of the next century or so. As for the religion of the *far* term – multiple centuries if not millennia – we will leave that to others.

But What If...

The reader might notice that our discussion of the history and future development of religion presumes a directional evolution, from pre-Axial to Axial to the still developing post-Axial spirituality. This presumes, of course, a certain stability for the human and broader Earth communities that will allow life on this planet and the human species in particular to continue to develop in the direction of increased complexity and increased consciousness. And yet, such continued stability is by no means guaranteed. Just as the main challenge to individual faith is the problem of theodicy, or the prevalence of pain and suffering in the world, similarly on a planetary scale any confidence in the continued evolutionary development of humanity, including our species' sense of the Sacred, must be tempered by the recognition of the possibility of catastrophic events on a scale never known since the emergence of humans, events which could destroy not only the species but all or most life on the planet. From global climate change to essential resource depletion to nuclear, chemical, or biological holocaust, the possibility of events that could destroy the human species and the entire biosphere is quite real and inevitably must taint any thoughtful person's perspective on the future. With a vision of such a gloomy future, how can one possibly take seriously the notion that human spirituality will continue to evolve in an expansive direction?

The answer is that there is no alternative. The evidence of 14 billion years of the history of the universe suggests that, while there are inevitable periods of chaos and destruction, the longer, unavoidable trend of the Universe is in the direction of increasing complexity, leading to increasing consciousness, including consciousness of the presence of Spirit in the Universe. That directionality is inevitable even if catastrophic events occur at particular places and times which interrupt the inevitable process that the Universe appears bound to follow toward the emergence of beings (such as humans) which have the capacity to attain consciousness of Spirit.[89]

From a human perspective, there is good reason for pessimism about the future of the species and even the planet. But such a perspective is an example of the epistemological parochialism which we have previously examined. Assessing the future from the point of view of the fate of the human species is an embarrassingly parochial point of view when one recognizes that the human species and the cognitive capacities that it has evolved are merely the capacities of a single tiny species existing on a single tiny planet for a very brief moment in cosmic history. Why should we judge the future based solely on the impact on that single species? Instead, we should exercise our unique capacity to look beyond our own narrow self-interest and consider the future on a larger scale. From that perspective, we have every reason to believe in the inevitability of the evolution toward increasing levels of complexity and consciousness, assured that if that process comes to a halt in the human species, it will begin again if Earth remains habitable to life, and if not it will continue at other places in the Universe, where species other than the human will evolve into beings with the capacity to know Spirit. As such, from a cosmic perspective, there is room only for optimism: We live in a universe in which the emergence of conscious beings is inevitable, and that consciousness eventually reaches a level of development at which there is awareness of Spirit. And if the evolution of such beings comes to an end at any given place and time, we can be assured that it will continue elsewhere. Religion, or the fundamental awareness of Spirit, might come to an end of its development in the human species and on the planet Earth, but surely it will emerge and evolve somewhere in the vastness of the Cosmos.

But Remember: A Period of Transition

In the previous pages we have presented a different way of thinking about religion, one that is fully compatible with a 21st century sensibility that is fully informed by the full range of human knowledge in the early 21st century. This way of looking at religion sees no conflict between religion and science, or religion and cross-cultural historical knowledge, or religion and any type of knowledge held by a thoughtful, well-informed, intelligent 21st century citizen. It *is* possible to be a religious/spiritual human being and not sacrifice one's moral or intellectual dignity, although – and this is our recurrent theme – that requires a radical adjustment to how we think about religion. If religion in future times is something which is perceived as fully compatible with contemporary scientific and moral sensibilities, it will indeed be a type of religion that differs significantly from what dominates the scene across the globe today.

Still, it's important to recognize that this religion of the future will not just magically make its appearance one day as a *fait accompli*, complete with new doctrines, rituals, institutional structures, and moral codes. The reader who asks where this new 21st century spirituality is must bear in mind that the evolutionary emergence of a new type of spirituality happens slowly, over a long period of time. As Ken Wilber, who is perhaps one of the most ardent supporters of the idea that we are transitioning to a new type of spirituality, pointedly reminds us, evolution, despite its long-term directionality and consistency, on a short-term basis (which in this case must be understood as thousands of years) tends to be a "meandering" process that often appears to be inoperative or moving in the wrong direction.[90]

With respect to the time frame of evolutionary change in the nature of human spirituality, consider that from the pre-Axial Age to the beginning of Axial Age religion, we see a span of at least 30,000 to 40,000 years. Hence, it would seem reasonable to expect that the transition from Axial to post-Axial spirituality might take a similarly long period of time, and given that (as many suggest) the first hints of a post-Axial spirituality did not appear until after the Renaissance, we should recognize that we are only in the early stages of the emergence of a post-Axial type of religion, and the best that we can do is look for glimpses of the emergence of this new way of thinking about, experiencing, and relating to the Sacred.

But glimpses of the emergence of a new type of spirituality are indeed evident and growing. Perhaps the appearance of an alternative spirituality of the sort that we are suggesting is slowly emerging as what will eventually become the "religion of the future" can clearly be seen as far back as the early 1800s in New England Transcendentalism, where the likes of Henry David Thoreau, Ralph Waldo Emerson, Bronson Alcott and others explicitly advocated a spirituality that rejected orthodox Christianity, separated itself from the confinements of existing denominations, and advocated a religion based not on ancient events or abstract dogma but rather on direct experience of the sacred, especially as found in the natural world. As Boller suggests, the Transcendentalist revolt against established American religion was an attempt "to replace old ways that no longer carried conviction" with a new spirituality.[91] In other words, Transcendentalism was a reflection of the movement from Axial to post-Axial religion.

This movement would continue in diverse expressions into the 20th century in both the Eastern and Western hemispheres. In the West we find the Jesuit priest/paleontologist, Teilhard de Chardin, developing a theology which is thoroughly grounded in an evolutionary understanding of the Cosmos, seeing no conflict between belief in the evolution of the physical universe and the presence of a spiritual reality behind that evolutionary process. Curiously, at about the same time that Teilhard was developing his theology in Europe and America, in India Aurobindo Ghose was creating a similar synthesis of science and religion.[92] The thought of both Teilhard and Aurobindo typifies what post-Axial spirituality is likely to look like, strongly asserting the reality of a spiritual dimension to the Cosmos, but doing so in a way that is radically removed from traditional Axial-based faith (whether Christian, Hindu, or other), and requiring no sacrifice of the intellect to affirm one's religious identity.

Similarly, we see the regular appearance of suggestive remarks from within the mainstream scientific community[93] and those considered on the "fringe,"[94] all defending a spiritual view of reality that can be embraced without hesitation by the 21st century thinker, although doing so requires the radical adjustment to how we look at traditional religion in a manner similar to what we have described in the previous pages.

In these and many other examples, we see a sense that the human species is moving (slowly) away from one mode of spiritual awareness (Axial) and into something new and different. We are indeed entering into a "Second Axial Age" or "post-Axial" spirituality, but we are in the early stages of that development and, as such, its contours remain quite nebulous and constantly changing. As Richard Tarnas states, "Ours is an age between worldviews, creative yet disoriented, a transitional era when the old cultural vision no longer holds and the new has not yet constellated. Yet we are not without signs of what the new might look like."[95]

At the present time, in the early stages of the emergence of a new spirituality, what we see is a rather chaotic mixture of diverse, unrelated, and sometimes contradictory spiritual perspectives. This reflects the reality that what is emerging is a bottom-up rather than a top-down movement. No one has captured this better than Robert Forman, in his work on what he has labeled "grassroots spirituality." Forman sees the early stages of movement toward a new religious perspective that aligns with what we have presented here, but he acknowledges that it's difficult to categorize or even identify exactly what that new religion is, since "it has developed in a spontaneous and disorganized way among many every day, ordinary people. Nobody has planned this growth. It is not coming from some religious authority or a Pope. No one is running the show."[96] Indeed, "We are still in the middle of, or at the tail end of, this period of a thousand new religions: the Age of Searching."[97]

Of course, at some point – perhaps decades or more likely even centuries from now – this new post-Axial spirituality will develop a structure, new rituals, new modes of authority, and new texts. It will have a name (or names). It will have leaders. It will have divisions and divisions within divisions, just as do existing Axial religions. No doubt the Protestant Reformation looked quite disorganized and messy during the first few decades after Luther posted his 95 Theses, but eventually it more or less coalesced in various structured expressions. The same is likely to happen with post-Axial religion, although the time frame for that development is likely far into the future.

Nonetheless, even though we find in the analyses of Tarnas, Forman, and many others who ponder the transition to the next phase of human spirituality a sense that things are rather muddled at present and difficult to predict in the future, the common theme that runs through all of these predictions is an understanding that religion is something that is evolving, and as the human species evolves in the coming centuries, the spiritual awareness of humanity will do the same. Rather than looking at religion as something that derives from past revelations and knowledge from ancient books, religion is seen as the product of the slow but progressive evolution of human spiritual awareness, a human capacity that has already evolved through the pre-Axial to Axial stage, and is beginning the next step in its evolution to a post-Axial stage.

Perhaps no contemporary figure has advocated for this evolutionary understanding of religion more than Ken Wilber. Revered by some and reviled by others, Wilber's remarkable output of books, articles, and a robust Internet presence over the past forty-plus years has led to a guru-like status among the rapidly growing "spiritual but not religious" population that identifies as religious but rejects the traditional Axial-based religion of the existing traditions. Wilber's appeal to this increasingly broad segment of the population can in part be attributed to his confidence in the forward moving trajectory of human evolutionary development, and, along with that, the forward evolution of human spirituality. Wilber presents a fairly detailed and sophisticated model of both human history and individual psychology, from which he deduces that humanity's capacity to experientially know Spirit evolves over time, as do all other components of human consciousness. Humans in the 21st century have a fuller knowledge of the nature of matter than did humans in 2100 BCE. Similarly, he argues, human awareness of the nature of spiritual reality has correspondingly changed, again in the direction of becoming fuller over the many centuries of human consciousness development, and, perhaps most importantly, the evolution of human consciousness of Spirit will continue to evolve. Although Wilber does not often use the language of the Axial model, he clearly is suggesting that just as human consciousness evolved from a pre-Axial to an Axial awareness of Spirit, likewise it will (and is already in the process of) evolving from an Axial to a post-Axial mode of Spiritual awareness.

Part of Wilber's appeal is the confidence with which he describes this process of evolutionary spiritual awareness. Speaking of the next step in this process, he boldly predicts "a supra-mental, superconscious singularity" in which there are "stunning new discoveries and evolutionary alternatives awaiting humans at this point in history."[98] Wilber also presents a very detailed model of the evolution of human consciousness. Some may challenge its presumption of non-dualism as the highest spiritual state and culmination of human spiritual development, and the evolutionary model first developed by Aurobindo (who is perhaps not sufficiently credited), but Wilber at least makes an attempt to articulate a fairly detailed model to account for not only the stages of human spiritual development that have already unfolded, but also the stages that will appear in the coming centuries (most recently in his massive 800 page *The Religion of Tomorrow*). Wilber also explores aspects of the religion of the future that are rarely examined, namely the broader sociocultural changes that will accompany the gradual widespread shift to a different mode of spirituality. If a culture is in large part the product of a worldview, or a model for thinking about what we are and how we are related to other beings, the natural world, and the cosmos at large, and if part of a worldview includes, and, some would argue, is deeply rooted in, our spirituality, then as the future spiritual consciousness spreads across a broader and broader expanse of the world's population, we should expect to see changes in humanity's worldview and, in more concrete terms, changes in the specific cultural institutions that will emerge from a new spiritual perspective. In other words, the religion of the future won't just be about religion, but rather will gradually produce a post-Axial array of cultural institutions, in which the economy, politics, education, the arts, social relationships, technology and science, and essentially all elements of human existence will reflect this post-Axial spiritual awareness and perspective.

But there's an even more mind-boggling aspect to this glimpse into a post-Axial future: What if *humans* change, in some very substantial ways, as well?

Granted, as we have examined throughout the course of this book, if humans remain as they are now, religion will nonetheless change dramatically. But if, as some speculate, humans evolve into something different, the changes in religion are inconceivable.

The notion that humanity might evolve into a radically different kind of being, perhaps even a different species, is suggested by a tantalizingly short remark by historian David Christian, who is certainly not known for wild speculation about matters concerning religion:

> Will new technologies allow humans to exchange ideas, thoughts, emotions, and images instantaneously and continuously? Creating something like a single, vast global mind? Will the noosphere partially detach itself from us humans and turn into a thin, unified layer of mind hovering over the biosphere? When, in all of this, will we decide that human history (as we understand it today) has ended because our species can no longer be described as *Homo sapiens*?[99]

Steve Taylor, who in contrast to Christian writes explicitly about the evolving nature of spirituality, offers a more specific suggestion of the possible future course of human relationship with Spirit:

> Eventually, assuming evolution continues, living beings with a more intense awareness than us will develop, and they will be aware of – and understand – more phenomena than us. They will have a more intense awareness of reality than using the same way that we have a more intense awareness than sheep – and their knowledge and understanding of the world will be correspondingly larger.[100]

Speculation on the future of the human species in the context of our recently acquired ability to radically and rapidly transform certain aspects of our existence and nature has generated an emerging field of thought known as transhumanism or post-humanism. The definitions of each label are still fluid and hardly used consistently by thinkers in this area, so for the sake of brevity and clarity we will use "post-human" to refer to the idea that the human species is on the path of moving radically beyond its current characteristics (trans-human) and headed toward the possibility of such a radical transformation that "human" needs to be replaced by a new name for a new species (hence, "post-human").

Post-humanists argue for a rapidly paced human-generated evolution that will be based on the dramatic progress that has been made in areas such as genetics, computer-brain interfaces, nanotechnology, and other technologies. The potential changes in aspects of human existence such as longevity, health and wellness, cognition, reproduction, and other areas have been explored in some detail by those who both defend and abhor the notion of a post-human species. Clearly, if humans develop the capacity to live much longer, with vastly enhanced health and physical abilities, with the cognitive processing ability of a powerful computer, and the capacity to program future humans in very precise ways through genetic engineering, the changes in not just the individuals that we now call "human," but also the changes in all aspects of what we call "society" will be enormous, and to us today, unimaginable. As noted above, Ken Wilber speculates about the broad range of social changes that would follow from a human population that has developed a new spirituality, but the changes would be exponentially greater if even the human species itself evolved into a radically different kind of being.

And if that happens, what will the religion or spirituality of the post-humans be like? How we perceive ourselves, others, nature, the Universe, reality – basically, every facet of human awareness – would change dramatically and changes in how we perceive Spirit would inevitably follow, perhaps even leading to a post-human post-post-Axial spirituality that bears little resemblance to that which we understand as "religion" today.

But caution is in order here, and perhaps the less speculation the better, given that any effort that we make to think about how post-humans think about Spirit would be done by humans – us – who almost by definition are confined to the perceptions and modes of reasoning to which we are currently limited. If the future is destined to evolve a post-human species, the nature of post-human spirituality will not be known until then.

In Closing

But enough said about the possibility of a post-human species at some point in the remote future: let's return to our present concern and the point of the entire book: how to think about religion *now*, in the 21st century.

As we have argued in various ways, *religion will persist* as we move into the 21st century and beyond, but it likely will persist in a significantly different expression than what humanity has seen for the past 2000 years. Religion rooted in Axial Age spirituality will almost certainly continue to decline, while a post-Axial spirituality will continue to expand and produce a believable, meaningful, viable, credible religion that will feature a more expansive, cosmic, non-anthropocentric understanding of Spirit/God; more emphasis on empirical experience of the sacred; less emphasis on adherence to ancient sacred texts and allegiance to religious institutional structures and authority; diminished interest in concrete, specific dogma and doctrine; recognition of the legitimacy of a plurality of ways of thinking about and experiencing the sacred; adherence to a sense of moral responsibility that expands our sense of moral obligation beyond the human to other species and life forms; and recognition that spirituality and science are not in conflict with each other.

So the fully-informed 21st century citizen can be religious without sacrificing intellectual or moral integrity, although that will mean thinking about Spirit in a very different way than the Axial spirituality that has dominated much of humanity's religions over the past 2500 or more years. This emerging but already present religion of the 21st century and beyond is only in the infancy stages of development. The specific nature of what such a post-Axial spirituality will be like (beyond the general characteristics that we've outlined) is hard to say, and how and why and in what outward manifestations it will emerge are equally hard to predict, given that we are in such early stages. Perhaps no one will intentionally design a program to bring it about (not unlike how Martin Luther never intended to bring about the vast, multidimensional religious tradition that constitutes Christian Protestantism). Perhaps, like the transition from pre-Axial animism to Axial monotheisms and monisms, it will spontaneously emerge from an evolving human consciousness, and the standard components of a structured religion (ritual, morals, texts, organizations) will just grow out of that, in fits and starts, with the usual conflicts, over time. But whatever form the spirituality of the 21st century and beyond takes, it surely will be one which believers can fully embrace, free from the intellectual and moral sacrifices that are required to sustain belief in the fading, Axial Age religions.

Author Biography

George Adams teaches in both Religious Studies and Philosophy at Susquehanna University in Selinsgrove, Pennsylvania, USA. He has taught a wide range of courses in World Religions, Philosophy of Religion, Religious Experience, Mysticism, Ethics, and related areas. Dr. Adams is a graduate of Fordham University in New York City, where he acquired his M.A. and Ph.D. degrees under the renowned eco-theologian and Teilhard scholar, Thomas Berry, and theologian of Comparative Religions and Sanskrit scholar, José Pereira. He is the author of two books, has published numerous scholarly articles, is a regular book reviewer for *Nova Religio*, and has presented papers at professional conferences.

Previous Titles

The Deathbed Sutra of the Buddha or Siddhartha's Regrets (Washington: O-Books, 2014)

The Structure and Meaning of Badarayana's Brahma Sutras (Delhi: Motilal Banarsidass, 1993)

Note to Readers

Thank you for purchasing *Thinking About Religion in the 21st Century. A New Guide for the Perplexed*. I hope that you will find it to be a convincing and well-argued exploration of the state of religion, both now and in the immediate future. Of course, forecasting the next stage in the evolution of religion is an enormous task, and I don't pretend to offer anything more than a brief glimpse of what that future, post-Axial religion might look like. I welcome readers to share their own ideas via my website at www.religionevolving.com., e-mailing me at *religionevolving@gmail.com*, or posting a review on relevant sites.

Endnotes

1. Kierkegaard, *Concluding Unscientific Postscript*, 133.

2. Since most readers of this book are likely to have been raised in a culture in which Christianity is the dominant religion and the Bible the most widely referenced sacred text, we will draw many of our examples from that context in order to operate on a terrain likely to be familiar to readers. In doing so, however, we are not suggesting that the Christian tradition is the only one that is in need of rethinking in the 21st century, and where appropriate, we will draw cases from other traditions.

3. While granting that physicalism, materialism, and naturalism are terms that are not necessarily identical, we will use them interchangeably to refer to the belief that 1) reality consists only of matter/energy/space/time – in other words, the Universe as recognized by traditional science; and 2) there exists no nonphysical "spiritual" reality of any sort.

4. "Modern," of course, has multiple meanings. But for the purposes of this book we will refer to the modern period as the one in which science, rationalism, and materialism have gradually gained ascendancy in the popular worldview of Western culture, and pre-modern as the preceding period during which a religious worldview held sway over most of the population. Roughly speaking, we are talking about pre-modern as anything before, and modern as anything after, the 15th to 16th centuries, with full blown modernism only reaching its dominance as a cultural and intellectual force in the 18th century and after.

5. The challenge of language is one of the first obstacles that we encounter when thinking about religion in the 21st century and beyond, and we should clarify the position

that we will take in this book on the use of language to describe that which is the object of and source of the spiritual sentiment. Given that the likely audience for this book is primarily Western readers, the use of "God" would seem to make sense. And yet, for reasons that will become apparent as we unfold our argument in the coming pages, "God" is a term which is also quite problematic, especially with regard to its anthropomorphic associations and the way in which God is characterized as an all-too-flawed human-like being in many sacred texts. Indeed, some would argue that it is precisely this concept of "God" that deters many would-be believers from openly identifying as "religious." The growing population of the "spiritual but not religious" believers often take pains to clarify that their spirituality is one that is based on belief in a spiritual dimension, but not a dimension that corresponds to the God of traditional Western theism, with its attributions of jealousy, vengefulness, violence, caprice, etc. But if we dispense with the word "God," with what language do we replace it? Options abound: the Sacred, the Transcendent, Spirit, Ultimate Reality, the Holy, Higher Power, Ground of Being, etc. Each word or phrase, however, carries with it its own strengths as well as limitations, and we could perhaps argue indefinitely regarding the right word for whatever "It" is. But that's illustrative of exactly what we hope to examine in this work: namely, the fact that we are in a period of transition from one type of spirituality to something quite different. As such, it will take time for a new language to develop to accurately and adequately describe the understanding of "Spirit" that is reflected in this emerging religious sentiment. For the purposes of the following pages, however, we will use all of the words, and perhaps even others, interchangeably. God, Spirit, the Sacred, Ultimate Reality, the Spiritual Dimension –

and more – will be used to refer to spiritual reality. In the absence of a new language, we will have to make use of existing language, however limited and problematic it might be.

6.   See, for example, the enormously popular works of Ken Wilber, Michael Singer, Deepak Chopra, Eckhart Tolle, and many others. While these and similar authors offer a wide range of perspectives, what they all share is a commitment to the belief that we are in a period of transition from an antiquated spirituality to a new form of spirituality that is still evolving.

7.   Case in point: Ken Wilber's writings on non-dualism. In defending his interpretation of pure non-dualism as the highest state of spiritual consciousness, he makes frequent reference to those ancient Hindu and Buddhist teachings that support his position, but doesn't even acknowledge the many schools of non-dualist thought (Ramanuja, Nimbarka, and more) that challenge his preferred interpretation. In essence, he is hiding the full picture from the reader who is unlikely to be familiar with the fact there is a broad spectrum of interpretations of non-dualism in Indic thought.

8.   Curiously, Wilber's work can be seen as an expression of both problems, given that, aside from the issue addressed in the previous note, his work is full of long and sometimes laborious footnotes.

9.   Perhaps best exemplified by Mircea Eliade, in classic works such as *Patterns in Comparative Religion*.

10. See Jaspers, *The Origin and Goal of History*. For a more recent summary, written for a general audience, of the key elements of Axial Age religions, see Karen Armstrong, *The Great Transformation: The Beginning of Our Religious Traditions*. Historian Robert Bellah has attempted a similar large-scale account of the historical development

of religion in his 2011 work, *Religion in Human Evolution: From the Paleolithic to the Axial Age.* Bellah's work, however, at times degenerates into a simple description of different traditions and perspectives, leaving out the evolutionary thread that ties them together.

11. Islam did not develop until the 7th century, but as indicated earlier, we are considering Islam as part of the Abrahamic family of religions, and as such its Abrahamic origins clearly reflect elements of Axial Age spirituality.

12. J.L. Schellenberg, *Evolutionary Religion,* 4.

13. See, for instance, multiple accounts in Biblical books such as Deuteronomy (20:10-19), Numbers (31:7-40), and Joshua (10:28-40).

14. Reza Aslan, *Zealot: The Life and Times of Jesus of Nazareth,* 31.

15. Both Eliade and Campbell were prolific authors. A good starting point for appreciating each would be Eliade's *Patterns in Comparative Religions* and Campbell's *The Hero with a Thousand Faces.*

16. See, for instance, Andrew Newberg, *Why God Won't Go Away: Brain Science and the Biology of Belief.*

17. In other words, ritual is not likely to disappear, but the forms that it will take might be radically different from the rituals that emerged from Axial religions. The development of post-Axial ritual is in its infancy and is not likely to proceed in any sort of defined manner until there is further development, refinement, and clarification of post-Axial belief, given that meaningful ritual is dependent on a bedrock of cognitive content, including a set of meaningful symbols, in order for it to have sufficient impact to be embraced by believers. We can see glimmers of such a movement toward a new belief system accompanied by new rituals in some of the spiritually-oriented communities of the environmental movement. The belief system coming out of this community includes a strong sense of planetary

consciousness, or our connection to and identity with the Earth as a whole (in contrast to identity as a particular tribe, ethnic group, nationality, or species). In groups that share such globally-oriented spiritual beliefs, we sometimes see communal gatherings for the performance of ritual in connection with the solstices, Earth Day, and other points in the calendar that acquire a new seriousness when spirituality becomes global. As time goes on, these rituals are likely to develop into more clearly defined and formal practices.

18. Bart Ehrman has written extensively (and with a clarity that makes the issues easy to grasp for lay readers) about the multiple versions of Christianity that competed for recognition during the first four centuries of the Christian era, and the process by which that multiplicity of Christianities came to be narrowed down to a single orthodoxy. See, for instance, his *Lost Christianities: The Battles for Scripture and the Faiths We Never Knew*.

19. As late as the mid-1600s, for example, four Quakers were hung in Boston merely for holding beliefs that differed from those of the dominant Puritanism of the Massachusetts Bay Colony.

20. See Richard Tarnas, *Cosmos and Psyche: Intimations of a New World View*, 35-42.

21. The tension between saying nothing and saying too much is wonderfully illustrated in the Buddhist account of the "unanswered questions" (variously numbered as 12, 14, or 16) and the Buddha's "Noble Silence" in response to these questions. These various accounts from the Pali sutras all describe how the Buddha's disciples, wishing to have a clearer understanding of his teaching, posed a series of metaphysical questions to him regarding the nature of reality: Is the world eternal or finite? Is the self the same as, or different from the body? Does an enlightened being

continue to exist after death or not? And so on. To the presumed disappointment of the disciples, the Buddha refused to answer these questions, on the grounds that speculation about such abstract matters was not conducive to the attainment of freedom from suffering. Nonetheless, reflecting the universal human need to say *something*, the subsequent Buddhist tradition produced an enormous amount of philosophical literature, quite in contrast to the silence of its founder! Indeed, the success of Buddhism as it spread beyond India to become a worldwide religion can be seen as made possible by the development of a comprehensive and detailed set of doctrines and philosophical arguments in support of those doctrines, without which there would not have been an identifiable "Buddhism" to be embraced by people throughout the world.

22. The slowly emerging symbols, language, beliefs, etc. that might eventually coalesce into an identifiable post-Axial religion is explored by Robert Forman in *Grassroots Spirituality: What It Is, Why It Is Here, Where It Is Going.*

23. For an interesting account of this development in higher education, see Tomoku Masuzawa, *The Invention of World Religions.*

24. For a thorough account of the migration (and transformation) of Asian spiritual traditions into American culture, see Philip Goldberg, *American Veda: From Emerson and the Beatles to Yoga and Meditation – How Indian Spirituality Changed the West.* Similarly, Rick Fields documents the history of the penetration of Buddhism in America in *How the Swans Came to the Lake: A Narrative History of Buddhism in America.*

25. All of which is not, of course, meant to lend credence to the tradition which asserts that Jesus lived in India. These legends are documented in Holger Kersten's *Jesus Lived in India: His Unknown Life Before and After the Crucifixion.*

26. Even a renowned, mainstream, conservative academic such as Robert Bellah has speculated on the idea that we are entering a new era of spirituality, a "second axial age" of sorts. See Bellah's *Religion in Human Evolution: From the Paleolithic to the Axial Age*, xix.

27. Indeed, there has developed an entire genre of works which all argue some version of the notion that contemporary science (by which is usually meant quantum physics) provides evidence of, if not proof of, some sort of spiritual dimension of existence (by which is usually meant some version of non-dualism). In a sense, this is an unfortunate development in that by stretching a legitimate observation (that there are parallels between *some* contemporary scientific observations and *some* religious beliefs) to quite indefensible limits (contemporary science provides *proof* about the existence of spiritual realities), these thinkers have tended to undermine any sense of intellectual legitimacy associated with systems of thought which attempt to incorporate ideas from both contemporary science and contemporary spirituality.

28. This theme was perhaps introduced almost fifty years ago with Fritjof Capra's *Tao of Physics*, a work much maligned by scientists and much praised by new believers.

29. Richard Feynman in Rosenblum and Kuttner, *Quantum Consciousness*, p. 80.

30. In the words of the father of quantum physics, Niels Bohr, "Anyone not shocked by quantum mechanics has not yet understood it." (Quoted in Rosenblum and Kuttner, *Quantum Consciousness*, p. 13.)

31. Accounts of the double-slit experiment can be found in any book on quantum physics, but for the non-scientist (such as myself) a particularly clear and easy-to-follow version can be found in Jim Al-Khalili's *Quantum: A Guide for the Perplexed*.

32. An excellent account of the role of consciousness (again, for the non-scientist) in quantum phenomena can be found in Philip Goff's *Galileo's Error: Foundations of a New Science of Consciousness*.

33. There is, of course, a long history to the philosophical notion that rather than perceiving reality directly, we perceive only that version of reality which our sensory capacities allow us to perceive. In the West, this was perhaps most carefully articulated by Immanuel Kant. In Buddhism, we find it in the much earlier schools of the Yogacara and Vijnanavada.

34. John Hick's extensive writing on religious pluralism touches on this issue.

35. Thomas Berry wrote extensively and eloquently about the need for the emergence of a "new story" to replace the myths of the Axial Age. For a summary of his wide-ranging work and an account of his profound influence on his students, see Tucker, Grim, and Angyal's *Thomas Berry: A Biography*.

36. See Huxley's *The Perennial Philosophy* and Smith's *The World's Religions*.

37. One might add that, in addition to differences between traditions, there is a wide range of diversity within each major tradition. Within Buddhism, for example, we have Hinayana and Mahayana, and within Mahayana we have, just as one example, Zen and Pure Land, and within Zen, we have Soto and Rinzai, and within Soto... and on and on the story goes.

38. Polls conducted by the Pew Research Center over the past 20 years have consistently found an increase in respondents who identify as "spiritual but not religious" accompanied by decreases in many of the mainline denominations. Also, for a fuller treatment of this phenomenon, see James Emery

White, *Rise of the Nones: Understanding and Reaching the Religiously Unaffiliated*.

39. The development of a sense of self and its religious implications are explored at length in Carl Jung's concept of individuation. Ken Wilber's model of the evolutionary stages of the development of consciousness examines the emergence of a sense of self in the evolution of consciousness. This theme is found throughout Wilber's works. See, for instance, his *Up from Eden: A Transpersonal View of Human Evolution*.

40. While Hindu Vedanta is overwhelmingly non-dualist, it should be noted that there are exceptions, in particular the Dvaita Vedanta school of Madhva.

41. This is the major theme of Philip Goff's *Galileo's Error: Foundations for a New Science of Consciousness*.

42. For an example of an extended work that treads ground back and forth between serious speculation and being a bit "out there," see Evan Harris Walker, *The Physics of Consciousness: The Quantum Mind and the Meaning of Life*.

43. Historians of science often assign to Isaac Newton the role of delivering a fatal blow to "god of the gaps" theology with the development of the laws of classical physics, which seemed to explain the movement of the heavenly bodies and other natural phenomena without any reference to a God. Such an observation would have appeared to be rather ridiculous to Newton, however, who remained a religious believer (although he had to hide his non-Trinitarian views) throughout his life, spending much of his later years more interested in theology and Biblical prophecy than in scientific studies. For an in-depth exploration of the role of religion in Newton's thought, see Rob Iliffe, *Priest of Nature: The Religious Worlds of Isaac Newton*.

44. The difficulty of defining consciousness is nicely summarized by Christof Koch in *Consciousness: Confessions of a Romantic Reductionist*, 32-34.

45. This is not meant to deny that gradations of consciousness clearly exist in different species and that consciousness in some nonhuman species has developed to the point of making possible an inner emotional life, memory, elementary rational deliberation, etc. The point that we are making is not whether or not a particular dimension of consciousness exists in a particular species, whether human, animal, or extraterrestrial, but rather the very nature of consciousness itself, regardless of the life form in which it is manifested.

46. This, of course, is an observation that goes back to Plato's theory of forms.

47. For a Buddhist perspective on the relationship between brain activity and consciousness, see the works of B. Alan Wallace such as *Contemplative Science: Where Buddhism and Neuroscience Converge* and *Hidden Dimensions: The Unification of Physics and Consciousness*.

48. In academic Philosophy, this position is represented by eliminative materialism, and has been articulated at length by Paul and Patricia Churchland. For a more general audience, a materialist understanding of consciousness can be found in the works of Daniel Dennett.

49. This is illustrated in the famous thought experiment known as "Mary's Room" by Frank Jackson, found in "Epiphenomenal Qualia" (1982) and extended in "What Mary Didn't Know" (1986).

50. Collectively and rather informally (and, at times, controversially), advocates of the position that the hard problem of consciousness cannot be resolved and that consciousness cannot be reduced to and comprehensively

explained by physical terms are known as the "New Mysterians," represented by Colin McGinn, Martin Gardner, Thomas Nagel, and many others (although it should be noted that not all philosophers who have been designated as new mysterians have agreed with such a designation).

51. Philosopher Thomas Nagel explores this point at length in his recent provocative and controversial work, *Mind and Cosmos: Why the Materialist Neo-Darwinian Conception of Nature is Almost Certainly False.*

52. This is hardly a new observation. Isaac Newton, for instance, used the experience of will to demonstrate the existence of a soul. See *Priest of Nature*, 103-110.

53. For a credible treatment of the relationship between quantum physics and consciousness, written for the lay reader, see Bruce Rosenblum and Fred Kuttner, *Quantum Enigma: Physics Encounters Consciousness.*

54. The initial, and still classic, treatment of the connections between quantum physics, consciousness, and spirituality, can be found in Fritjof Capra's *The Tao of Physics*. Gary Zukav's *The Dancing Wu Li Masters* covers similar territory in a more restrained manner. More recently, the quantum-consciousness-spirituality connection is covered by Robert Lanza in *Biocentrism: How Life and Consciousness are the Keys to Understanding the True Nature of the Universe.*

55. From the "founding father" of the quantum physics revolution, Niels Bohr ("Anyone not shocked by quantum mechanics has not yet understood it"), to the renowned late 20th century physicist Richard Feynman ("Nobody understands quantum mechanics"), admissions of the bizarre picture of reality presented by quantum theory abound.

56. One attempt to articulate a new model that accounts for the primary role of consciousness is panpsychism, or the

theory that consciousness in some form is present in all of reality, not just in humans, and not just in living creatures. According to panpsychism, consciousness goes, so to speak, all the way down, present in the smallest particle or quantum of energy. Panpsychism has ancient origins, but has been tentatively suggested by some contemporary thinkers in the scientific and philosophical communities. For an introduction, see David Skrbina, *Panpsychism in the West*, or Peter Ells, *Panpsychism: The Philosophy of the Sensuous Cosmos*. Also see the works of the prolific contemporary idealist philosopher Bernardo Kastrup, including *Science Ideated*.

57. See, for instance, Immanuel Kant's well-known "argument from morality," presented as a rational justification for belief in God.

58. William James adopts this position in his classic work, *The Varieties of Religious Experience*.

59. There are, of course, exceptions within Christianity. For example, in both the Pentecostal tradition in Protestantism and the medieval mystical tradition within Catholicism we find an emphasis on the importance of direct experience of God.

60. Schleiermacher's two major works that relate to our discussion are *On Religion: Speeches to Its Cultured Despisers* and *The Christian Faith*.

61. Rudolf Otto, *The Idea of the Holy: An Inquiry Into the Non-Rational Factor in the Idea of the Divine and Its Relation to the Rational*. Also see Otto's classic comparative work, *Mysticism East and West*.

62. Many editions of James' classic work have been published, but readers who are new to James might refer to the Centenary Edition of *The Varieties of Religious Experience*.

63. See James, *The Varieties of Religious Experience*, 294-296.

64. Pew polls on religion can be found at https://www.pewforum.org/2019/10/17/in-u-s-decline-of-christianity-continues-at-rapid-pace/

65. The theme of the evolution of human consciousness, including the projection of an increased sensibility to spiritual experiences, especially those of the non-dual type, is a theme running throughout the work of Ken Wilber. See, for example, his *A Brief History of Everything*, 137-243. One of the earliest advocates of an evolutionary view of consciousness and religion, writing in the first half of the twentieth century, was the French priest and paleontologist, Pierre Teilhard de Chardin, known mostly for *The Phenomenon of Man*.

66. Although it now seems somewhat dated in places, one of the earliest anthologies of first-person accounts of mystical experiences, Richard Maurice Bucke's *Cosmic Consciousness*, remains a good starting point for readers new to the study of mysticism.

67. The primary theme of Ralph Waldo Emerson's poem, *Give All to Love*, might be human love and loss, but the closing lines ("When half-gods go, The Gods arrive") certainly convey a spiritual sentiment that runs throughout his work. See Brooks Atkinson, ed., *The Selected Writings of Ralph Waldo Emerson*, 773-775.

68. While this notable observation is attributed to Epicurus, it's doubtful that the attribution is accurate.

69. From David Hume's *Dialogues Concerning Natural Religion*, as found in Steven Cahn, *Reason and Religions: Philosophy Looks at the World's Religious Beliefs*.

70. The challenge of finding a convincing theodicy becomes even greater when viewed in the context of not just the suffering experienced by humans, but the suffering experienced by *all sentient beings*. Buddhism and Jainism demonstrate a sensitivity to this nonhuman dimension

of suffering to an extent that is not found in the Western religions.

71. The free will theodicy takes for granted that human beings can only exist as free-willed beings who sometimes choose evil over good. But critics of this theodicy ask *why* this should necessarily be the case. If God is indeed omnipotent, could he not have created humans with *both* the capacity to make free choices and a free will that always makes that choice a choice of the good, as would appear to be the case with God?

72. Some would argue that, in his moving short fictional account of the death of a small child in the presence of its mother, Dostoevsky provides a challenge to theodicies that is far more convincing than any of the complex arguments presented by centuries of philosophers and theologians. See the "Rebellion" chapter in Dostoevsky's *The Brothers Karamazov*, 204-213.

73. As Kierkegaard puts it in *The Concept of Dread*, "terror, perdition, annihilation, dwell next door to every man... and every dread which alarms may the next instant become a fact," p. 140.

74. See Pierre Teilhard de Chardin, *The Phenomenon of Man*. For a shorter summary of Teilhard's vision, see his essay, "My Fundamental Vision," in *Toward the Future*.

75. Nick Cave, "Fireflies," from the Nick Cave and the Bad Seeds album, *Ghosteen* (2019).

76. Daniel Matt, *God and the Big Bang: Discovering Harmony Between Science and Spirituality*, 157.

77. Taylor, *Spiritual Science*, 2.

78. Sean Kelly, *Coming Home: The Birth and Transformation of the Planetary Era*, 153.

79. Laszlo, *Quantum Shift in the Global Brain*, 116.

80. J.L. Schellenberg, *Evolutionary Religion*, 77.

81. For an excellent account of the multiple ways in which "Christian" was defined in the first four centuries after Jesus, see Bart Ehrman, *Lost Christianities: The Battles for Scripture and the Faiths We Never Knew.*

82. Lynn White, "The Historical Roots of Our Ecological Crisis," *Science* 155 (10 March 1967): 1203-1207.

83. See Shantideva, *The Bodhicharyavatara,* chapter 10.

84. In Wing-Tsit Chan, *A Source Book in Chinese Philosophy,* chapter 35.

85. Laszlo, *Quantum Shift in the Global Brain,* 125.

86. Duane R. Bidwell, *When One Religion Isn't Enough: The Lives of Spiritually Fluid People.*

87. Quoted in David Lewis-Williams, *Conceiving God: The Cognitive Origin and Evolution of Religion,* 10.

88. Transhumanism/Posthumanism is rapidly moving from the academic fringe to mainstream, as seen for instance with the establishment of the *Journal of Posthuman Studies* through Penn State University Press.

89. See Schellenberg's discussion of the likelihood of continued development of human spirituality even in the context of potentially catastrophic events in *Evolutionary Religion,* 31 ff.

90. Ken Wilber, *The Religion of Tomorrow,* 649.

91. Paul Boller, *American Transcendentalism, 1830-1860,* xx.

92. See Teilhard de Chardin, *The Phenomenon of Man* and Sri Aurobindo, *The Life Divine* and *The Future Evolution of Man.*

93. From Werner Heisenberg during the formative years of quantum physics in the early 20th century to contemporary figures such as Freeman Dyson and others, we find leading edge scientists offering speculative musings about the nature of spiritual reality.

94. As found, for instance, in the many works of Ervin Laszlo and Rupert Sheldrake.

95. Tarnas, *Cosmos and Psyche,* 26.

96. Robert Forman, *Grassroots Spirituality: What It Is, Why It Is Here, Where It Is Going*, 26.

97. Forman, *Grassroots Spirituality*, 208.

98. Wilber, *The Religion of Tomorrow*, 213.

99. David Christian, *Origin Story: A Big History of Everything*, 302.

100. Taylor, *Spiritual Science*, 226.

References

Al-Khalili, Jim. *Quantum: A Guide for the Perplexed*. London: Weidenfeld and Nicolson, 2003.

Armstrong, Karen. *The Great Transformation: The Beginning of Our Religious Traditions*. New York: Anchor Books, 2007.

Aslan, Reza. *Zealot: The Life and Times of Jesus of Nazareth*. New York: Random House, 2014.

Atkinson, Brooks. *The Selected Writings of Ralph Waldo Emerson*. New York: The Modern Library, 1964.

Aurobindo, Sri. *The Future Evolution of Man*. Twin Lakes, WI: Lotus Press, 1990.

Aurobindo, Sri. *The Life Divine*. Twin Lakes, WI: Lotus Press, 1990.

Bellah, Robert. *Religion in Human Evolution: From the Paleolithic to the Axial Age*. Cambridge: Belknap/Harvard, 2011.

Bidwell, Duane R. *When One Religion Isn't Enough: The Lives of Spiritually Fluid People*. Boston: Beacon Press, 2018.

Boller, Paul F. *American Transcendentalism, 1830-1860: An Intellectual Inquiry*. New York: G.P. Putnam's Sons, 1974.

Bucke, Richard Maurice. *Cosmic Consciousness*. New York: Penguin Books, 1969.

Cahn, Steven M. *Reason and Religions: Philosophy Looks at the World's Religious Beliefs*. Boston: Wadsworth, 2014.

Campbell, Joseph. *The Hero with a Thousand Faces*. Novato, CA: New World Library, 2008.

Capra, Fritjof. *The Tao of Physics*. Boulder: Shambhala, 1975.

Chalmers, David. *The Character of Consciousness*. London: Oxford University Press, 2010.

Chan, Wing-Tsit. *A Source Book in Chinese Philosophy*. Princeton: Princeton University Press, 1963.

Christian, David. *Origin Story: A Big History of Everything*. New York: Little, Brown Spark, 2018.

Dostoevsky, Fyodor. *The Brothers Karamazov*. New York: W.W. Norton, 2011.

Ehrman, Bart. *Lost Christianities: The Battles for Scripture and the Faiths We Never Knew*. London: Oxford University Press, 2005.

Eliade, Mircea. *Patterns in Comparative Religion*. New York: World Publishing, 1972.

Ells, Peter. *Panpsychism: The Philosophy of the Sensuous Cosmos*. Washington: O-Books, 2011.

Fields, Rick. *How the Swans Came to the Lake: A Narrative History of Buddhism in America*. Boston: Shambhala, 1992.

Forman, Robert. *Grassroots Spirituality: What It Is, Why It Is Here, Where It Is Going*. Charlottesville, VA: Imprint Academic, 2004.

Fowler, James W. *Stages of Faith: The Psychology of Human Development and the Quest for Meaning*. New York: Harper Collins, 1995.

Goff, Philip. *Galileo's Error: Foundations for a New Science of Consciousness*. London: Rider, 2019.

Goldberg, Philip. *American Veda: From Emerson and the Beatles to Yoga and Meditation – How Indian Spirituality Changed the West*. Easton: Harmony Press, 2013.

Hick, John. *God Has Many Names*. Louisville: Westminster/John Knox Press, 1980.

Huxley, Aldous. *The Perennial Philosophy*. New York: Harper Perennial, 2009.

Iliffe, Rob. *Priest of Nature: The Religious Worlds of Isaac Newton*. New York: Oxford University Press, 2017.

James, William. *The Varieties of Religious Experience: A Study in Human Nature*. New York: Routledge, 2002.

Jaspers, Karl. *The Origin and Goal of History*. London: Routledge, 2021.

Kastrup, Bernardo. *Science Ideated: The fall of matter and the contours of the next mainstream scientific worldview*. Washington: Iff Books, 2021.

Kelly, Sean. *Becoming Gaia: On the Threshold of Planetary Initiation.* Olympia, WA: Integral Imprint, 2021.

Kelly, Sean M. *Coming Home: The Birth and Transformation of the Planetary Era.* Great Barrington, MA: Lindisfarne Books, 2010.

Kersten, Holger. *Jesus Lived in India: His Unknown Life Before and After the Crucifixion.* Boston: Element Books, 1994.

Kierkegaard, Soren. *The Concept of Dread.* Princeton: Princeton University Press, 1957.

Kierkegaard, Soren. *Concluding Unscientific Postscript.* Princeton: Princeton University Press, 1941.

Koch, Christof. *Consciousness: Confessions of a Romantic Reductionist.* Cambridge, MA: MIT Press, 2012.

Lanza, Robert. *Biocentrism: How Life and Consciousness are the Keys to Understanding the True Nature of the Universe.* Dallas: Benbella Books, 2009.

Laszlo, Ervin. *The Intelligence of the Cosmos: Why Are We Here? New Answers from the Frontiers of Science.* Rochester, VT: Inner Traditions, 2017.

Laszlo, Ervin. *Quantum Shift in the Global Brain: How the New Scientific Reality Can Change Us and Our World.* Rochester, VT: Inner Traditions, 2008.

Lewis-Williams, David and David Pearce. *Inside the Neolithic Mind: Consciousness, Cosmos, and the Realm of the Gods.* London: Thames and Hudson, 2018.

Masuzawa, Tomoko. *The Invention of World Religions.* Chicago: University of Chicago Press, 2005.

Matt, Daniel C. *God and the Big Bang: Discovering Harmony Between Science and Spirituality.* Nashville: Jewish Lights, 2016.

Nagel, Thomas. *Mind and Cosmos: Why the Materialist Neo-Darwinian Conception of Nature is Almost Certainly False.* New York: Oxford University Press, 2012.

Newberg, Andrew. *Why God Won't Go Away: Brain Science and the Biology of Belief.* New York: Ballantine Books, 2001.

Otto, Rudolf. *The Idea of the Holy*. New York: Oxford University Press, 1976.

Otto, Rudolf. *Mysticism East and West*. New York: Macmillan, 1970.

Rosenblum, Bruce and Fred Kuttner. *Quantum Enigma: Physics Encounters Consciousness*. New York: Oxford University Press, 2006.

Schellenberg, J.L. *Evolutionary Religion*. New York: Oxford University Press, 2013.

Schellenberg, J.L. *Religion After Science: The Cultural Consequences of Religious Immaturity*. Cambridge: Cambridge University Press, 2019.

Schleiermacher, Friedrich. *On Religion: Speeches to Its Cultured Despisers*. Cambridge: Cambridge University Press, 1988.

Shantideva. *The Bodhicharyavatara*. Translated by the Padmakara Translation Group. Boston: Shambhala, 1967.

Skrbina, David. *Panpsychism in the West*. Cambridge, MA: MIT Press, 2017.

Smith, Huston. *Forgotten Truth. The Common Vision of the World's Religions*. San Francisco: Harper Collins, 1976.

Tallis, Raymond. *Aping Mankind: Neuromania, Darwinitis and the Misrepresentation of Humanity*. New York: Routledge, 2016.

Tarnas, Richard. *Cosmos and Psyche: Intimations of a New World View*. New York: Plume Books, 2006.

Taylor, Steve. *Spiritual Science: Why Science Needs Spirituality to Make Sense of the World*. London: Watkins, 2018.

Teilhard de Chardin, Pierre. *Activation of Energy: Enlightening Reflections on Spiritual Energy*. New York: Harcourt, 1976.

Teilhard de Chardin, Pierre. *The Heart of Matter*. New York: Harcourt, 1976.

Teilhard de Chardin, Pierre. *The Phenomenon of Man*. New York: Harper Torchbooks, 1961.

Teilhard de Chardin, Pierre. *Toward the Future*. New York: Harcourt, 1973.

Tucker, Mary Evelyn, John Grim, and Andrew Angyal. *Thomas Berry: A Biography*. New York: Columbia University Press, 2019.

Walker, Evan Harris. *The Physics of Consciousness*. New York: Basic Books, 2000.

Wallace, B. Alan. *Contemplative Science: Where Buddhism and Neuroscience Converge*. New York: Columbia University Press, 2007.

Wallace, B. Alan. *Hidden Dimensions: The Unification of Physics and Consciousness*. New York: Columbia University Press, 2007.

White, James Emery. *The Rise of the Nones: Understanding and Reaching the Religiously Unaffiliated*. Ada, MI: Baker Books, 2014.

White, Lynn. "The Historical Roots of Our Ecological Crisis." *Science* 155:1203-1207, 1967.

Wilber, Ken. *A Brief History of Everything*. Boston: Shambhala, 1996.

Wilber, Ken. *The Religion of Tomorrow: A Vision for the Future of the Great Traditions*. Boulder: Shambhala, 2017.

Wilber, Ken. *Sex, Ecology, Spirituality: The Spirit of Evolution*. Boston: Shambhala, 1995.

Wilber, Ken. *Up from Eden: A Transpersonal View of Human Evolution*. Wheaton, IL: Quest Books, 1996.

Zukav, Gary. *The Dancing Wu Li Masters: An Overview of the New Physics*. New York: Harper One, 1979.

IFF
BOOKS

ACADEMIC AND SPECIALIST

Iff Books publishes non-fiction. It aims to work with authors
and titles that augment our understanding of the human
condition, society and civilisation, and the world or universe
in which we live. If you have enjoyed this book, why not tell
other readers by posting a review on your preferred book site.
Recent bestsellers from Iff Books are:

Why Materialism Is Baloney
How true skeptics know there is no death and fathom
answers to life, the universe, and everything
Bernardo Kastrup
A hard-nosed, logical, and skeptic non-materialist
metaphysics, according to which the body is in mind,
not mind in the body.
Paperback: 978-1-78279-362-5 ebook: 978-1-78279-361-8

The Fall
Steve Taylor
The Fall discusses human achievement versus the issues of war,
patriarchy and social inequality.
Paperback: 978-1-78535-804-3 ebook: 978-1-78535-805-0

Brief Peeks Beyond
Critical essays on metaphysics, neuroscience,
free will, skepticism and culture
Bernardo Kastrup
An incisive, original, compelling alternative to current
mainstream cultural views and assumptions.
Paperback: 978-1-78535-018-4 ebook: 978-1-78535-019-1

Framespotting
Changing how you look at things changes how you see them
Laurence & Alison Matthews
A punchy, upbeat guide to framespotting. Spot deceptions
and hidden assumptions; swap growth for growing up.
See and be free.
Paperback: 978-1-78279-689-3 ebook: 978-1-78279-822-4

Is There an Afterlife?
David Fontana
Is there an Afterlife? If so what is it like? How do Western
ideas of the afterlife compare with Eastern? David Fontana
presents the historical and contemporary evidence for
survival of physical death.
Paperback: 978-1-90381-690-5

Nothing Matters
a book about nothing
Ronald Green
Thinking about Nothing opens the world to everything by
illuminating new angles to old problems and stimulating
new ways of thinking.
Paperback: 978-1-84694-707-0 ebook: 978-1-78099-016-3

Panpsychism
The Philosophy of the Sensuous Cosmos
Peter Ells
Are free will and mind chimeras? This book, anti-materialistic
but respecting science, answers: No! Mind is foundational
to all existence.
Paperback: 978-1-84694-505-2 ebook: 978-1-78099-018-7

Punk Science
Inside the Mind of God
Manjir Samanta-Laughton
Many have experienced unexplainable phenomena; God,
psychic abilities, extraordinary healing and angelic encounters.
Can cutting-edge science actually explain phenomena
previously thought of as 'paranormal'?
Paperback: 978-1-90504-793-2

The Vagabond Spirit of Poetry
Edward Clarke
Spend time with the wisest poets of the modern age and of the
past, and let Edward Clarke remind you of the importance of
poetry in our industrialized world.
Paperback: 978-1-78279-370-0 ebook: 978-1-78279-369-4

Readers of ebooks can buy or view any of these bestsellers
by clicking on the live link in the title. Most titles are
published in paperback and as an ebook. Paperbacks
are available in traditional bookshops. Both print and
ebook formats are available online. Find more titles and
sign up to our readers' newsletter at
www.collectiveinkbooks.com/non-fiction